Other books by Michael Levine

The Corporate Address Book
The Music Address Book

Coming in mid 1991
from Perigee Books

The Environmental Address Book

THE

ADDRESS

BOOK

How to Reach Anyone Who *Is* Anyone

MICHAEL LEVINE

A Perigee Book

Perigee Books
are published by
The Putnam Publishing Group
200 Madison Avenue
New York, NY 10016

Every effort has been made to provide the most current mailing addresses. Addresses, however, do change, and neither publisher nor author are responsible for misdirected or returned mail.

Library of Congress Cataloging-in-Publication Data

Levine, Michael, date.
The address book : how to reach anyone who is anyone /
Michael Levine.
p.   cm.
ISBN 0-399-51621-2
1. United States—Social registers.   2. United States—
Directories.   3. Celebrities—Directories.   4. Associations,
Institutions, etc.—United States—Directories.
5. Associations, institutions, etc.—Directories.   I. Title.
E154.5.L48   1991   90-7719 CIP
917.3'0025—dc20

Printed in the United States of America
1   2   3   4   5   6   7   8   9   10

This book is printed on acid-free paper.

∞

Acknowledgments

"Friendship is the only cement that will hold the world together."

I'm lucky. I get to say publicly to special people in my life, whom I love, how much they mean to me.

My literary agent, Alice Martell, and her assistant, Sheila Core.

At Putnam, Adrienne Ingrum, Ginger Marino, Laura Shepherd, and Eugene Brissie.

My father, Arthur O. Levine.

My special friends, Bart Andrews, Rana Bendixen, Sue Bennett, Ken Bostic, Bill Calkins, Susan Gauthier, Richard Imprescia, Bette Geller Jackson, Richard Lawson, Karen L'Heureux, Nancy Mager, John McKillop, Evadne Morakis, Dennis Prager, Heidi Rotbart, Joshua Trabulus, and Erline White.

My office family, Gabrielle Abrams, Jeff Albright, Amanda Cagan, Marla Capra, Kim Davis, Kim Kaiman, Karen Lindstrom, Suzette Mir, Monique Moss, Tresda Redburn, Marcee Rondan, Mitchell Schneider, Jane Singer, Alex Soffer, Laura Sterrett, Jeff Sullivan, Roz Wolf, Julie Wheeler, and Staci Wolfe.

My business associates, Laura Herlovich, Pierre Lehu, Dan Pine, Myrna Post, and Joy Sapieka.

Special thanks to Sal Manna, Alison Taylor, and Kathleen Conner for their invaluable help in research.

This book is dedicated with deep appreciation
to my two dearest lifelong friends,
Richard Imprescia (friend since 1963) and
John McKillop (friend since 1972).

Foreword by Robin Leach

Dear friends:

Over the years, I've had the pleasure of dallying with the royally rich and fantastically famous, and escorting millions and millions of viewers on tantalizing television tours of their lavish life-styles. Perhaps some of you have thought, "That fellow Leach must be mighty lucky to hobnob with everyone who's anyone." Well, I am lucky. Although the opulent opportunities to visit those whose champagne wishes and caviar dreams have come true may not be in your own future, you can still rub letters with them, if not elbows.

Super-wealthy or mega-powerful, you now know where to write them, thanks to the addresses in this inexpensive (that shall be the last time you hear that word from me) volume. You can tell them what you think, ask them what you will, chat with them—perhaps even more than I can. Will you receive a reply? Try and see.

Mentioned here in Mr. Levine's books are the important, the useful, the outrageous, and indeed both the great and the small. Enjoy!

Operation Address Book

There are several million names not appearing in this address book, but they may be among the most important people of all: the countless dedicated men and women serving in our armed forces around the world. There's nothing that means more to our troops than a letter from home, and though most of them certainly correspond with their families, they also enjoy hearing from other Americans as well. This year, more than 200,000 servicemen and women will participate in the America Remembers Campaign, which delivers letters, packages, baked goods, and other precious reminders of home.

You can participate. The following are several addresses you can write to that guarantee your letter or package will reach our defenders of freedom at their lonely outposts. Please take the time to write them.

America Remembers the Army
c/o Commander
2nd ACR
Attn: S-5/PAO
APO New York, NY 09093

America Remembers 435th Tactical Air Wing
c/o 435th TAW
Rhein-Mein Air Base
APO New York, NY 09057

America Remembers U.S. Forces in Korea
c/o Chaplain
APO San Francisco, CA 96202

America Remembers the Forrestal (CV-59)
c/o Commander, Forrestal
(CV-59)
ATTN: PAO
FPO Miami, FL 34080-2730

America Remembers Enterprise (CVN-65)
c/o Commander Enterprise
(CVN-65)
ATTN: PAO
FPO San Francisco, CA 96636-2610

America Remembers the Marines
c/o Camp Foster USO
P.O. Box 743
FPO Seattle, WA 98774

Introduction

Earlier this year, I proudly accepted an invitation to deliver a speech at the Harvard Business School. Never having visited an Ivy League school, I wasn't quite sure what to expect. The audience of America's best and brightest took me completely by surprise—and damn near gave the faculty a collective heart attack—when they stood and cheered my concluding observation: "Some ideas are so stupid, only intellectuals can believe them."

I came to appreciate this truism about ten years ago when I first approached New York's publishing elite with my admittedly simple idea to create a series of address books. One by one, they peered down from their thrones, rejecting the idea as "far too simple," and suggesting that in this hurry-up world, only fools would be naive enough to write to people they didn't know.

Finally, Putnam saw its worth, and today, it is estimated over 1,500,000 letters have been successfully delivered, thanks to the best-selling series of address books.

I've heard from desperate medical patients who have received help from blood donors thanks to the book, from lost lovers reunited, from consumers battling and beating corporate villains, and, of course, from fans hearing from their heroes.

By the way, last year I visited the White House, and never in my life did I feel prouder than when I saw *The Address Book* on the desks in several executive offices.

Yes, the address book was a simple idea; an idea that works. But, how can you make it work for you?

How can you make sure the notable receives your letter? The number-one reason mail to notables is left unanswered is that it is addressed improperly and never reaches its intended destination. A letter addressed simply to "Barbra Streisand, Hollywood, California" will find its way only to the dead-letter file of the post office. The complete, accurate addresses in this book will get your mail to the offices, agents, studios, managers, or even homes of the addressees, and I have been unable to find one notable, no matter how busy or important, who doesn't personally read some of his or her mail—even the president of the United States. That doesn't mean notables read and answer every single piece, but it should offer encouragement to people who write to them.

Politicians have a standard rule of thumb: for every letter they receive, they estimate that one hundred people who didn't take the time to write are thinking the same thought as the letter expresses. So you can calculate the effect of your single letter by multiplying it by one hundred! And all entertainment figures keep a close watch on their mail. It is a real indication of what people are thinking and feeling. Often, the notable is surrounded by a small group of associates who tend to isolate the star from the public. Your letter helps break down this barrier. Amazing things have been accomplished with letters as long as they have the proper mailing address.

Here are several important things to remember in writing notables: always include a self-addressed stamped envelope. This is the single most important factor in writing a letter if you want a response. Because of the unusually high volume of mail notable people receive, anything you can do to make it easier for them to respond is going to work in your favor. Keep your letters short and to the point. Notables are usually extremely busy people, and long letters tend to be set aside for "future" consideration. For instance, if you want an autographed picture of your favorite TV personality, don't write three pages of prose to explain your request.

Make your letter as easy to read as possible. This means type it or, at the very least, handwrite it very neatly. Avoid crayons, markers, or even pencils. And don't forget to leave some margins on the paper.

And, be sure to include your name and address (even on all materials that you include with your letter) in the event the materials are separated from your letter. You would be amazed how many people write letters without return addresses and then wonder why they never hear from the person to whom they wrote.

Never send food to notables. Due to spoilage and security matters, it cannot be eaten anyway. (Would you eat a box of homemade brownies given to you by a total stranger?) If you send gifts, don't wrap them in large boxes with yards of paper, string, and tape around them. (They may not have a crowbar on hand.) Again, don't forget to include your name and address on all material you send. Of course, don't send—or ask for—money.

In writing to corporation heads, remember most of them rose to their lofty positions because they were better problem-solvers than their company peers. Good corporation heads are zealous about finding solutions to written complaints (especially if you have sent copies of your complaint letters to appropriate consumer organizations). A recent survey of corporation heads showed that 88 percent of all letters of complaint were resolved. Therefore, the old adage, "When you have a problem, go to the top," appears to be accurate. Likewise, corporation executives greatly appreciate hearing good news (satisfaction, extra service, helpful employees, and so forth). (See *The Corporate Address Book: The Complete Directory to Who's Who and What's What in American Business Today,* Perigee Books, 1987.)

But nowhere is it written that mail should only be filled with praise and congratulations. You may enjoy shaking a fist at your favorite villain, so I have included infamous people in my book.

Most people are usually very kind and sincere in their letters. They write what they would say or ask if they had the opportunity to do so in person. This is especially true of children, who are extremely honest. On the other hand, infamous people and others who are out of favor with the public predictably receive hostile and angry letters.

Most of the people, famous and infamous, listed in *The Address Book* are movers and shakers, and thus highly transient, changing their addresses far more often than the average person. Their mail is usually forwarded to them, but occasionally a letter may be returned to the sender. If this should happen to your letter, first check to make sure that you have copied the address correctly. If you wish to locate another address for the person to whom you are writing, begin your search by writing to him or her in care of the company or association with which they may have been most recently associated. For example, if a musician or singer has last recorded an album with a specific record company, write in care of that company; a sports figure might be contacted through the last team he or she was associated with; an author through his most recent publisher; and so forth.

According to 1987 statistics, about 90 million pieces of mail land in the dead-letter pile because the carrier couldn't make out the address, so write clearly.

Remember, *a person who writes to another makes more impact than ten thousand who are silent.*

—Michael Levine
Los Angeles, CA

A

**Aames, Willie
(William Upton)**
113 N. Robertson Blvd.
Los Angeles, CA 90048
Actor

Aaron, Betsy
c/o CBS News
524 W. 57th St.
New York, NY 10019
Television journalist

**Aaron, Hank
(Henry)**
c/o Atlanta Braves
P.O. Box 4064
Atlanta, GA 30302
Baseball homerun king

Abba
Box 26072, S-100 41
Stockholm, Sweden
Pop group

Abbado, Claudio
Piazzetta Bosil
20121 Milan, Italy
Classical conductor

Abbott, George
1270 6th Ave.
New York, NY 10020
Broadway producer

Abbott, Jim
c/o California Angels
2000 State College Blvd.
Anaheim, CA 92806
Baseball pitcher

Abbott, Robert Tucker, Dr.
c/o American Malacologists
P.O. Box 2255
Melbourne, FL 32901
Zoologist

**Abbott and Costello Fan
    Club**
P.O. Box 262
Carteret, NJ 07008
Billy Wolfe, president

Abbott Laboratories
Robert A. Schoellhorn, chairman
Abbott Park Rt. 137
North Chicago, IL 60064
Drug manufacturer

**ABC, Inc.
(American Broadcasting
    Companies)**
77 W. 66th St.
New York, NY 10023
John B. Sias, president

Abdul, Paula
9830 Wilshire Blvd.
Beverly Hills, CA 90212
Singer/dancer/choreographer

**Abdul-Jabbar, Kareem
(Lew Alcindor)**
1875 Century Park E. (#1200)
Los Angeles, CA 90067
All-time basketball scorer

Abe, Mitsuyuki
Kyoto University Radiology
Dept.
Kawahara-cho, Shogoin, Sakyo-
ku
Kyoto 606, Japan
Radiology expert

A Better Chance
Charles K. Gleason, vice
president
419 Boylston St.
Boston, MA 02116
Recruits minorities for schools

Abraham, F. Murray
9301 Wilshire Blvd. (#312)
Beverly Hills, CA 90210
Actor

Abramovitz, Max
930 5th Ave.
New York, NY 10021
Architect

**Academy of Motion Picture
Arts & Sciences**
8949 Wilshire Blvd.
Beverly Hills, CA 90211
Presents Academy Awards

Accuracy In Media
Reed Irvine, chairman
1275 K Street NW.
Washington, DC 20005
Media watchdogs

AC/DC
11 Leonminster Rd., Morden
Surrey SM4 England
Rock band

Ace Hardware Corp.
2200 Kensington Court
Oak Brook, IL 60521
Theodore Costoff, chairman

Acid Rain Foundation
1410 Varsity Dr.
Raleigh, NC 27606
Dr. Harriet S. Stubbs, executive
director

Acme Machine Co.
2901 Fremont Ave. S.
Minneapolis, MN 55408
Carl A. Carlson, chairman

A.C. Nielsen
N. Eugene Harden, president
Nielsen Plaza
Northbrook, IL 60062
Television ratings company

ACT-UP
Larry Kramer, founder
496-A Hudson St. (#64)
New York, NY 10014
*AIDS Coalition To Unleash
Power*

**Actors and Others for
Animals**
Earl Holliman, president
5510 Cahuenga Blvd.
N. Hollywood, CA 91601
Animal rights group

Acuff, Roy
2510 Franklin Rd.
Nashville, TN 37204
Country singer

Adams, Cindy
c/o N.Y. Post
210 South St.
New York, NY 10002
Entertainment columnist

**Adams, Don
(Yarmy)**
P.O. Box 1228
Aspen, CO 81611
Agent 86 on "Get Smart"

**Adams, Richard Newbold,
Dr.**
University of Texas
Department of Anthropology
Austin, TX 78712
Anthropologist

Adjani, Isabelle
c/o Phonogram
89 Boulevard Auguste Blanqui
75013 Paris, France
Actress

**Adler, Larry
(Lawrence Cecil)**
c/o Bakewell
118 Tottenham Court Rd.
London W1 England
Harmonica player

Adler, Mortimer J.
Inst. for Philosophical Research
101 E. Ontario St.
Chicago, IL 60611
Philosopher

Adoptees in Search
P.O. Box 41016
Bethesda, MD 20814
Ronald P. Shepard, secretary

Advanced Micro Devices
901 Thompson Pl.
Sunnyvale, CA 94086
W.J. Sanders III, chairman

Advocate, The
Robert McQueen/Gerry Kroll,
editors
P.O. Box 4371
Los Angeles, CA 90078
National gay newsmagazine

Aerosmith
P.O. Box 4668
San Francisco, CA 94101
Fan club for rock group

Aetna Life and Casualty Co.
151 Farmington Ave.
Hartford, CT 06156
James T. Lynn, chairman

**Afghan Freedom Fighters
Fund**
P.O. Box 693
Boulder, CO 80306

Afghanistan Embassy
2341 Wyoming Ave. NW.
Washington, DC 20008
Alishah Masood, chargé d'affairs

AFL-CIO
Lane Kirkland, president
815 16th St. NW.
Washington, DC 20006
Union

African Methodist Episcopal Zion Church
8605 Caswell Ct.
Raleigh, NC 27612
William Milton Smith, senior bishop

A Frog From Wisconsin
c/o Hall
138 Frog Hollow Rd.
Churchville, PA 18966
Contortionist

AFS Intercultural Programs
William M. Dyal, Jr., president
313 E. 43rd St.
New York, NY 10017
Student exchange programs

Aga Khan IV
Aiglemont, Gouvieux
Chantilly, France
Muslim religious leader

Agassi, Andre
c/o Int. Managment Group
One Erieview Plaza
Cleveland, OH 44114
Tennis star

Agnos, Art
400 Van Ness Ave. (#200)
San Francisco, CA 94102
Mayor of San Francisco

Ahenakew, David Frederick
Assembly of First Nations
222 Queen St.
Ottawa, ON Canada
KIP 5V9
National Indian chief

Aiello, Danny
10000 Santa Monica Blvd. (#305)
Los Angeles, CA 90067
Actor

Aikman, Troy
c/o Dallas Cowboys
One Cowboys Parkway
Irving, TX 75063
Football quarterback

Aircraft Owners and Pilots Assoc.
421 Aviation Way
Frederick, MD 21701
John Baker, president

Akihito
The Imperial Palace
1-1 Chiyoda-ku
Tokyo, Japan
Emperor of Japan

Al-Anon Family Group
P.O. Box 862
Midtown Station
New York, NY 10018
Alcoholics self-help group

Al-Assad, Hafez
Office of the President
Damascus, Syria
President of Syria

Alabama
818 19th Ave. South
Nashville, TN 37203
Country music group

Alabama Space and Rocket Center
Tranquility Base
Huntsville, AL 35807
Edward O. Buckbee, director

Albano, Captain Lou
P.O. Box 3859
Stamford, CT 06905
Professional wrestler

Albee, Edward
14 Harrison St.
New York, NY 10013
Playwright

Albert, Eddie
(Edward Albert Heimberger)
9000 Sunset Blvd. (#1200)
Los Angeles, CA 90069
Actor

Albert, Marv
c/o NBC Sports
30 Rockefeller Plaza (#720F)
New York, NY 10112
Sportscaster

Albert, Prince
Palais de Monaco
Boite Postal 518
98015 Monte Carlo, Monaco
Crown Prince of Monaco

Alcoholics Anonymous
P.O. Box 459
Grand Central Station
New York, NY 10017
John Bragg, general manager

Alcott, Amy Strum
1250 Shoreline Dr. (#200)
Sugar Land, TX 77478
Golfer

Alda, Alan
(Alphonso D'Abruzzo)
100 Universal City Plaza (#507)
Universal City, CA 91608
Actor

Aldredge, Theoni Vachliotis
890 Broadway
New York, NY 10003
Fashion designer

Alexander, Jane
(Quigley)
1350 6th Ave.
New York, NY 10019
Actress

Alexander, Shana
c/o Doubleday
245 Park Ave.
New York, NY 10017
Author/social commentator

Alexander Graham Bell
Assoc. for the Deaf
3417 Volta Place NW.
Washington, DC 20007

Alf
8660 Hayden Pl.
Culver City, CA 90230
Alien television star

Ali, Muhammad
(Cassius Marcellus Clay)
P.O. Box 187
Berrien Springs, MI 49103
Boxing legend

Allen, Betty
Harlem School of the Arts
645 St. Nicholas Ave.
New York, NY 10030
Mezzo-soprano

Allen, Debbie
c/o "A Different World"
4024 Radford (Bldg. 4)
Studio City, CA 91604
Actress/director/dancer

17

Allen, Jay Presson
c/o Lewis Allen Productions
1500 Broadway
New York, NY 10036
Playwright

Allen, Karen
151 El Camino Dr.
Beverly Hills, CA 90212
Actress

Allen, Marcus
c/o L.A. Raiders
332 Center St.
El Segundo, CA 90245
Football player

Allen, Mel
Yankee Stadium
Bronx, NY 10451
Sportscaster

**Allen, Steve (Stephen
Valentine Patrick
William)**
15201 Burbank Blvd.
Van Nuys, CA 91411
Humorist/songwriter/author

**Allen, Woody
(Allen Konigsberg)**
c/o Rollins/Joffe
130 W. 57th St.
New York, NY 10019
Film director/actor/writer

Alley, Kirstie
10390 Santa Monica Blvd. (#310)
Los Angeles, CA 90025
"Cheers" actress

Allied-Signal Inc.
Columbia Rd. & Park Ave.
Morristown, NJ 07962
Edward L. Hennessy, CEO

Allred, Gloria
6380 Wilshire Blvd. (#1404)
Los Angeles, CA 90048
Feminist attorney

Allstate Insurance Co.
Allstate Plaza
Northbrook, IL 60062
Donald F. Craib, Jr., chairman

Alonso, Maria Conchita
8500 Wilshire Blvd. (#801)
Beverly Hills, CA 90211
Actress

Alpern, Mathew, Dr.
3545 Woodland Rd.
Ann Arbor, MI 48104
Physiological optician

Alpert, Herb
1416 N. La Brea Ave.
Hollywood, CA 90028
Musician

Alpo Petfoods
P.O. Box 2187
Allentown, PA 18001
Franklin W. Krum, CEO

Alt, Carol
8500 Melrose Ave. (#210)
Los Angeles, CA 90069
Model

Altman, Jeff
151 El Camino Dr.
Beverly Hills, CA 90212
Comedian

Altman, Robert B.
502 Park Ave. (15G)
New York, NY 10022
Film director

**Aluminum Co. of America
(ALCOA)**
1501 Alcoa Bldg.
Pittsburgh, PA 15219
Paul H. O'Neill, CEO

Alzado, Lyle
151 El Camino Dr.
Beverly Hills, CA 90212
Former football star

**Alzheimer's Disease and
Related Disorders Assoc.**
70 E. Lake St.
Chicago, IL 60601

Amana Refrigeration
Amana, IA 52204
Henry J. Meyer, CEO

**Amateur Athletic Union
(AAU)**
3400 W. 86th St.
Indianapolis, IN 46268

**Amateur Softball
Association**
2801 N.E. 50th St.
Oklahoma City, OK 73111

Ambler, Eric
c/o Campbell, Thomson &
McLaughlin
31 Newington Green
London NI6 9PY England
Author

AMC Theatres
S.H. Durwood, CEO
106 W. 14th St.
Kansas City, MO 64105
Movie theater company

**Ameche, Don
(Dominic Felix)**
2121 Ave. of the Stars
Los Angeles, CA 90067
Actor

America's Cup
Sail America
1904 Hotel Circle North
San Diego, CA 92108

America's Most Wanted
c/o 20th Century Fox TV
P.O. Box 900
Beverly Hills, CA 90201
Crime hunt television series

American Airlines
P.O. Box 619616
Dallas, TX 75261
Robert L. Crandall, CEO

**American Association for
Marriage and Family
Therapy**
1717 K Street NW. (#407)
Washington, DC 20006
Bonnie Hilton Green,
spokesperson

**American Association of
Individual Investors**
625 N. Michigan Ave. (#1900)
Chicago, IL 60611
James B. Cloonan, president

American Association of Retired Persons (AARP)
1909 K St. NW.
Washington, DC 20049

American Atheists
P.O. Box 140195
Austin, TX 78714
Dr. Madalyn Murray O'Hair, founder

American Automobile Association (AAA)
8111 Gatehouse Rd.
Falls Church, VA 22047
Richard F. Hebert, managing director

American Bandstand Memory Club
c/o David Fress
P.O. Box 131
Adamstown, PA 19501
Fan club

American Baptist Association
P.O. Box 1050
Texarkana, TX 75504
Ken Ashlock, president

American Bar Association (ABA)
750 N. Lake Shore Dr.
Chicago, IL 60611
Jill Wine-Banks, executive vice president

American Bar Assoication Center for Professional Responsibility
750 N. Lake Shore Dr.
Chicago, IL 60611
Jeanne P. Gray, director

American Battle Monuments Commission
200 Massachusetts Ave. NW.
Washington, DC 20314
Gen. Andrew J. Goodpaster, chairman

American Bible Society
1865 Broadway
New York, NY 10023
James Wood, president

American Cancer Society
90 Park Ave.
New York, NY 10017

American Chiropractic Association
1701 Clarendon Blvd.
Arlington, VA 22209
Ms. Leslie L. Frank, spokesperson

American Express Co.
American Express Plaza
New York, NY 10004
James D. Robinson III, chairman

American Fed. of Radio and Television Artists (AFTRA)
260 Madison Ave.
New York, NY 10016
Performers' union

American Film Institute
2021 N. Western Ave.
Los Angeles, CA 90027
Jean Firstenberg, director

**American Friends Service
Committee**
Paul E. Brink, director
1501 Cherry St.
Philadelphia, PA 19102
Quaker peace organization

American Fur Industry
363 7th Ave. (7th floor)
New York, NY 10001
Sandra Blye, executive vice
president

American Heart Association
7320 Greenville Ave.
Dallas, TX 75231

American Hockey League
218 Memorial Ave.
West Springfield, MA 01089
Gordon C. Anziano, vice
president

**American Immigration
Control Foundation**
P.O. Box 525
Monterey, VA 24465
John C. Vinson, president

**American Indian
Scholarships**
4520 Montgomery Blvd. NE
(#1-B)
Albuquerque, NM 87109
Lorraine P. Edmo, president

American Ireland Fund
150 Federal St. 25th floor
Boston, MA 02110
William J. McNally, executive
director

**American Kennel Club
(AKC)**
51 Madison Ave.
New York, NY 10010
Louis Auslander, chairman

American Legion
700 N. Pennsylvania St.
Indianapolis, IN 46204

American Lung Association
1740 Broadway
New York, NY 10019

**American Medical
Association
(AMA)**
535 N. Dearborn St.
Chicago, IL 60610
William C. Garrett, executive
vice president

**American Museum of
Historial Documents**
3601 W. Sahara Ave., Promenade
Las Vegas, NV 89102

**American Museum of
Natural History**
Central Park West at 79th St.
New York, NY 10024
Robert G. Goelet, president

American Numismatic Society
Leslie A. Elam, CEO
Broadway and 155th St.
New York, NY 10032
Coin collectors

American Philatelic Society
P.O. Box 8000
State College, PA 16803
Stamp collectors

American Political Items Collectors
P.O. Box 340339
San Antonio, TX 78234
Joseph D. Hayes, president

American Red Cross
150 Amsterdam Ave.
New York, NY 10023
Delbert C. Staley, chairman

American Smokers Alliance
Dave Brenton, president
3401 West End Ave. (#560)
Nashville, TN 37203
Defends rights of smokers

American Society of Dowsers
Brainerd St.
Danville, VT 05828

American Society of Inventors
134 Narbeth Ave. (#101)
Narberth, PA 19072

American Sports Collectibles
P.O. Box 475
Horsham, PA 19044
Buck Lane, president

American Stock Exchange
86 Trinity Pl.
New York, NY 10006
Arthur Levitt, Jr., chairman

American Telephone & Telegraph Co. (AT&T)
550 Madison Ave.
New York, NY 10022
C.L. Brown, CEO

American Youth Soccer Organization (AYSO)
5403 W. 138th St.
Hawthorne, CA 90250

Americans for Decency
P.O. Box 218
Staten Island, NY 10302
Paul J. Gangemi, founder

Amin, Idi
Manama, Bahrain
Ex-dictator of Uganda

Amis, Kingsley
c/o Jonathan Clowes and Co.
22 Prince Albert Rd.
London NW1 England
Author

Amis, Martin Louis
c/o A.D. Peters
10 Buckingham St.
London WC2 England
Novelist

Amnesty International
John G. Healy, executive director
322 8th Ave.
New York, NY 10001
Worldwide justice organization

Amoco Corp.
200 E. Randolph Dr.
Chicago, IL 60601
Richard M. Morrow, CEO

Amory, Cleveland
200 W. 57th St.
New York, NY 10019
Author/animal rights activist

Amway Corp.
7575 E. Fulton Rd.
Ada, MI 49301
Richard De Vos, president

AMTRAK
W. Grayham Claytor, Jr.,
  chairman
60 Massachusetts Ave. NE.
Washington, DC 80002
American train corporation

Anderson, DuWayne Marlo
c/o Texas A&M University
305 E. Bizzell Hall
College Station, TX 77843
Polar scientist

Anderson, Harry
9830 Wilshire Blvd.
Beverly Hills, CA 90212
Actor/comedian/magician

Anderson, Ivan Delos
1060 Flamingo Rd.
Laguna Beach, CA 92651
*Sells art via Home Shopping
  Network*

Anderson, Jack
1531 P Street NW.
Washington, DC 20005
Investigative journalist

Anderson, Laurie
c/o Original Artists
129 W. 69th St.
New York, NY 10023
Multi-media artist

Anderson, Loni
151 El Camino Dr.
Beverly Hills, CA 90212
Actress

Anderson, Louie
8033 Sunset Blvd. (#605)
Los Angeles, CA 90046
Comedian

**Anderson, Lynn
(Rene)**
818 18th Ave. South
Nashville, TN 37203
Country singer

Anderson, Marian
40 W. 57th St.
New York, NY 10019
Opera singer

**Anderson, Sparky
(George Lee)**
c/o Detroit Tigers
Tiger Stadium
Detroit, MI 48126
Baseball manager

Anderson, Theodore Wilbur
Dept. of Statistics, Sequoia Hall
Stanford, CA 94305
Statistician

**Andre the Giant
(Roussimoff)**
P.O. Box 3859
Stamford, CT 06905
Professional wrestler

Andrea Doria Search Team
10 E. 63rd St.
New York, NY 10021

Andretti, Mario
53 Victory Ln.
Nazareth, PA 18064
Racecar driver

**HRH The Prince Andrew
(Albert Christian Edward)**
Buckingham Palace
London SW1 England
The duke of York

Andrews, Bart
7510 Sunset Blvd. (#100)
Los Angeles, CA 90046
"I Love Lucy" expert

**Andrews, Julie
(Julia Wells)**
11777 San Vicente Blvd. (#501)
Los Angeles, CA 90049
Actress/singer

Andrews, V.C.
c/o Pocket Books
1230 6th Ave.
New York, NY 10020
Science fiction author

Andrus, Cecil D.
State Capitol
Boise, ID 83720
Governor of Idaho

**Andy Griffith Show Rerun
Watchers**
27 Music Sq. E. (#146)
Nashville, TN 37202
James H. Clark, president

Angelou, Maya
c/o Random House
201 E. 50th St.
New York, NY 10017
Author/poet

Angelyne
7764 Hollywood Blvd. (#2)
Los Angeles, CA 90046
Celebrity celebrity

**Anglo American Corp. of
South Africa, Ltd.**
P.O. Box 61587
Marshalltown, RSA 2107
Gavin W.H. Relly, chairman

**Anheuser-Busch Companies,
Inc.**
August A. Busch III, chairman
One Busch Pl.
St. Louis, MO 63118-1852
Brewmeister

Animal Rights International
P.O. Box 214
Planetarium Station
New York, NY 10024
Henry Spira, spokesperson

Anka, Paul
P.O. Box 100
Carmel, CA 93921
Singer

**Ann-Margret
(Olsson)**
9830 Wilshire Blvd.
Beverly Hills, CA 90212
Actress

HRH The Princess Anne
(Elizabeth Alice Louise)
Gatcombe Park
Gloucestershire, England
Daughter of Queen Elizabeth II

Annenberg, Walter
P.O. Box 98
Rancho Mirage, CA 92270
Publishing executive

Annesley, Hugh
Chief Constable
Brooklyn, Knock Rd.
Belfast, Northern Ireland
Royal Ulster Constabulary

Anorexics and Bulimics
Anonymous
4500 E. Pacific Coast Hwy.
(#330)
Long Beach, CA 90804
Dr. Adel A. Eldahmy, founder

Another World Viewer
Alliance
Suzanne Leonard, president
71 Berry St.
Pittsburgh, PA 15205
Soap opera fan club

Ant, Adam
(Stuart Goddard)
45-53 Sinclair Rd.
London W14 England
Singer/actor

Antekeier, Kristopher
7510 Sunset Blvd. (#100)
Los Angeles, CA 90046
"Greatest Show on Earth"
ringmaster

Anton, Susan
151 El Camino Dr.
Beverly Hills, CA 90212
Actress/singer

Antonioni, Michelangelo
Via Vincenzo Tiberio 18
00191 Rome, Italy
Film director

Apple Computer
20525 Mariana Ave.
Cupertino, CA 95104
John Sculley, president

Applegate, Christina
c/o "Married . . . With Children"
1438 N. Gower St.
Los Angeles, CA 90028
Actress

Aquino, Corazon Cojuangco
Malacanang Palace, Metro
Manila, Philippines
President of the Philippines

Arad, Moshe
3541 International Dr. NW.
Washington, DC 20008
Israeli ambassador to U.S.

Arafat, Yassir
(Muhammad Abed Ar'ouf)
Palais Essasada La Marsa
Tunis, Tunisia
Palestinian leader

Archer, Jeffrey Howard
c/o Pocket Books
1230 6th Ave.
New York, NY 10020
Author/former British politician

Archer, Jules
404 High St.
Santa Cruz, CA 95060
Current affairs author

Archerd, Army
c/o Daily Variety
5760 Wilshire Blvd.
Los Angeles, CA 90036
Hollywood journalist

Arens, Moshe
49 Hagderat
Savyon, Israel
Israeli politician

Ariyan, Stephen, Dr.
Yale University
New Haven, CT 06510
Plastic surgeon

Arizona Reenactors
  Association
Terrence C. Leavey, advisor
4758 West Caron St.
Glendale, AZ 85302
Reenacts Civil War battles

Arkoff, Samuel Z.
9200 Sunset Blvd. (PH 3)
Los Angeles, CA 90069
Film producer

Arledge, Roone
c/o ABC
1330 6th Ave.
New York, NY 10019
Television executive

Armani, Giorgio
650 5th Ave.
New York, NY 10019
Fashion designer

Armatrading, Joan
c/o Running Dog Management
27 Queensdale Pl.
London W11 England
Jazz/Pop singer

Armchair Detective
  Magazine
129 W. 56th St.
New York, NY 10019
Michael Seidman, publisher

Armenian Church of
  America
13010 Hathaway Dr.
Wheaton, MD 20906
Bishops T. Manoogian/V.
  Hovsepian

Armitage, Karole
225 Lafayette St. (#1102)
New York, NY 10012
Dancer/choreographer

Armour, Richard
894 W. Harrison Ave.
Claremont, CA 91711
Humorist

Armstrong, Neil
31 N. Broadway
Lebanon, OH 45036
First man to walk on the moon

Arnaz, Desi, Jr.
P.O. Box 2000
Ojai, CA 93023
Actor

Arnaz, Lucie Desiree
9255 Sunset Blvd. (#1115)
Los Angeles, CA 90069
Actress

Arness, James
(Aurness)
P.O. Box 49004
Los Angeles, CA 90049
"Gunsmoke" actor

Arnold, Danny
9200 Sunset Blvd. (#920)
Los Angeles, CA 90069
Television producer

Arpel, Adrien
521 5th Ave.
New York, NY 10175
Cosmetics queen

Arquette, Rosanna
9830 Wilshire Blvd.
Beverly Hills, CA 90212
Actress

Arrow, Kenneth
(Joseph)
Dept. of Economics, Stanford
   Univ.
Stanford, CA 94305
Economist

Art and Antiques
89 5th Ave.
New York, NY 10003
Jefferey Schaire, editor

Art Institute of Chicago
Michigan Ave. & Adams St.
Chicago, IL 60603
Bowen Blair, president

Artforum Magazine
65 Bleecker St.
New York, NY 10012
Ida Panicelli, editor

Arthur, Beatrice
(Bernice Frankel)
151 El Camino Dr.
Beverly Hills, CA 90212
Actress

Arts & Entertainment Cable
   Network
5455 Wilshire Blvd. (#1715)
Los Angeles, CA 90036

Arum, Bob
(Robert)
919 Third Ave.
New York, NY 10022
Boxing promoter

As the World Turns Fan
   Club
212 Oriole Dr.
Montgomery, NY 12549
Deanne Turco, executive officer

Ash, Mary Kay Wagner
8787 Stemmons Freeway
Dallas, TX 75247
Cosmetics leader

Ashe, Arthur Robert
c/o ProServ
888 17th St. NW.
Washington, DC 20006
Former tennis star

Ashkenazy, Vladimir
c/o ICM
40 W. 57th St.
New York, NY 10019
Classical pianist

Ashley, Elizabeth
(Cole)
151 El Camino Dr.
Beverly Hills, CA 90212
Actress

Ashram, The
P.O. Box 8009
Calabasas, CA 91302
Spa

Asimov, Isaac
10 W. 66th St. (#33A)
New York, NY 10023
Author

Ask a Silly Question
Kathleen Conner, president
P.O. Box 1950
Hollywood, CA 90078
Research company

Aslett, Don
311 S. 5th Ave.
Pocatello, ID 83204
Home cleaning expert

Asner, Edward
10100 Santa Monica Blvd. (#700)
Los Angeles, CA 90210
Actor/activist

ASPCA (American Society for the Prevention of Cruelty to Animals)
441 E. 92nd St.
New York, NY 10128
John F. Kullberg, president

Aspin, Les
2336 Rayburn House Office Bldg.
Washington, DC 20515
Congressman from Wisconsin

Assante, Armand
RD #1, Box 561
Campbell Hall, NY 10916
Actor

Association for Retarded Citizens
2501 Avenue J
Arlington, TX 76006
V.K. Tashjian, president

Association for Voluntary Surgical Contraception
122 E. 42nd St.
New York, NY 10168

Association to Save Madonna From Nuclear War
228 McCormick (#3)
Cincinnati, OH 45219
Demands nuke-free zone for Madonna

Astin, Patty Duke
(Anna Marie)
9100 Sunset Blvd. (#300)
Los Angeles, CA 90069
Actress

Astley, Rick
c/o David Anthony
649 Knutsford Rd., Latchford
Warrington,
Cheshire WA4 1JJ England
Pop singer

Astor, Brooke
c/o Vincent Astor Foundation
405 Park Ave.
New York, NY 10022
Socialite

Atari Corp.
1196 Borregas Ave.
Sunnyvale, CA 94088
Jack and Sam Tramiel, chairmen

Atlanta Braves
P.O. Box 4064
Atlanta, GA 30302
Ted Turner, owner

Atlanta Falcons
Suwanee Rd.
Suwanee, GA 30174
Rankin M. Smith, chairman

Atlanta Hawks
One CNN Center, South Tower
(#405)
Atlanta, GA 30303
Stan Kasten, general manager

Atlantic Magazine
8 Arlington St.
Boston, MA 02216
William Whitworth, editor

**Atlantic Richfield Co.
(ARCO)**
515 S. Flower St.
Los Angeles, CA 90071
Lowdrick M. Cook, CEO

A Touch of Days
Sally Ann Morris, president
116 Boston Ave.
North Arlington, NJ 07032
"Days Of Our Lives" fan club

**Attenborough, Richard
(Samuel), Sir**
Old Friars
Beaver Lodge, Richmond Green
Surrey, England
Film director/actor

Atwood, Margaret Eleanor
c/o Oxford University Press
70 Wynford Dr.
Don Mills, ON Canada M3C 1J9
Author

Au Pair in America
c/o Amer. Inst. for Foreign
Study
102 Greenwich Ave.
Greenwich, CT 06830
Lauren Kratouil, director

AuCoin, Les
2159 Rayburn House Office Bldg.
Washington, DC 20515
Congressman from Oregon

Audubon Magazine
950 3rd Ave.
New York, NY 10022
Les Line, editor

Audubon Society
P.O. Box 2666
Boulder, CO 80322

**Auerbach, Red
(Arnold Jacob)**
c/o Boston Celtics
150 Causeway St.
Boston, MA 02114
Basketball executive/coach

Austin, Tracy Ann
c/o Advantage International
1025 Thomas Jefferson NW.
Washington, DC 20007
Tennis star

Australian Embassy
1601 Massachusetts Ave. NW.
Washington, DC 20036
F. Rawdon Dalrymple,
ambassador

Auto Racing Digest
990 Grove St.
Evanston, IL 60201
Michael Herbert, editor

Autry, Gene
(Orvon)
P.O. Box 710
Los Angeles, CA 90078
Singer/baseball executive

Avalon, Frankie
(Avallone)
3800 Barham Blvd. (#303)
Los Angeles, CA 90068
Singer

Avedon, Richard
407 E. 75th St.
New York, NY 10021
Photographer

Avengers, The
114 Dartmouth St.
Burslem, Stoke-on-Trent
Staffordshire ST6 1HE England
Dave Rogers, fan club pres.

Aviado, Domingo M., Dr.
152 Parsonage Hill Rd.
Short Hills, NJ 07078
Pharmacologist/toxicologist

Avildsen, John Guilbert
200 E. 90th St. (#27D)
New York, NY 10128
Film director

Avis, Inc.
900 Old Country Rd.
Garden City, NY 11530
Joseph V. Vittoria, CEO

Avon Books
105 Madison Ave.
New York, NY 10016
Carolyn Reidy, president

Avon Products
9 W. 57th St.
New York, NY 10019
James E. Preston, CEO

Axthelm, Pete
c/o NBC Sports
30 Rockefeller Plaza
New York, NY 10112
Sportcaster

Axton, Hoyt
3135 Cedarwood Dr. (#614)
Tahoe City, CA 95730
Country singer/actor

Aykroyd, Daniel Edward
9200 Sunset Blvd. (#428)
Los Angeles, CA 90069
Actor

Azenberg, Emanuel
165 W. 46th St.
New York, NY 10036
Theatrical producer

B

Babilonia, Tai
8730 Sunset Blvd. (6th floor)
Los Angeles, CA 90069
Ice skating star

Bacall, Lauren
(Betty Joan Perske)
1350 6th Ave.
New York, NY 10019
Actress

Bacardi Corp.
P.O. Box G 3549
San Juan, Puerto Rico 00936
Manuel Luis del Valle, CEO

Back Valley Public Library
Dot Byrd, librarian
Oliver Springs, TN 37840
World's smallest library

Backpacker Magazine
33 E. Minor St.
Emmaus, PA 18098
John Viehman, editor

Backstage Magazine
330 W. 42nd St.
New York, NY 10036
Richard Mueller, editor

Bacon, Kevin
8436 W. 3rd St. (#650)
Los Angeles, CA 90048
Actor

Bad Attitude Magazine
The Baroness, editor
P.O. Box 110
Cambridge, MA 02139
Lesbian sex magazine

Baez, Joan
P.O. Box 1026
Menlo Park, CA 94025
Folk singer

Bailey, F. Lee
109 State St.
Boston, MA 02109
Attorney

Bailey, Frederick Eugene,
Jr., Dr.
c/o Union Carbide Corp.
Tech Center
South Charleston, WV 25303
Polymer scientist

Baio, Scott
P.O. Box 5617
Beverly Hills, CA 90210
Actor

Bajor, Jim
P.O. Box 090309
Rochester Hills, MI 48309
New age musician

Baker, Anita
c/o BNB
9545 Wilshire Blvd.
Beverly Hills, CA 90212
Jazz/pop singer

Baker, James Addison, III
2201 C Street NW.
Washington, DC 20520
Secretary of State

Baker, R. Robinson, Dr.
Johns Hopkins Hospital
Baltimore, MD 21205
Thoracic cancer surgeon

Baker Street Journal
Phillip Shreffler, editor
Fordham University Box L
Bronx, NY 10458
Sherlock Holmes magazine

Bakker, Jim
(James Orsen)
c/o Federal Medical Center
2110 Center St. E.
Rochester, MN 55904
Disgraced televangelist

Bakker, Tammy Faye
  LaValley
P.O. Box 790788
Orlando, FL 32869
Wife of Jim Bakker

Balch, Charles M., Dr.
Anderson Hospital & Tumor
  Inst.
Houston, TX 77025
Skin cancer surgeon

Bald-Headed Men of
  America
P.O. Box 1466
Morehead City, NC 28557
John T. Capps, III, founder

Baldrige, Letitia
c/o Rawson Associates
866 3rd Ave.
New York, NY 10022
Etiquette expert

Baldwin, Alec
14755 Ventura Blvd. (#1-170)
Sherman Oaks, CA 91403
Actor

Baldwin, David S., Dr.
20 E. 68th St.
New York, NY 10021
Kidney specialist

Baldwin Piano & Organ Co.
1801 Gilbert Ave.
Cincinnati, OH 45202
Harold Smith, president

Ballantine/Fawcett/Ivy
  Books
201 E. 50th St.
New York, NY 10022
Robert B. Wyatt/Leona Nevler,
  editors

Ballard, Robert Duane
Woods Hole Oceanographic
  Institute
Woods Hole Road
Woods Hole, MA 02543
Discoverer of the Titanic

Ballroom Dancing Times
Clerkenwell Green
London EC1R OBE England
Mary Clark, editor

Bally Manufacturing Corp.
8700 W. Bryn Mawr
Chicago, IL 60631
Robert E. Mullane, CEO

Baltimore Orioles
Memorial Stadium
Baltimore, MD 21218
Roland Hemond, general
    manager

Balukas, Jean
c/o Billiards Congress
14 S. Linn St.
Iowa City, IA 52240
Women's pool champ

Bananarama
40 Weymouth St.
London W1 England
Pop group

Bancroft, Ann
(Anna Maria Italiano)
P.O. Box 900
Beverly Hills, CA 90213
Actress

Bangles, The
4455 Torrance Blvd.
Torrance, CA 90503
Rock band fan club

Bangs, Richard
c/o SOBEK
P.O. Box 7007
Angels Camp, CA 95222
Adventurer

Bani-Sadr, Abolhassan
Auvers-Sur-Oise, France
Exiled Iranian leader

Bank of America
555 California St.
San Francisco, CA 94104
Richard M. Rosenberg, CEO

Banks, Ernie
P.O. Box 24302
Los Angeles, CA 90024
Former baseball great

Bantam Books
666 5th Ave.
New York, NY 10103
Linda Grey, president

Baraka, Amiri
(Everett LeRoi Jones)
13 Belmont Ave.
Newark, NJ 07103
Author

Barbarians, The
(David/Peter Paul)
2210 Wilshire Blvd. (#726)
Santa Monica, CA 90403
Actors/bodybuilders

Barber, Red
3013 Brookmont Dr.
Tallahassee, FL 32312
Sportscaster

Barbie, Klaus
St. Joseph Prison
Lyons, France
Nazi war criminal

Barbie and Ken
5150 Rosecrans Ave.
Hawthorne, CA 90250
Doll and hunk

Bardis, Panos Demetrios, Dr.
University of Toledo
Bancroft St.
Toledo, OH 43606
Sociologist

Bardot, Brigitte (Camille Javal)
La Madrique, Aix-en-Provence
Saint Tropez, France
Actress

Barkin, Ellen
8899 Beverly Blvd.
Los Angeles, CA 90048
Actress

Barkley, Charles
c/o Philadelphia 76ers
P.O. Box 25040
Philadelphia, PA 19147
Basketball star

Barnard, Christiaan, Dr.
S. Cross Dr., Constantia,
Cape Town, Republic of South
   Africa
Heart surgeon

Barnes, Clive
45 W. 60th St. (#8A)
New York, NY 10023
Theater critic

Barnett, Arthur Doak
c/o Johns Hopkins University
Massachusetts Ave. NW.
Washington, DC 20036
China expert

Barr, Roseanne
8436 W. 3rd St. (#650)
Los Angeles, CA 90048
Comedienne/actress

Barrett, Ron
c/o National Lampoon
635 Madison Ave.
New York, NY 10022
Cartoonist

Barrett, Rona
P.O. Box 1410
Beverly Hills, CA 90213
Hollywood journalist

Barry, Lynda J.
c/o L.A. Weekly
P.O. Box 29905
Los Angeles, CA 90029
*"Ernie Pook's Comeek"
   cartoonist*

Barry, Marion Shepilou, Jr.
District Bldg.
14th and E Sts.
Washington, DC 20004
*Former mayor of Washington,
   D.C.*

Barrymore, Drew
3960 Laurel Canyon Blvd. (#159)
Studio City, CA 91604
Actress

Bartel, Paul
8899 Beverly Blvd.
Los Angeles, CA 90048
Film director

Bartender Magazine
P.O. Box 158
Liberty Corner, NJ 07938
Jaclyn W. Foley, editor

Barty, Billy John
1930 Century Park W. (#303)
Los Angeles, CA 90067
Actor/little people activist

Baryshnikov, Mikhail
9830 Wilshire Blvd.
Los Angeles, CA 90212
Ballet dancer/actor

Basil, Toni
9595 Wilshire Blvd. (#505)
Los Angeles, CA 90212
Musicvideo choreographer/singer

Basinger, Kim
P.O. Box 1305
Woodland Hills, CA 91364
Actress

Bass, Saul
7039 W. Sunset Blvd.
Los Angeles, CA 90028
Graphic designer/filmmaker

Bass N' Gal
Sugar Ferris, president
2007 Roosevelt
Arlington, TX 76013
Fisherwomen's organization

Bateman, Jason
P.O. Box 333
Woodland Hills, CA 91365
Actor

Bateman, Justine
3960 Laurel Canyon Blvd. (#193)
Studio City, CA 91604
Actress

Bateman, Robert McLellan
c/o Center Court
Venice, FL 34292
Painter of animal subjects

Battle, Kathleen
c/o Columbia Artists
165 W. 57th St.
New York, NY 10019
Opera soprano

Bauer, Steven
8033 Sunset Blvd. (#102)
Los Angeles, CA 90046
Actor

Bauer, William J.
U.S. Court of Appeal
Seventh Circuit
Chicago, Il 60604
Chief Judge

Baulieu, Etienne-Emile, Dr.
Hopital de Bicetre
94 Bicetre, France
Developer of RU-486, the "abortion pill"

Bayer USA
500 Grant St., One Mellon Ctr.
Pittsburgh, PA 15219
Konrod M. Weis, president

Bayh, Evan
State Capitol
Indianapolis, IN 46204
Governor of Indiana

Bazell, Robert
c/o NBC News
30 Rockefeller Plaza
New York, NY 10112
Science journalist

Beach Boys, The
101 Mesa Lane
Santa Barbara, CA 93109
Pop group

Beastie Boys, The
1750 N. Vine St.
Hollywood, CA 90028
Rappers

Beatrice/Hunt-Wesson Foods
55 E. Monroe St.
Chicago, IL 60603
Frederick B. Rentschler,
   president

Beatrix, Queen
(Wilhelmina Armgard)
Binnen Huf 19
The Hague 2513 AA, The
   Netherlands
Queen of The Netherlands

Beatts, Anne
555 W. 57th St. (#1230)
New York, NY 10019
Writer

Beatty, Warren
(Beaty)
1849 Sawtelle (#500)
Los Angeles, CA 90069
Actor

Becker, Boris
Nusslocher Strasse 51, 6906
   Leiman
Baden, Germany
Tennis star

Becker, Donald P., Dr.
UCLA School of Medicine
Los Angeles, CA 90024
Neurosurgeon

Bedelia, Bonnie
8899 Beverly Blvd.
Los Angeles, CA 90048
Actress

Bee Gees
(Barry, Maurice, Robin)
P.O. Box 8179
Miami Beach, FL 33139
Pop singers

Beene, Geoffrey
550 7th Ave.
New York, NY 10018
Fashion designer

Beer Can Collectors of
   America
747 Merus Court
Fenton, MO 63026
Marcia Bulterbaugh, president

Beer Drinkers of America
150 Paularino Ave.
Costa Mesa, CA 92626
Bill Schreiber, executive director

Begley, Ed, Jr.
8899 Beverly Blvd.
Los Angeles, CA 90048
Actor

Beilenson, Anthony C.
1025 Longworth House Office
  Bldg.
Washington, DC 20515
Congressman from California

Bela Lugosi Society
330 G St. SW
Ardmore, OK 73401
Graydon Rhodes, executive
  director

Belafonte, Harry
P.O. Box 1700
Ansonia Station
New York, NY 10023
Singer

Bell, George
c/o Toronto Blue Jays
Exhibition Stadium
Toronto, ON Canada
Baseball player

Belli, Melvin
3052 Pacific Ave.
San Francisco, CA 94115
Attorney

Bellisario, Donald P.
c/o Universal Studios
100 Universal City Plaza
Universal City, CA 91608
Television producer

Bellow, Saul
c/o Committee on Social Thought
1126 E. 59th St., U. of Chicago
Chicago, IL 60637
Novelist

Belushi, Jim
9830 Wilshire Blvd.
Beverly Hills, CA 90212
Actor

Belzer, Richard
151 El Camino Dr.
Beverly Hills, CA 90212
Comedian

**Ben and Jerry's Homemade
  Ice Cream**
P.O. Box 240
Waterbury, VT 05676
Ben Cohn/Jerry Greenfield

Bench, Johnny
P.O. Box 2486
Cincinnati, OH 45201
Former baseball great

Benetton, Luciano
Via Chiesa Ponzano 24
31050 Ponzano Veneto (TV)
Italy
Clothing manufacturer

Benihana
8685 NW. 53rd Terr.
Miami, FL 33166
R.H. Aoki, founder

Benitez, Jellybean
9830 Wilshire Blvd.
Beverly Hills, CA 90212
Music producer

Benjamin, Richard
222 N. Canon Dr. (#202)
Beverly Hills, CA 90210
Actor/film director

Benji
c/o Frank Inn
30227 Hasley Canyon Rd.
Castaic, CA 91384
Canine actor

Bennett, Tony
(Anthony Benedetto)
9000 Sunset Blvd. (12th floor)
Los Angeles, CA 90069
Singer

Bennett, William John
1600 Pennsylvania Ave. NW.
Washington, DC 20500
Director, National Drug Control
   Policy

Benoit, Joan
P.O. Box 1200
Portland, ME 04104
Marathon runner

Benton, Barbi
(Barbara Klein)
P.O. Box 7114
Pasadena, CA 91109
Celebrity

Benton, Robert
c/o ICM
40 W. 57th St.
New York, NY 10019
Film director/writer

Bentsen, Lloyd Millard, Jr.
708 Hart Bldg.
Washington, DC 20510
Senator from Texas

Berenger, Tom
P.O. Box 1842
Beaufort, SC 29901
Actor

Beresford, Bruce
151 El Camino Dr.
Beverly Hills, CA 90212
Film director

Berg, Paul, Dr.
Stanford University
School of Medicine
Stanford, CA 94305
Nobel Prize biochemist

Bergen, Candace
c/o Shukovsky/English
4000 Warner Blvd.
Burbank, CA 91522
Actress

Bergman, (Ernst) Ingmar
c/o Svensk Filmindustri
Kungsgatan 36
Stockholm, Sweden
Film director

Berkoff, Steven
9255 Sunset Blvd. (#515)
Los Angeles, CA 90069
Actor

Berkowitz, David
Sullivan Correctional Facility
Fallsburg, NY 12733
"Son of Sam" serial murderer

Berle, Milton
(Mendel Berlinger)
151 El Camino Dr.
Beverly Hills, CA 90212
Comedian

Bernhard, Sandra
10100 Santa Monica Blvd.
   (#1600)
Los Angeles, CA 90067
Comedienne

Bernsen, Corbin
9000 Sunset Blvd. (12th floor)
Los Angeles, CA 90069
Actor

Bernstein, Carl
40 W. 57th St.
New York, NY 10019
Watergate journalist

Bernstein, Jay
1888 Century Park E. (#622)
Los Angeles, CA 90067
TV producer/show biz manager

Bernstein, Leonard
24 W. 57th St.
New York, NY 10019
Classical conductor

**Berra, Yogi
(Lawrence Peter)**
P.O. Box 288
Houston, TX 77001
Baseball coach/former star

**Berry, Chuck
(Charles Edward Anderson)**
Berry Park, Buckner Rd.
Wentzville, MO 63385
Rock 'n' roll guitarist

Berry, Wendell
c/o North Point Press
850 Talbot Ave.
Albany, CA 94706
Poet/farmer

Bertinelli, Valerie
151 El Camino Dr.
Beverly Hills, CA 90212
Actress

Bertles, John, Dr.
St. Luke's Hospital Center
New York, NY 10025
Sickle cell anemia specialist

Bertolucci, Bernardo
Via del Babuino 51
Rome, Italy
Film director

Bessie Smith Society
c/o Prof. Michael Roth
Franklin and Marshall College
Lancaster, PA 17604
Late blues singer's fan club

Bethlehem Steel Corp.
8th and Eaton Aves.
Bethlehem, PA 18016
Walter F. Williams, CEO

Better Homes and Gardens
1716 Locust St.
Des Moines, IA 50336
David Jordan, editor

Better Vision Institute
230 Park Ave.
New York, NY 10169
Dr. Bonnie Sugar, spokesperson

Beutler, Ernest, Dr.
Scripps Clinic
La Jolla, CA 92037
Anemia specialist

B.F. Goodrich Co.
3925 Embassy Pkwy.
Akron, OH 44313
John D. Ong, CEO

B-52's, The
c/o Direct Management
945A N. La Cienega Blvd.
Los Angeles, CA 90069
Rock group

Bhutto, Benazir
Office of the Prime Minister
Islamabad, Pakistan
Prime Minister of Pakistan

Bible-Science Association
2911 E. 42nd St.
Minneapolis, MN 55406
Creationist advocates

Bic Pen Corporation
500 Bic Dr.
Milford, CT 06460
Bruno Bich, president

Biden, Joseph R., Jr.
221 Senate Russell Bldg.
Washington, DC 20510
Senator from Delaware

Big Beautiful Woman Magazine
19611 Ventura Blvd. (#200)
Tarzana, CA 91356
Carole Shaw, editor

Big Bird
c/o Children's Television
  Workshop
One Lincoln Plaza
New York, NY 10023
"Sesame Street" character

Big Brothers/Big Sisters
230 N. 13th St.
Philadelphia, PA 19107
Thomas M. McKenna, executive
  director

Biglieri, Edward, Dr.
U. of California Medical Center
San Francisco, CA 94143
Endocrinology specialist

Big Man's Fan Club
P.O. Box 162
Benton, KY 42025
Clarence Clemons fan club

Bikel, Theodore
Money Hill Rd.
Georgetown, CT 06829
Folk singer

Bill, Tony
73 Market St.
Venice, CA 90291
Film director

Billingsley, Barbara
P.O. Box 1320
Santa Monica, CA 90402
Beaver Cleaver's "mom"

Bing Crosby Historical Society
P.O. Box 216
Tacoma, WA 98401
Ken Twiss, president

Binney & Smith, Inc.
P.O. Box 431
Easton, PA 18044
Makers of Crayola Crayons

Bird, Larry Joe
c/o Boston Celtics
150 Causeway St.
Boston, MA 02114
Basketball star

Bird, Rose Elizabeth
P.O. Box 51376
Palo Alto, CA 94306
Attorney/commentator

Birnbaum, Stephen
c/o Tribune Media Services
64 E. Concord St.
Orlando, FL 32801
Travel columnist

Birney, Meredith Baxter
10100 Santa Monica Blvd.
(#1600)
Los Angeles, CA 90067
Actress

Bishop, Joey
(Joseph Abraham Gottlieb)
c/o Greshler
9200 Sunset Blvd.
Los Angeles, CA 90069
Comedian

Bisset, Jacqueline
8899 Beverly Blvd.,
Los Angeles, CA 90048
Actress

Bixby, Bill
9046 Sunset Blvd. (#201)
Los Angeles, CA 90069
Actor

Black, Barbara Aronstein
Columbia University Law School
New York, NY 10027
Law school dean

Black, Karen
(Ziegeler)
10000 Santa Monica Blvd. (#305)
Los Angeles, CA 90067
Actress

Black, Shirley Temple
c/o McGraw-Hill
11 W. 19th St.
New York, NY 10011
Ambassador to Czechoslovakia

Black & Decker Corp.
701 E. Joppa Rd.
Towson, MD 21204
Nolan D. Archibald, CEO

Black Enterprise Magazine
130 5th Ave.
New York, NY 10011
Earl G. Graves, publisher

Blackmun, Harry A.
U.S. Supreme Court Bldg.
One 1st Street NE.
Washington, DC 20543
Supreme Court Justice

Black Rock Coalition
Don Eversley, executive officer
P.O. Box 1054
Cooper Station
New York, NY 10276
Black rock musicians group

Blackstone, Harry, Jr.
P.O. Box 3819
La Mesa, CA 92044
Magician

Blackwell, Mr.
(Richard Sylvan Seltzer)
719 Los Angeles St.
Los Angeles, CA 90014
Announces worst-dressed list

Blades, Ruben
1674 Broadway (#703)
New York, NY 10019
Musician/actor

41

Blair, Linda
1930 Century Park W. (#303)
Los Angeles, CA 90067
Actress

Blakely, Susan
2121 Ave. of the Stars (#950)
Los Angeles, CA 90067
Actress

Blanchard, Nina
7060 Hollywood Blvd. (#1000)
Los Angeles, CA 90028
Models' Agent

**Blass, Bill
(William Ralph)**
550 7th Ave.
New York, NY 10021
Fashion designer

Bloch, Henry Wollman
4410 Main St.
Kansas City, MO 64111
H&R Block, president

Block, Herbert
c/o Washington Post
1150 15th St. NW.
Washington, DC 20071
Political cartoonist

Block, Lawrence
3750 Estero Blvd.
Fort Myers Beach, FL 33931
Author

Block, Susan
8306 Wilshire Blvd. (#1047)
Beverly Hills, CA 90211
Singles expert

Bloom, Allan
1126 E. 59th St.
Chicago, IL 60637
Education author

Bloomingdales
59th St. & Lexington Ave.
New York, NY 10022
Marvin S. Traub, CEO

Blues Foundation
352 Beale St.
Memphis, TN 38103
Promotes blues music

Blue Suede News
Bill Cooper, editor
P.O. Box 11384
Bradenton, FL 34282
Newsletter on the '50s and '60s

Bochco, Steven
4024 Radford Ave.
Studio City, CA 91604
Television producer

Body Positive
263A W. 19th St. (#107)
New York, NY 10011
Newsletter for those with AIDS

Boeing
7755 E. Marginal Way S.
Seattle, WA 98108
Frank A. Shrontz, chairman

Boesak, Allan Aubrey, Rev.
150 Route de Ferney
1211 Geneva 20, SWI
Anti-apartheid activist

Bogdanovich, Peter
c/o Camp and Peiffer
2040 Ave. of the Stars
Los Angeles, CA 90067
Film director

B'nai B'rith International
1640 Rhode Island Ave. NW.
Washington, DC 20036
Thomas Neumann, executive vice
   president

Boggs, Wade Anthony
c/o Boston Red Sox
24 Yawkey Way
Boston, MA 02215
Baseball star

Bogosian, Eric
1350 6th Ave.
New York, NY 10019
Playwright/actor

Boise Cascade
One Jefferson Sq.
Boise, ID 83728
Jon H. Miller, president

Boitano, Brian
c/o Leigh Steinberg
2737 Dunleer Pl.
Los Angeles, CA 90064
Ice skating star

Bok, Derek
Office of the President
Massachusetts Hall, Harvard U.
Cambridge, MA 02138
University president

Bol, Manute
c/o Golden State Warriors
Oakland Coliseum Arena
Oakland, CA 94621
Basketball shot blocker

Bolton, Michael
c/o Contemporary
   Communications
155 E. 55th St.
New York, NY 10022
Pop singer

Bombeck, Erma
1703 Kaiser Ave.
Irvine, CA 92714
Humorist

Bond, Alan
89 Watkins Rd.
Dalkeith 6009 Australia
Yacht racing executive

Bonet, Lisa
8322 Beverly Blvd. (#202)
Los Angeles, CA 90027
Actress

Bonham Carter, Helena
c/o Lantz
888 7th Ave.
New York, NY 10106
Actress

Bon Jovi
P.O. Box 4843
San Francisco, CA 94101
Rock band's fan club

Bono
(Paul Hewson)
Four Windmill Lane
Dublin 2, Ireland
Singer with U2

Bono, Sonny
(Salvatore)
250 W. Camino Buena Vista Park
Palm Springs, CA 92262
Mayor of Palm Springs/singer

Boone, Pat
(Charles Eugene)
9255 Sunset Blvd. (#519)
Los Angeles, CA 90069
Singer

Boorman, John
The Glebe, Annamoe
County of Wicklow, Ireland
Film director

Borden
277 Park Ave.
New York, NY 10172
Romeo J. Ventres, CEO

Borg, Bjorn Rune
c/o Int. Management Group
Pier House, Strand on the Green
Chiswick, London W4 3NN
   London
Ex-tennis star

Borgnine, Ernest
(Ermes Borgnino)
13111 Ventura Blvd.
Studio City, CA 91604
Actor

Bork, Robert Heron
c/o American Enterprise
   Institute
1150 17th St. NW.
Washington, DC 20012
Former judge

Boskin, Michael J.
Old Executive Office Bldg.
Washington, DC 20500
Chairman, Council of Economic
   Advisors

Bosley, Tom
2121 Ave. of the Stars (#410)
Los Angeles, CA 90067
Actor

Boston Bruins
150 Causeway St.
Boston, MA 02114
Harry Sinden, general manager

Boston Celtics
150 Causeway St.
Boston, MA 02114
Don Gaston, chairman

Boston Globe
135 Morrissey Blvd.
Boston, MA 02107
John S. Driscoll, editor

Boston Marathon
17 Main St.
Hopkinton, MA 01748

Boston Red Sox
Fenway Park
24 Yawkey Way
Boston, MA 02215
Haywood Sullivan, president

Bostwick, John, III, Dr.
Emory University Clinic
Atlanta, GA 30322
Breast surgeon

Bosworth, Brian
c/o Seattle Seahawks
11220 Northeast 53rd St.
Kirkland, WA 98033
Football's "Boz"

**Botha, Roelof Frederik
(Pik)**
c/o Ministry of Foreign Affairs
Union Bldg., Private Bag X152
Pretoria 0001 Republic of South
   Africa
South African politician

Boulez, Pierre
Postfach 22
Baden Baden, Germany
Classical composer/conductor

Bowhunters Who Care
P.O. Box 269
Columbus, NE 68601
C.A. Saunders, president

**Bowie, David
(David Robert Jones)**
641 5th Ave. (#22-Q)
New York, NY 10022
Rock singer

Boxcar Willie
1300 Division St. (#103)
Nashville, TN 37203
Blues singer

Boxleitner, Bruce
151 El Camino Dr.
Beverly Hills, CA 90212
Actor

**Boycott McDonald's
   Coalition**
Heather Schofield, president
P.O. Box 1836
Boston, MA 02205
Boycott to preserve the rainforest

Boyer, Randall
8 Mustang Court
Florissant, MO 63033
Look-alike for Stooges' Curley

**Boy George
(George Alan O'Dowd)**
153 George St.
London W1 England
Pop singer

Boyle, Peter
1700 Broadway
New York, NY 10019
Actor

Boy Scouts of America
1325 Walnut Hill Lane
Irving, TX 75015
Ben H. Love, Chief Scout

Boy's Life Magazine
P.O. Box 152079
Irving, TX 75015
William B. Norris, editor

Bozo the Clown
5455 Wilshire Blvd. (#2200)
Los Angeles, CA 90036
Larry Harmon, creator

Bradbury, Ray
c/o Bantam Books
666 5th Ave.
New York, NY 10103
Fantasy author

Brademas, John, Dr.
New York University
New York, NY 10011
University president

Bradley, Bill
731 Senate Hart Bldg.
Washington, DC 20510
Senator from New Jersey

Bradley, Ed
c/o CBS News
524 W. 57th St.
New York, NY 10019
Television journalist

Bradley, Tom
200 N. Spring St.
Los Angeles, CA 90012
Mayor of Los Angeles

Bradshaw, Terry
P.O. Box 227
Gordonville, TX 76254
Sportscaster/former football great

Brady, Nicholas F.
1500 Pennsylvania Ave. NW.
Washington, DC 20220
Secretary of the Treasury

Braga, Sonia
8899 Beverly Blvd.
Los Angeles, CA 90048
Actress

Braille, Inc.
205 Worchester Court (#C-3)
Falmouth, MA 02542
Joan B. Rose, executive director

Branagh, Kenneth
c/o Marmont Management
308 Regent St., Langham House
London W1 England
Actor/film director

Brandauer, Klaus Maria
Bartensteingasse 819
A-1010 Vienna, Austria
Actor

Branson, Richard
c/o Virgin Ltd.
95 Ladbroke Grove
London W11 England
*Entertainment
    executive/adventurer*

Breathed, Berke
1150 15th St. NW.
Washington, DC 20071
"Outland" cartoonist

**Brennan, William Joseph,
    Jr.**
U.S. Supreme Court Bldg.
One 1st St. NE.
Washington, DC 20543
Retired Supreme Court Justice

Brett, George
c/o Kansas City Royals
Royals Stadium
Kansas City, MO 64141
Baseball star

**Brett, Jeremy
(Huggins)**
151 El Camino Dr.
Beverly Hills, CA 90212
Actor/author

Brickell, Edie (& New Bohemians)
c/o Geffen Records
9130 Sunset Blvd.
Los Angeles, CA 90069
Rock group

Brickman, Paul M.
10100 Santa Monica Blvd.
(#1600)
Los Angeles, CA 90067
Film director/writer

Bride's Magazine
350 Madison Ave.
New York, NY 10017
Barbara D. Tober, editor

Bridges, Beau
(Lloyd Vernet Bridges III)
9830 Wilshire Blvd.
Beverly Hills, CA 90212
Actor

Bridges, Jeff
9830 Wilshire Blvd.
Beverly Hills, CA 90212
Actor

Briggs, Joe Bob
P.O. Box 33
Dallas, TX 75221
Drive-in movie critic

Brimley, Wilford
9830 Wilshire Blvd.
Beverly Hills, CA 90212
Actor

Brinkley, David
c/o ABC News
1717 DeSales St. NW.
Washington, DC 20036
Television journalist

Brinks
Thorndal Circle
Darien, CT 06820
D.L. Marshall, chairman

Brisco-Hooks, Valerie
P.O. Box 21053
Long Beach, CA 90801
Track athlete

Bristol-Meyers Co.
345 Park Ave.
New York, NY 10154
Richard L. Gelb, chairman

British Petroleum Co.
Britannica House, Moor Lane
London EG2Y 9BU England
Peter Walters, CEO

Brittany, Morgan
(Suzanne Cupito)
2029 Century Park E. (#3250)
Los Angeles, CA 90067
Actress

Broccoli, Albert Romolo
c/o Gand, Tyre and Brown
6400 Sunset Blvd.
Los Angeles, CA 90028
"James Bond" film producer

Brodie, H. Keith, Dr.
Duke University
Durham, NC 27706
University president

Brodsky, Joseph
Mt. Holyoke Dept. of Literature
South Hadley, MA 01075
Nobel Prize poet

Brokaw, Norman
151 El Camino Dr.
Beverly Hills, CA 90212
Talent agent

Brokaw, Tom
c/o NBC News
30 Rockefeller Plaza
New York, NY 10112
Television journalist

Brolin, James
10100 Santa Monica Blvd.
(#1600)
Los Angeles, CA 90067
Actor

Bronson, Charles
(Buchinski)
c/o Paul Kohner
9169 Sunset Blvd.
Los Angeles, CA 90069
Actor

Brook, Peter Stephen Paul
c/o C.I.R.T.
9 Rue Du Cirque
75008 Paris, France
Theater director

Brooks, Albert
(Einstein)
c/o Moress-Nanas
2128 Pico Blvd.
Santa Monica, CA 90405
Film director/actor/writer

Brooks, Jack
2449 Rayburn House Office Bldg.
Washington, DC 20515
Congressman from Texas

Brooks, Mel
(Melvin Kaminsky)
P.O. Box 900
Beverly Hills, CA 90213
Film actor/director

Brosnan, Pierce
9830 Wilshire Blvd.
Beverly Hills, CA 90212
Actor

Brothers, Joyce, Dr.
151 El Camino Dr.
Beverly Hills, CA 90212
Psychologist

Brower, David Ross
Earth Island Institute
Fort Mason Center
San Francisco, CA 94123
Environmentalist

Brown, Blair
9000 Sunset Blvd. (12th floor)
Los Angeles, CA 90069
Actress

Brown, Bobby
18653 Ventura Blvd. (#707)
Tarzana, CA 91356
Pop singer

Brown, Bobby, Dr.
(Robert)
350 Park Ave.
New York, NY 10022
American League president

Brown, Bryan
9830 Wilshire Blvd.
Beverly Hills, CA 90212
Actor

Brown, Charlie
One Snoopy Place
Santa Rosa, CA 95401
"Peanuts" star

Brown, Georg Sanford
P.O. Box 69453
Los Angeles, CA 90069
Actor/director

Brown, Helen Gurley
c/o Cosmopolitan Magazine
224 W. 57th St.
New York, NY 10019
Magazine editor

Brown, Henry
P.O. Box 69
Benton, LA 71006
*America's toughest district
   attorney*

Brown, James
c/o Brothers Management
141 Dunbar Ave.
Fords, NJ 08863
R&B singer

**Brown, Jerry
(Edmund Gerald)**
329 Bryant St. (#3C)
San Francisco, CA 94107
Politician

Brown, Jim
2040 Ave. of the Stars (4th floor)
Los Angeles, CA 90067
Actor/former football great

Brown, Julie
2400 Broadway (#100)
Santa Monica, CA 90404
Comedienne

Brown, Julie
c/o MTV
1775 Broadway
New York, NY 10019
Club MTV veejay

Brown, Larry
c/o San Antonio Spurs
600 E. Market (#102)
San Antonio, TX 78205
Basketball coach

Brown, Lester
Worldwatch Institute
1776 Massachusetts Ave. NW.
Washington, DC 20036
Environmentalist

Brown, Michael S., Dr.
5323 Harry Hines Blvd.
Dallas, TX 75235
Nobel Prize geneticist

Brown, Rita Mae
c/o Julian Bach
747 3rd Ave.
New York, NY 10017
Author

Browne, Dik
c/o King Features Syndicate
245 E. 45th St.
New York, NY 10017
"Hagar the Horrible" cartoonist

Browne, Jackson
9830 Wilshire Blvd.
Beverly Hills, CA 90212
Pop singer

49

Brubaker, Richard, Dr.
Mayo Clinic
Rochester, MN 55905
Glaucoma specialist

Brubeck, David Warren
P.O. Box 216
Wilton, CT 06897
Jazz musician

Brundtland, Gro Harlem
P.O. Box 8001, Dept. N-0030
Oslo 3, Norway
Prime Minister of Norway

Brunswick Corp.
One Brunswick Plaza
Skokie, IL 60077
Jack F. Reichert, CEO

Brustein, Robert A.
c/o Loeb Drama Center
64 Brattle St.
Cambridge, MA 02138
Theater critic/artistic director

Brzezinski, Zbigniew K.
1800 K Street NW. (#400)
Washington, DC 20006
Foreign affairs expert

Buchanan, Patrick Joseph
1017 Savile Lane
McLean, VA 22101
Political commentator

Buchanon, James McGill, Dr.
P.O. Box G
Blacksburg, VA 24063
Nobel Prize economist

Buchwald, Art
2000 Pennsylvania Ave. NW.
Washington, DC 20006
Political humorist

Buchwald, Henry, Dr.
U. of Minnesota Hospitals
Minneapolis, MN 55455
Obesity surgery specialist

Buckley, William Frank, Jr.
c/o National Review
150 E. 35th St.
New York, NY 10016
Political commentator

Buddhist Churches of America
1710 Octavia St.
San Francisco, CA 94109
Seigen H. Yamaoka, bishop

Buddy Holly Memorial Society
3022 56th St.
Lubbock, TX 79413

Budget Rent-A-Car
200 N. Michigan Ave.
Chicago, IL 60601
Clifton E. Haley, CEO

Buffalo Bills
One Bills Drive
Orchard Park, NY 14127
Ralph C. Wilson Jr., president

Buffalo Sabres
Memorial Auditorium
Buffalo, NY 14202
Gerry Meehan, general manager

Buffett, Jimmy
P.O. Box 480
Snowmass, CO 81654
Singer/author

Bugliosi, Vincent
9300 Wilshire Blvd. (#470)
Beverly Hills, CA 90210
Attorney

Bumpers, Dale
229 Senate Dirksen Bldg.
Washington, DC 20510
Senator from Arkansas

Bundys, The (Al, Peg, Kelly, Bud, and Buck)
10201 W. Pico Blvd.
Los Angeles, CA 90035
"Married . . . With Children"

Bunny, Bugs
c/o Warner Bros.
4000 Warner Blvd.
Burbank, CA 91522
"Eh, what's up, Doc?"

Burger King
17777 Old Cutler Rd.
Miami, FL 33157
Barry J. Gibbons, CEO

Burke, Delta Ramona Leah
P.O. Box 25909
Los Angeles, CA 90025
Actress

Burlington Industries
3330 W. Friendly Ave.
Greensboro, NC 27410
Frank S. Greenberg, CEO

Burnett, Carol
10601 Wilshire Blvd. (#501)
Los Angeles, CA 90024
Comedienne

**Burns, George
(Nathan Birnbaum)**
c/o Irving Fine
1100 N. Alta Loma Rd.
Los Angeles, CA 90069
Comedian

Burpee Seed Co.
300 Park Ave.
Warminster, PA 18974
William N. Englehart, president

Burr, Raymond
P.O. Box 678
Geyserville, CA 95441
"Perry Mason" actor.

Burroughs Wellcome Co.
3030 Cornwallis Rd.
Research Triangle Pk, NC 27709
Theodore E. Haigler, Jr.,
president

Burroughs, William Seward
c/o Grove Weidenfeld
841 Broadway
New York, NY 10003-4793
Author

Burrows, James
5555 Melrose Ave. (D-208)
Los Angeles, CA 90038
Television director

Burstyn, Ellen
(Edna Rae Gilhooley)
P.O. Box 217
Palisades, NY 10964
Actress

Burton, Lance
151 El Camino Dr.
Beverly Hills, CA 90212
Magician

Burton, LeVar (Levardis
Robert Martyn, Jr.)
9301 Wilshire Blvd. (#312)
Beverly Hills, CA 90210
Actor

Buscaglia, Leo, Dr.
P.O. Box 488
Glenbrook, NV 89413
Author/self-esteem expert

Busey, Gary
151 El Camino Dr.
Beverly Hills, CA 90212
Actor

Busfield, Timothy
9744 Wilshire Blvd. (#308)
Beverly Hills, CA 90212
Actor

Bush, Barbara Pierce
The White House
1600 Pennsylvania Ave.
Washington, DC 20500
First Lady

Bush, George Herbert
Walker
The White House
1600 Pennsylvania Ave.
Washington, DC 20500
President of the United States

Business Week
1221 6th Ave.
New York, NY 10020
Stephen B. Shepard, editor

Buss, Jerry Hatten, Dr.
c/o Great Western Forum
P.O. Box 10
Inglewood, CA 90306
L.A. Lakers owner

Buster Brown Apparel
2001 Wheeler Ave.
Chattanooga, TN 37406
Kent C. Robinson, CEO

Butcher, Susan
c/o Iditarod Visitors Bureau
P.O. Box 251
Nome, AL 99762
Dog sled champion

Buthelezi, Gatsha
Mangosuthu
Ashpenaz Nathan
Private Bag X01, Ulundi 3838
Kwazulu, Republic of South
Africa
Zulu chief

Butkus, Dick
151 El Camino Dr.
Beverly Hills, CA 90212
Actor/former football great

Butterworth, Robert A., Dr.
P.O. Box 76477
Los Angeles, CA 90076
Child and teen psychologist

**Button, Dick
(Richard)**
250 W. 57th St. (#1818)
New York, NY 10107
Ice skating commentator

Byrd, Robert C.
311 Senate Hart Bldg.
Washington, DC 20510
Senator from West Virginia

Byrne, David
1775 Broadway (#700)
New York, NY 10019
Rock musician

Byron Society
259 New Jersey Ave.
Collingswood, NJ 08108
Fans of Lord Byron

C

Caan, James
c/o Martin Licker
9025 Wilshire Blvd. (#313)
Beverly Hills, CA 90211
Actor

Caen, Herb
c/o San Francisco Chronicle
925 Mission St.
San Francisco, CA 94103
Newspaper columnist

Caesar, Sid
c/o Korman Contemporary
132 Lasky Dr.
Beverly Hills, CA 90212
Comedian

Caesar's World
Henry Gluck, chairman
1801 Century Park E.
Los Angeles, CA 90067
Gambling casino

Cage, John
101 W. 18th St.
New York, NY 10011
Avant-garde composer

Cage, Nicolas
(Nicholas Coppola)
151 El Camino Dr.
Beverly Hills, CA 90212
Actor

Caine, Michael
(Maurice Micklewhite)
c/o ICM
388-396 Oxford St.
London W1 England
Actor

Calgary Flames
P.O. Box 1540, Station M
Calgary, AL Canada
T2P 3B9
Cliff Fletcher, general manager

California Angels
P.O. Box 2000
Anaheim, CA 92803
Gene Autry, owner

California Raisins
c/o Will Vinton
1400 NW 22nd Ave.
Portland, OR 97210
Dancing raisins

Calloway, Cab
(Cabell)
1040 Knollwood Rd.
White Plains, NY 10603
Musician

Cameron, Kirk
P.O. Box 2592
Hollywood, CA 90078
Actor

Campbell, Levin H.
U.S. Court of Appeal
First Circuit
Boston, MA 02109
Chief Judge

Candy, John
8899 Beverly Blvd.
Los Angeles, CA 90048
Comic actor

Cannell, Stephen Joseph
7083 Hollywood Blvd.
Hollywood, CA 90028
Television producer

**Cannon, Dyan
(Samile Diane Friesen)**
9830 Wilshire Blvd.
Beverly Hills, CA 90212
Actress

Canseco, Jose
c/o Oakland Athletics
Oakland-Alameda County
  Coliseum
Oakland, CA 94621
Baseball slugger

CAP BOOK INC.
700 Exchange St.
Rochester, NY 14608
Hard-to-place kids to adopt

Capital Cities/ABC
77 W. 66th St.
New York, NY 10023
Daniel B. Burke, chairman

Capshaw, Kate
9830 Wilshire Blvd.
Beverly Hills, CA 90212
Actress

Cara, Irene
P.O. Box 135
Massapequa Park, NY 11762
Actress/singer

Car and Driver Magazine
151 Broadway
New York, NY 10036
Don Sherman, editor

Caray, Harry
c/o Chicago Cubs
Wrigley Field
Chicago, IL 60613
Sports announcer

Cardin, Pierre
59 Rue du Faubourg-Saint
  Honore
75008 Paris, France
Fashion designer

**CARE (Cooperative for
  American Relief
  Everywhere)**
660 1st Ave.
New York, NY 10016

**Carlin, George Denis
  Patrick**
901 Bringham Ave.
Los Angeles, CA 90049
Comedian

Carlisle, Belinda
11500 San Vicente Blvd.
Los Angeles, CA 90049
Pop singer

Carl's Jr.
1200 N. Harbor Blvd.
Anaheim, CA 92801
Carl N. Karcher, Jr., chairman

Carmel, Peter C., Dr.
Neurological Institute
Columbia-Presbyterian Hospital
New York, NY 10032
Pediatric neurosurgeon

Carner, Joanne Gunderson
1250 Shoreline Dr. (#200)
Sugar Land, TX 77478
Golfer

Carney, Art (Arthur William Matthew Carney)
RR # 20, Box 911
Westbrook, CT 06498
Actor

Carol Burnett Fund for Responsible Journalism
U. of Hawaii
2550 Campus R, Crawford 208
Honolulu, HI 96822
John Luter, chairman

Caroline, Princess (Grimaldi)
Grimaldi Palace
Monte Carlo, Monaco
Jetsetter

Caron, Leslie Clair Margaret
c/o Hugh J. Alexander
235 Regent St. (4th floor)
London W1R 8RU England
Actress

Carpenter, John
8383 Wilshire Blvd. (#840)
Beverly Hills, CA 90211
Film director

Carpenter, Karen
P.O. Box 823
Burbank, CA 91503
Fan club for late singer

Carr, Allan
439 N. Bedford Dr. (#1000)
Beverly Hills, CA 91210
Film producer

Carr, Jane
c/o Plant and Froggatt
4 Windmill St., Julian House
London W1 England
"Dear John" actress

Carr, Vikki (Florencia Bisenta de Casillas Martinez Cardona)
8961 Sunset Blvd.
Los Angeles, CA 90069
Singer

Carradine, David
132 Lasky Dr.
Beverly Hills, CA 90212
Actor

Carradine, Robert
2121 Ave. of the Stars (#950)
Los Angeles, CA 90067
Actor

Carrillo, Pedro
P.O. Box 87
West Lebanon, NY 12195
High-wire artist

Carroll, Diahann (Carol Diahann Johnson)
P.O. Box 2999
Beverly Hills, CA 90068
Actress

**Carsey/Warner Productions
(Marcy/Tom)**
4024 Radford Ave. (#3)
Studio City, CA 91604
Television producers

Carson, Johnny
3000 W. Alameda Ave.
Burbank, CA 91523
Talk show host

**Carter, Dixie
(Holbrook)**
10100 Santa Monica Blvd.
(#1600)
Los Angeles, CA 90067
Actress

**Carter, Jimmy
(James Earl, Jr.)**
c/o The Carter Center
1 Copenhill
Atlanta, GA 30307
Former president

Carter, Joe
c/o San Diego Padres
9449 Friars Rd., San Diego
Stadium
San Diego, CA 92120
Baseball player

Carter, Nell
10100 Santa Monica Blvd.
(#1600)
Los Angeles, CA 90067
Singer/actress

**Carter, Nick
(Michael Angelo Avallone,
Jr.)**
80 Hilltop Blvd.
East Brunswick, NJ 08816
Mystery author

Cartier-Bresson, Henri
c/o Helen Wright
135 E. 74th St.
New York, NY 10021
Photographer

Cartland, Barbara
Camfield Pl., Hatfield
Hertfordshire, England
Romance novelist

**Cartoon/Fantasy
Organization**
Randall Stakey, chairman
P.O. Box 18261
San Antonio, TX 78218
Fans of Japanese cartoons

Carvey, Dana
30 Rockefeller Plaza (#1700)
New York, NY 10019
Comedian

Casey, Robert
State Capitol
Harrisburg, PA 17120
Governor of Pennsylvania

**Cash, Johnny
(and June Carter Cash)**
9000 Sunset Blvd. (#1200)
Los Angeles, CA 90069
Country's "Man in Black"

Cash, Rosanne
1775 Broadway (7th floor)
New York, NY 10019
Country singer

Cashman, Terry
c/o Lifesong
94 Grand Ave.
Englewood, NJ 07631
Baseball's songwriter

Cassidy Class (David, Shaun, Patrick, and Ryan)
825 Oak Grove Rd. (#20)
Concord, CA 54518
Fan club for Cassidy family

Cassidy, Joanna
10351 Santa Monica Blvd. (#211)
Los Angeles, CA 90025
Actress

Cassini, Oleg
3 W. 57th St.
New York, NY 10019
Fashion designer

Castelli, Leo
420 W. Broadway
New York, NY 10012
Art gallery owner

Castro Ruz, Fidel
c/o Palacio del Gobierno
Havana, Cuba
Premier of Cuba

Caterpillar, Inc.
100 N.E. Adams St.
Peoria, IL 61629
G.A. Schafer, CEO

Cat Fanciers' Association
Thomas H. Dent, executive
    director
1309 Allaire Ave.
Ocean, NJ 07712
World's largest cat registry

Cates, Phoebe
9830 Wilshire Blvd.
Beverly Hills, CA 90212
Actress

Cauthen, Steve
Barry Hills
Lambourne, England
Jockey

Cavanaugh, John, Dr.
c/o Dept. of Psychology
Bowling Green State University
Bowling Green, OH 43403
Memory expert

Cavazos, Lauro
400 Maryland Ave. SW.
Washington, DC 20202
Secretary of Education

Cavett, Dick
151 El Camino Dr.
Beverly Hills, CA 90212
Talk show host

CBS Television
51 W. 52nd St.
New York, NY 10019
Lawrence Alan Tisch, chairman

Celebrity Source
Rita Tateel, president
8033 Sunset Blvd. (#1108)
Los Angeles, CA 90046
Finds celebrities for charities

Celeste, Richard
State House
Columbus, OH 43215
Governor of Ohio

Cemetery Consumers Service Council
P.O. Box 3574
Washington, DC 20007
Robert M. Fells, chairman

Center for Excellence in Government
20 F St. NW.
Washington, DC 20001
Mark A. Abrahamson, executive
director

Center for Holocaust Studies
1610 Avenue J
Brooklyn, NY 11230
Prof. Yaffa Eliach, director

Center for Scientific Creation
5612 N. 20th Place
Phoenix, AZ 85016
Walter T. Brown, Jr., director

Central Committee for Conscientious Objection
2208 South St.
Philadelphia, PA 19146

Central Intelligence Agency (CIA)
Washington, DC 20505
William Hedgcock Webster,
director

Chamberlain, Richard
9830 Wilshire Blvd.
Beverly Hills, CA 90212
Actor

Chambers, Tom
c/o Phoenix Suns
2910 N. Central Ave.
Phoenix, AZ 85012
Basketball player

Chamorro, Violeta Barrios de
Oficina del Presidente
Managua, Nicaragua
President of Nicaragua

Champagne News and Information
355 Lexington Ave.
New York, NY 10017
Irving Smith Kogan, director

Chancellor, John William
c/o NBC News
30 Rockefeller Plaza
New York, NY 10020
Television journalist

Chandrasekhan, Subrahmanyan, Dr.
Lab for Astrophysics and Space
933 E. 56th St.
Chicago, IL 60637
Nobel Prize physicist

Chaney, John
c/o McGonigle Hall
Temple University
Philadelphia, PA 19122
Basketball coach

Changing Times Magazine
1729 H St. NW.
Washington, DC 20006
Theodore J. Miller, editor

Channing, Carol
151 El Camino Dr.
Beverly Hills, CA 90212
Musical comedy star

Channing, Stockard
(Susan Stockard)
8899 Beverly Blvd.
Los Angeles, CA 90048
Actress

Chapman, Mark David
Attica State Prison
Attica, NY 14011
Assassin of John Lennon

Chapman, Tracy
c/o Lookout
506 Santa Monica Blvd.
Santa Monica, CA 90401
Singer/songwriter

Charles, Prince (Philip Arthur George Mountbatten-Windsor)
Kensington Palace
London W8 England
Heir to throne of England

Charles, Ray
(Ray Robinson)
c/o CBS Records
1801 Century Park W.
Los Angeles, CA 90067
Soul singer

Charlie the Tuna
c/o Star-Kist Foods
582 Tuna St.
Terminal Island, CA 90731
"Sorry, Charlie!"

Charlotte Hornets
Two First Union Center (#2600)
Charlotte, NC 28282
George Shinn, president

Charo
151 El Camino Dr.
Beverly Hills, CA 90212
Singer/entertainer

Charron, Peggy
Action for Children's Television
46 Austin St.
Newtonville, MA 02160
Activist

Chase, Chevy
2916 Main St. (#200)
Santa Monica, CA 90405
Actor/comedian

Chase Manhattan
Chase Manhattan Plaza
New York, NY 10018
Willard C. Butcher, chairman

Chast, Roz
P.O. Box 4203
New York, NY 10017
"New Yorker" cartoonist

Chavez, Cesar Estrada
P.O. Box 62, La Paz
Keene, CA 93531
United Farm Workers, president

Cheap Trick
315 W. Gorham St.
Madison, WI 53703
Rock band

Checker, Chubby
(Ernest Evans)
1650 Broadway (#1011)
New York, NY 10019
Rock 'n' roll star

Cheerleaders, The
2901 S. Las Vegas Blvd.
Las Vegas, NV 89109
Female professional wrestlers

Cheerleading Foundation
10600 Barkley
Overland Park, KS 66212
Randy Neil, president

Chen, Joan
10100 Santa Monica Blvd.
(#1600)
Los Angeles, CA 90067
Actress

Cheney, Victor T.
P.O. Box 10
Ozone Park, NY 11417
Advocates castration of rapists

Cher
(Cherilyn Sarkasian)
9200 Sunset Blvd. (#1001)
Los Angeles, CA 90069
Actress/singer

Cherry, Neneh
9830 Wilshire Blvd.
Beverly Hills, CA 90212
Pop singer

Chevron Corp.
225 Bush St.
San Francisco, CA 94104
George M. Keller, chairman

Chicago
80 Universal City Plaza (#400)
Universal City, CA 91608
Rock band

Chicago, Judy
c/o ACA Contemporary
41 E. 57th St.
New York, NY 10022
Painter

Chicago Bears
250 N. Washington
Lake Forest, IL 60045
Edward W. McCaskey, chairman

Chicago Black Hawks
1800 W. Madison St.
Chicago, IL 60612
Bob Pulford, general manager

Chicago Bulls
980 N. Michigan Ave. (#1600)
Chicago, IL 60611
Jerry Reinsdorf, chairman

Chicago Cubs
Wrigley Field
Clark and Addison Sts.
Chicago, IL 60613
Jim Frey, general manager

Chicago Tribune
435 N. Michigan Ave.
Chicago, IL 60611
James Squires, editor

Chicago White Sox
Comiskey Park
323 W. 35th St.
Chicago, IL 60616
Jerry Reinsdorf/Eddie Einhorn,
owners

**Chickamauga and
  Chattanooga**
National Military Park
P.O. Box 2128
Fort Oglethorpe, GA 30742
Civil War museum

**Chicken, The
(Ted Giannoulas)**
P.O. Box 2000
San Diego, CA 92102
Sporting events quack-up

Child, Desmond
1780 Broadway (#1208)
New York, NY 10019
Songwriter

Child, Julia McWilliams
c/o WGBH-TV
125 Western Ave.
Boston, MA 02134
Cooking expert

**Childbirth Without Pain
  Assoc.**
20134 Snowden
Detroit, MI 48235

Children of Ageing Parents
2761 Trenton Rd.
Levittown, PA 19056
Mirca Leberti, executive director

Children's Defense Fund
122 C St. NW.
Washington, DC 20001
Marian Wright Edelman,
  president

Chin, Gilbert Yukyu, Dr.
c/o AT&T Bell Labs
600 Mountain Ave.
Murray Hill, NJ 07974
Metallurgist

Chirac, Jacques Rene
Hotel de Ville
Paris RP, France 75196
Politician

Cho-Delle, Nomi
2509 N. Campbell (#91)
Tucson, AZ 85719
Handwriting analyst

Chocolate Lovers of America
P.O. Box 4121
Laguna Beach, CA 92652
Howard Levin, president

Chomsky, (Avram) Noam
Dept. of Linguistics & Philosophy
77 Massachusetts Ave.
Cambridge, MA 02139
Theoretical linguist

Chong, Rae Dawn
P.O. Box 5356
New York, NY 10150
Actress

Chow, Raymond
8 Hammer Hill Rd.
Kowloon, Hong Kong
Film company executive

Christian Science Monitor
One Norway St.
Boston, MA 02115
Katherine Fanning/Earl Foell,
  editors

Christie, Julie
8899 Beverly Blvd.
Los Angeles, CA 90048
Actress

Christo (Javacheff)
48 Howard St.
New York, NY 10013
Artist

Christopher, Warren
611 W. 6th St.
Los Angeles, CA 90017
Attorney

Chung, Connie (Constance Yu-Hwa)
c/o NBC
30 Rockefeller Plaza
New York, NY 10112
Television journalist

Church Lady, The
c/o NBC-TV
30 Rockefeller Plaza
New York, NY 10112
Hostess of "Church Chat"

Church of Christ, Scientist
175 Huntington Ave.
Boston, MA 02115
Pearline B. Thompson, president

Church of Jesus Christ of Latter-Day Saints
50 E. North Temple St.
Salt Lake City, UT 84150
Ezra Taft Benson, president

Church of Monday Night Football
P.O. Box 2127
Santa Barbara, CA 93120
"Reverend" Rick Slade

Church of the Lutheran Brethren
707 Crestview Dr.
West Union, IA 52175
Rev. Robert Overgard, Sr., president

Church of the Nazarene
6401 The Paseo
Kansas City, MO 64131
B. Edgar Johnson, general secretary

Church's Fried Chicken
1333 S. Clearview Pkwy.
Jefferson, LA 70121
Alvin C. Copeland, chairman

Churchill Downs
700 Central Ave.
Louisville, KY 40208
Kentucky Derby racetrack

Cicciolina
Via Europa 300
Rome, Italy
Porn star/politician

Cigarette Pack Collectors
61 Searle St.
Georgetown, MA 01833
Richard Elliott, spokesperson

Cigna Corporation
One Logan Sq.
Philadelphia, PA 19103
Wilson H. Taylor, chairman

Cimino, Michael
151 El Camino Dr.
Beverly Hills, CA 90212
Film director

Cincinnati Bengals
200 Riverfront Stadium
Cincinnati, OH 45202
Paul Brown, general manager

Cincinnati Reds
Riverfront Stadium
Cincinnati, OH 45202
Marge Schott, owner

Cirque du Soleil
1217 Notre-Dame St. E.
Montreal, QU Canada
H2L 2R3
Circus

Citicorp
399 Park Ave.
New York, NY 10022
John S. Reed, chairman

**Citizens Against Foreign
Control of America**
P.O. Box 3528
Montgomery, AL 36109
June Collier-Mason, chairman

**Citizens Against
Government Waste**
1511 K St. NW. (#643)
Washington, DC 20005
Alan L. Keyes, president

**Citizens Committee for the
Right to Keep and Bear
Arms**
12500 NE 10th Pl., Liberty Park
Bellevue, WA 98005
Joe Friend, executive director

Citizens for Law & Order
P.O. Box 13089
Oakland, CA 94661

Civil Air Patrol
Maxwell Air Force Base
Montgomery, AL 36112
Brig. Gen. Carl Miller, USAF
(Ret.)

**Civil War Round Table of
New York**
Roy B. Greenfield, president
P.O. Box 3485
New York, NY 10185
Experts on Civil War

**Claiborne, Liz
(Elizabeth Claiborne
Ortenberg)**
1441 Broadway
New York, NY 10018
Fashion designer

Clancy, Tom
c/o G.P. Putnam's Sons
200 Madison Ave.
New York, NY 10016
Thriller author

Clapton, Eric
9830 Wilshire Blvd.
Beverly Hills, CA 90212
Rock guitarist

Clark, Charles
U.S. Court of Appeal
Fifth Circuit
New Orleans, LA 70130
Chief Judge

Clark, Dick
3003 W. Olive Ave.
Burbank, CA 91505
"World's Oldest Teenager"

Clark, Jack
c/o San Diego Padres
9449 Friars Rd.
San Diego, CA 92120
Baseball player

Clark, Mary Higgins
210 Central Park S.
New York, NY 10019
Author

Clark, Petula
P.O. Box 498
Quakertown, PA 18951
Pop singer

Clark, Will
c/o San Francisco Giants
Candlestick Park, Bay Shore
San Francisco, CA 94124
Baseball star

Clarke, Arthur Charles
25 Barnes Pl.
Colombo 7, Sri Lanka
Novelist

Clarke, Martha
c/o Sheldon Soffer
130 W. 56th St.
New York, NY 10019
Dancer

Claus, Santa (also Mrs.
Claus, Elves & Reindeer)
North Pole, 30351
Official Postal Service address

Clay, Andrew Dice
(Silverstein)
163 Joralemon St. (#1508)
Brooklyn, NY 11201
Comedian's fan club

Clay, Bill
(William)
2470 Rayburn House Office Bldg.
Washington, DC 20515
Congressman from Missouri

Clayburgh, Jill
9830 Wilshire Blvd.
Beverly Hills, CA 90212
Actress

Clean Air Working Group
818 Connecticut Ave. NW.
  (#900)
Washington, DC 20006
William D. Fay, administrator

Cleary, Beverly Atlee
c/o William Morrow & Co.
105 Madison Ave.
New York, NY 10016
Children's author

Cleese, John
8 Clarendon Rd.
London W11 3AA England
Comic actor

Clemens, Roger
c/o Boston Red Sox
24 Yawkey Way
Boston, MA 02215
Baseball pitcher

Clements, William P., Jr.
State Capitol
Austin, TX 78711
Governor of Texas

Cleveland Browns
Cleveland Stadium
Cleveland, OH 44114
Arthur Modell, president

Cleveland Cavaliers
The Coliseum
2923 Streetsboro Rd.
Richfield, OH 44286
Wayne Embry, general manager

Cleveland Indians
Municipal Stadium
Cleveland, OH 44114
John McNamara, manager

Cliff, Jimmy
c/o Victor Chambers
51 Lady Musgrave Rd.
Kingston, Jamaica
Reggae singer

Cline, Patsy
P.O. Box 244
Dorchester, MA 02125
Late singer's fan club

**Clinton, Bill
(William J.)**
State Capitol
Little Rock, AK 72201
Governor of Arkansas

Close, Del
8457 Melrose Pl. (#200)
Los Angeles, CA 90069
Comedy teacher

Close, Glenn
9830 Wilshire Blvd.
Beverly Hills, CA 90212
Actress

Clothe America
Kenneth Sitomer, president
1411 Broadway
New York, NY 10018
Donates clothes to the homeless

Club Med
40 W. 57th St.
New York, NY 10019
Jacques Ganin, president

**Coalition Against Lyrics
Legislation**
1155 21st St. NW. (#1000)
Washington, DC 20036

Cobb, Randall "Tex"
2121 Ave. of the Stars (#410)
Los Angeles, CA 90067
Actor/former pugilist

Coca-Cola Company
One Coca-Cola Plaza NW.
Atlanta, GA 30313
Donald R. Keough, president

**Cocker, Joe
(John)**
c/o QBQ
48 E. 50th St.
New York, NY 10022
Rock singer

**Coen, Ethan and Joel
(aka Roderick James)**
445 N. Bedford Dr. (PH)
Beverly Hills, CA 90210
Film directors/writers

Cohen, Stanley
Dept. of Genetics S-337
Stanford U. School of Medicine
Stanford, CA 94305
Nobel Prize geneticist

Colbert, Claudette
(Lily Claudette Chauchoin)
Bellerive, St. Peter
Barbados, British West Indies
Actress

Cole, Natalie
c/o Capitol Records
1750 N. Vine St.
Hollywood, CA 90028
Pop singer

Coleman, A. Michael
28 Brookhaven Blvd.
Port Jefferson Stn., NY 11776
America's #1 bill collector

Coleman, Dabney W.
8899 Beverly Blvd.
Los Angeles, CA 90048
Actor

Coles, Robert Martin, Dr.
P.O. Box 674
Concord, MA 01742
Child psychiatrist

Colgate-Palmolive
300 Park Ave.
New York, NY 10022
Keith Crane, chairman

College Board, The
Donald Stewart, president
45 Columbus Ave.
New York, NY 10023
Gives college admissions tests

Collins, Jackie
c/o Simon & Schuster
1230 6th Ave.
New York, NY 10020
Author

Collins, Joan Henrietta
c/o Judy Bryer
15363 Mulholland Dr.
Los Angeles, CA 90077
Actress

Collins, Judy Marjorie
P.O. Box 1296
New York, NY 10025
Pop singer

Collins, Phil
Shalford
Surrey, England
Rock musician

Colonial Warriors United
Richard A. Sensale, president
34 Figurehead Lane (#4)
Quincy, MA 02169
"Battlestar Galactica" fans

**Color Association of the
  U.S.**
343 Lexington Ave.
New York, NY 10016
Forecasts fashion colors

Commission on Civil Rights
1121 Vermont Ave. NW.
Washington, DC 20425
William B. Allen, chairman

**Committee on the Present
  Danger**
C.D. Dillon, spokesperson
905 16th St. NW.
Washington, DC 20006
Think tank on U.S./U.S.S.R.

Committee to Abolish Sport Hunting
P.O. Box 43
White Plains, NY 10605
Luke A. Dommer, chairman

Communist Party, U.S.A.
235 W. 23rd St.
New York, NY 10011
Gus Hall, chairman

Companions of Doctor Who Fan Club
P.O. Box 724002
Atlanta, GA 30339
Glyn Davis, president

COMSAT (Communications Satellite Corp.)
950 L'Enfant Plaza SW.
Washington, DC 20024
Irving Goldstein, chairman

Concannon, Gary
2990 Redhill Ave.
Costa Mesa, CA 92626
Rolls-Royce repair

Conde Nast's Traveler Magazine
360 Madison Ave.
New York, NY 10017
Tom Florio, editor

Condon, Richard
c/o Harold Matson Agency
276 5th Ave.
New York, NY 10001
Author

Congress of Racial Equality
Immigration Service
1457 Flatbush Ave.
Brooklyn, NY 11210
Cicely Morris, director

Conner, Dennis Walter
c/o San Diego Yacht Club
1011 Anchorage Lane
San Diego, CA 92106
America's Cup skipper

Connery, Sean (Thomas)
9830 Wilshire Blvd.
Beverly Hills, CA 90212
Actor

Connoisseur Magazine
224 W. 57th St.
New York, NY 10019
Thomas Hoving, editor

Connors, Chuck (Kevin Joseph)
8306 Wilshire Blvd. (#252)
Beverly Hills, CA 90211
"Rifleman" actor

Connors, Jimmy (James Scott)
c/o ProServ
888 17th St. NW.
Washington, DC 20006
Tennis star

Conrad, Barnaby
3530 Pine Valley Dr.
Sarasota, FL 34239
Bullfighter/author/painter

Conrad, Robert
(Conrad Robert Falk)
21316 Pacific Coast Hywy.
Malibu, CA 90265
Actor

Conroy, Pat
c/o Houghton Mifflin
2 Park St.
Boston, MA 02109
The Prince of Tides *author*

Conservative Digest
   Magazine
National Press Bldg. (#800)
Washington, DC 20045
Scott Stanley, editor

Conservatree Paper Co.
10 Lombard St. (#250)
San Francisco, CA 94111
Susan Kinsella, spokesperson

Constantine, King
4 Linnell Drive, Hampstead Way
London NW11 England
Exiled King of Greece

Consumer Information
   Center
P.O. Box 100
Pueblo, CO 81002
Publisher of government info.

Consumer Product Safety
   Commission
5401 Westbard Ave.
Bethesda, MD 20207
Anne Graham, chairman

Conte, Silvio O.
2300 Rayburn House Office Bldg.
Washington, DC 20515
Congressman from
   Massachusetts

Conti, Tom
(Thomas Antonio)
c/o Chatton & Linnet
Shaftsbury Ave.
London W1 England
Actor

Continental Basketball
   Assoc.
(CBA)
425 S. Cherry St.
Denver, CO 80222

Conway, Tim
c/o Phillip Weltman
425 S. Beverly Dr.
Beverly Hills, CA 90212
Comedian

Conyers, John, Jr.
2426 Rayburn House Office Bldg.
Washington, DC 20515
Congressman from Michigan

Cooder, Ry
c/o Warner Bros. Records
3300 Warner Blvd.
Burbank, CA 91510
Musician

Cook, Peter Edward
c/o Wright and Webb
10 Soho Sq.
London W1 England
Comic actor

Cooke, (Alfred) Alistair
1150 5th Ave.
New York, NY 10028
American Englishman

Cooke, Jack Kent
Kent Farms
Middleburg, VA 22117
Business leader

Cooley, Denton, Dr.
Texas Heart Institute
Houston, TX 77025
Heart surgeon

**Cooper, Alice
(Vincent Furnier)**
8033 Sunset Blvd (#745)
Los Angeles, CA 90046
Rock star

Cooper, Jackie
c/o Contemporary Artists
132 Lasky Dr.
Beverly Hills, CA 90210
Actor/film director

Coors
Adolph Coors Co.
East of Town
Golden, CO 80401
Jeffrey H. Coors, president

Copeland, Miles
c/o Firstar Management
194 Kensington Park Rd.
London W11 England
Music executive

Copland, Aaron
c/o Boosey and Hawkes
24 W. 57th St.
New York, NY 10019
Composer

Copperfield, David
9107 Wilshire Blvd. (#500)
Beverly Hills, CA 90210
Magician

Coppola, Francis Ford
Zoetrope Studios
916 Kearny St.
San Francisco, CA 94133
Film director

Corcoran Gallery of Art
17th St. and New York Ave.
NW.
Washington, DC 20006
Michael Botwinick, director

Cordero, Angel T., Jr.
P.O. Box 90
Jamaica, NY 11411
Jockey

**Corea, Chick
(Armando)**
2635 Griffith Park Blvd.
Los Angeles, CA 90039
Jazz musician

Corman, Roger William
c/o New Horizons Productions
11600 San Vicente Blvd.
Los Angeles, CA 90049
Film producer

Cornelius, Don
9255 Sunset Blvd. (#420)
Los Angeles, CA 90039
"Soul Train" host

**Corporation for Public
Broadcasting**
1111 16th St. NW.
Washington, DC 20036
Donald Ledwig, president

Cosby, Bill
P.O. Box 808
Greenfield, MA 01301
Comedian

Cosmetic Ingredient Review
1110 Vermont Ave. NW. (#810)
Washington, DC 20005
Dr. Robert L. Elder, director

Cosmopolitan Magazine
224 W. 57th St.
New York, NY 10019
Helen Gurley Brown, editor

Cossette, Pierre
8899 Beverly Blvd.
Los Angeles, CA 90048
Entertainment producer

**Costa-Gavras
(Henri Constantin)**
244 Rue St. Jacques
Paris, France
Film director

Costas, Bob
c/o NBC Sports
30 Rockefeller Plaza
New York, NY 10112
Sportscaster

**Costello, Elvis (Declan
Patrick Aloysius
McManus)**
Western House, Harlequin Ave.
Brentford, Middlesex TW8 9EW
  England
Rock musician

Costner, Kevin
151 El Camino Dr.
Beverly Hills, CA 90212
Actor

Count Dracula Fan Club
29 Washington Sq. W. (PH H)
New York, NY 10011
Dr. Ann Hart, executive
  secretary

Country Music Association
P.O. Box 22299
Nashville, TN 37202

Cousins, Norman
c/o Saturday Review
214 Massachusetts Ave. NE.
  (#460)
Washington, DC 20002
Author

Cousteau, Jacques-Yves
930 W. 21st St.
Norfolk, VA 23517
Undersea explorer

Cox, Archibald
P.O. Box 393
Wayland, MA 01778
Attorney

Cox, Courtney
8600 Melrose Ave.
Los Angeles, CA 90069
Actress

Cox, Frank D., Dr.
905 Mission Canyon Rd.
Santa Barbara, CA 93105
Marriage and family educator

Coyote, Peter
121 N. San Vicente Blvd.
Beverly Hills, CA 90211
Actor

Craig, Jenny
445 Marine View Dr. (#300)
Del Mar, CA 92014
Diet expert

Craig, Roger
c/o San Francisco 49ers
711 Nevada St.
Redwood City, CA 94061
Football star

Cram, David L., Dr.
350 Parnassus Ave.
San Francisco, CA 94117
Psoriasis specialist

Crane, Philip M.
1035 Longworth House Office
Bldg.
Washington, DC 20515
Congressman from Illinois

Cranston, Alan
112 Senate Hart Bldg.
Washington, DC 20510
Senator from California

Craven, Wes
c/o Henri Bollinger
9200 Sunset Blvd. (#418)
Los Angeles, CA 90069
Horror film director

Crawford, Christina
3530 Pine Valley Dr.
Sarasota, FL 34239
Author of Mommie Dearest

Crawford, Cindy
345 N. Maple Dr. (#183)
Beverly Hills, CA 90210
Model

**Crawford, Michael
(Dumbell-Smith)**
c/o Duncan Heath
162-170 Wardour St, Paramount
House
London W1 England
"Phantom of the Opera" star

Crenna, Richard
9830 Wilshire Blvd.
Beverly Hills, CA 90212
Actor

Crenshaw, Ben
c/o U.S. Golf Association
Liberty Corners Rd.
Far Hills, NJ 07931
Golfer

Crichton, (John) Michael
1750 14th St. (#C)
Santa Monica, CA 90404
Author/film director

Cricket Magazine
Marianne Carus, editor
315 5th St.
Peru, IL 61354
Children's magazine

**Criminal Justice Legal
Foundation**
Michael Rushford, president
2131 L Street
Sacramento, CA 95812
Victims' rights organization

Criser, Marshall M.
University of Florida
Gainesville, FL 32611
University president

Crist, Judith Klein
180 Riverside Dr.
New York, NY 10024
Film critic

Cristiani, Alfredo
Office of the President
Casa Presidential
San Salvador, El Salvador
President of El Salvador

Cronkite, Walter Leland, Jr.
c/o CBS News
524 W. 57th St.
New York, NY 10019
Television journalist

**Cronyn, Hume
(Hume Blake)**
8899 Beverly Blvd.
Los Angeles, CA 90048
Actor

Crosby, David
1588 Crossroads of the World
Hollywood, CA 90028
Rock star

Crosby, Norm
P.O. Box 48779
Los Angeles, CA 90048
Comedian

Crown Books
500 5th Ave.
Landover, MD 20785
Robert M. Haft, president

Crucial Concepts
Izzy Siev, editor
P.O. Box 10
Ozone Park, NY 11417
*Journal dealing with crime
  issues*

**Cruise, Tom (Thomas Cruise
  Mapother IV)**
c/o Mailman
4708 Vesper Ave.
Sherman Oaks, CA 91403
Fan club

Cryer, Jon
10000 W. Washington Blvd.
  (#3018)
Culver City, CA 90232
Actor

Crystal, Billy
c/o Rollins
801 Westmount Dr.
Los Angeles, CA 90069
Comedian

Cunningham, Randall
c/o Philadelphia Eagles
Broad St. and Pattison Ave.
Philadelphia, PA 19148
Football quarterback

Cunningham, William, Dr.
University of Texas
Austin, TX 78712
University president

Cuomo, Mario Matthew
State Capitol
Albany, NY 12224
Governor of New York

Cure, The
200 W. 57th St. (#1403)
New York, NY 10019
Rock group

Curry, Tim
31/32 Soho Square
London W1 England
Actor

Curtin, Jane Therese
11726 San Vicente Blvd. (#300)
Los Angeles, CA 90049
Comic actress

Curtis, Jamie Lee
8436 W. 3rd St. (#650)
Los Angeles, CA 90048
Actress

Curtis, Tony
(Bernard Schwartz)
1900 Ave. of the Stars (#2440)
Los Angeles, CA 90067
Actor

Cusack, Joan
8457 Melrose Pl. (#200)
Los Angeles, CA 90069
Actress

Cusack, John
8457 Melrose Pl. (#200)
Los Angeles, CA 90069
Actor

Cyert, Richard M., Dr.
Carnegie Mellon University
Pittsburgh, PA 15213
University president

D

D'Abo, Olivia
10100 Santa Monica Blvd.
(#1600)
Los Angeles, CA 90067
Actress

Dads Against Discrimination
P.O. Box 8525
Portland, OR 97207
Victor Smith, president

Dafoe, Willem
9830 Wilshire Blvd.
Beverly Hills, CA 90212
Actor

Dahl, Roald
c/o Gipsy House
Great Missenden
Buckinghamshire HP16 OPB
   England
Author

Dailey, Janet
P.O. Box 2197
Branson, MO 65616
Romance novelist

Daily Variety
5700 Wilshire Blvd.
Los Angeles, CA 90036
Peter P. Pryor, editor

Dairy Queen
P.O. Box 35286
Minneapolis, MN 55435
Michael P. Sullivan, CEO

Dakin
3220 Sacramento
San Francisco, CA 94115
Henry S. Dakin, chairman

**Dalai Lama (Bstan'dzin-
   ryga-mtsho)**
c/o Thekchen Choeling
McLeod Ganj, 176219
Dharamsala
Himachal Pradesh, India
Religious leader of Tibet

Daley, Richard M.
Office of the Mayor
121 N. La Salle St.
Chicago, IL 60602
Mayor of Chicago

Dallas Cowboys
One Cowboys Parkway
Irving, TX 75063
Jimmy Jones, owner

Dallas Mavericks
Reunion Arena
777 Sports St.
Dallas, TX 75207
Donald Carter, owner

Dalton, Timothy
c/o James Sharkey
15 Golden Square
London W1 England
Actor

Daltrey, Roger
9255 Sunset Blvd. (#505)
Los Angeles, CA 90069
Rock singer/actor

Daly, Chuck
c/o Detroit Pistons
3777 LaPeer Rd.
Auburn Hills, MI 48057
Basketball coach

Daly, Robert
c/o Warner Bros. Film Company
4000 Warner Blvd.
Burbank, CA 91522
Entertainment executive

Daly, Tyne
2121 Ave. of the Stars (#410)
Los Angeles, CA 90067
Actress

D'Amato, Alfonse
520 Senate Hart Bldg.
Washington, DC 20510
Senator from New York

Damian, Michael
9000 Sunset Blvd. (12th floor)
Los Angeles, CA 90069
Actor

Damon, Stuart
9169 Sunset Blvd.
Los Angeles, CA 90069
Actor

D'Angelo, Beverly
151 El Camino Dr.
Beverly Hills, CA 90212
Actress

Dangerfield, Rodney
(Jacob Cohen)
1888 Century Park E. (#600)
Los Angeles, CA 90067
Comedian

Daniels, Jeff
c/o Hildy Gottlieb
40 W. 57th St.
New York, NY 10019
Actor

Daniels, William David
10000 Santa Monica Blvd. (#305)
Los Angeles, CA 90067
Actor

Dannemeyer, William E.
2351 Rayburn House Office Bldg.
Washington, DC 20515
Congressman from California

Danner, Blythe Katharine
9000 Sunset Blvd. (#315)
Los Angeles, CA 90069
Actress

Danning, Sybil
9300 Wilshire Blvd. (#410)
Beverly Hills, CA 90212
Actress

Danson, Ted
9830 Wilshire Blvd.
Beverly Hills, CA 90212
Actor

Danza, Tony
8899 Beverly Blvd.
Los Angeles, CA 90048
Actor

D.A.R.E.
(Drug Abuse Resistance
Education)
150 N. Los Angeles St. (#439)
Los Angeles, CA 90012

Dark Shadows,
The World of
Kathleen Resch
President
P.O. Box 1766
Temple City, CA 91780
Fan club

Darman, Richard
Old Executive Office Bldg.
Washington, DC 20500
Director, Management and
Budget

Daroff, Robert B., Dr.
University Hospitals
Cleveland, OH 44106
Neuro-ophthalmologist

Data General Corp.
4400 Computer Dr.
Westboro, MA 01580
Edson De Castro,
president

Daughters of the American
Revolution (DAR)
1776 D St. NW.
Washington, DC 20006
Mrs. Raymond F. Fleck,
president

D'Aviano, Jean Benoit
Guillaume Marie Robert
Louis Antoine Adolphe
Marc
Grand Ducal Palace
Luxembourg
Grand Duke of Luxembourg

Davis, Al
c/o L.A. Raiders
332 Center St.
El Segunda, CA 90245
Football team owner

Davis, Clifton
P.O. Box 69453
Los Angeles, CA 90069
Actor/singer

Davis, Clive
6 W. 57th St.
New York, NY 10019
Arista Records, president

Davis, Eric
c/o Cincinnati Reds
Riverfront Stadium
Cincinnati, OH 45202
Baseball star

Davis, Geena
211 S. Beverly Dr. (#201)
Beverly Hills, CA 90212
Actress

Davis, Jim
Oak Tree Computing
23250 Dolorosa St.
Woodland Hills, CA 91367
Personal computer consultant

Davis, Jim (James Robert)
c/o United Features Syndicate
200 Park Ave.
New York, NY 10166
"Garfield" creator

Davis, John S., Dr.
U. of Virginia Medical Center
Charlottesville, VA 22908
Arthritis specialist

Davis, Mark
c/o Kansas City Royals
Royals Stadium
Kansas City, MO 64141
Baseball reliever

Davis, Michael
801 Westmount Dr.
Los Angeles, CA 90069
Juggler/comedian

Davis, Miles
c/o Ted Kurland
173 Brighton Ave.
Boston, MA 02134
Jazz trumpeter

Dawson, Andre
c/o Chicago Cubs
Clark and Addison Sts.
Chicago, IL 60613
Baseball's "Hawk"

Dawson, Mary Ruth
c/o Carnegie Museum
4400 Forbes Ave.
Pittsburgh, PA 15213
Museum curator

**Day, Doris
(Von Kappelhoff)**
P.O. Box 223163
Carmel, CA 93922
Actress/animal rights activist

Day-Lewis, Daniel
c/o Julian Belfrage
60 St. James's St.
London SW1 England
Actor

**Dean, Jimmy
(Seth Ward)**
1341 W. Mockingbird Ln.
   (#1100E)
Dallas, TX 75247
Country singer/businessman

Dean, Morton Nissan
c/o ABC News
47 W. 66th St.
New York, NY 10023
Television journalist

DeBakey, Michael Ellis, Dr.
Baylor College of Medicine
1200 Moursund Ave.
Houston, TX 77030
Heart surgeon

DeBarge, El
6255 Sunset Blvd. (#624)
Los Angeles, CA 90028
Pop singer

DeBartolo, Ed
c/o San Francisco 49ers
711 Nevada St.
Redwood City, CA 94061
Football team owner

De Becker, Gavin
11684 Ventura Blvd. (#440)
Studio City, CA 91604
Expert on safety from obsessive
fans

DeBeer, Zacharias Johannes
P.O. Box 6946
Johannesburg, Republic of South
   Africa
Business leader

Debreu, Gerard, Dr.
University of California
Department of Economics
Berkeley, CA 94720
Nobel Prize economist

Decker, Mary Teresa
c/o Athletics West
3968 W. 13th Street
Eugene, OR 97402
Track athlete

DeConcini, Dennis
328 Senate Hart Bldg.
Washington, DC 20510
Senator from Arizona

Dee, Ruby
(Ruby Ann Wallace)
10000 Santa Monica Blvd. (#305)
Los Angeles, CA 90067
Actress

Dees, Rick
c/o KIIS-FM
6255 Sunset Blvd.
Los Angeles, CA 90028
Disc jockey

Def Leppard
P.O. Box 670
Old Chelsea Station
New York, NY 10113
Hard rock band

Deford, Frank
c/o The National
15 W. 52nd St.
New York, NY 10019
Sportswriter

De Havilland, Olivia Mary
B.P. 156
75764 Paris Cedex 1B, France
Actress

Deighton, Len
Fairymount, Blackrock, Dundalk
County Louth, Ireland
Spy thriller novelist

DeKlerk, Frederik Willem
House of Assembly
Cape Town 0001 Republic of
   South Africa
Prime Minister of South Africa

de Kooning, Willem
P.O. Box 1437
East Hampton, NY 11973
Painter

De la Renta, Oscar
Brook Hill Farm
Skiff Mountain Rd.
Kent, CT 10009
Fashion designer

De Laurentiis, Dino
Via Della Vasca Navale 58
Rome, Italy
Film executive

DeLillo, Don
c/o Viking Penguin
375 Hudson St.
New York, NY 10014
Author

Dell Publishing Co.
666 5th Ave.
New York, NY 10103
Carole Baron, president

Dellums, Ronald V.
2136 Rayburn House Office Bldg.
Washington, DC 20515
Congressman from California

Delors, Jacques Lucien Jean
Comm. of European Communities
200 Rue de la Loi
1049 Brussels, Belgium

DeLuise, Dom
151 El Camino Dr.
Beverly Hills, CA 90212
Actor

DeLuise, Peter
151 El Camino Dr.
Beverly Hills, CA 90212
Actor

Demme, Jonathan
9000 Sunset Blvd. (#1115)
Los Angeles, CA 90069
Film director

Democratic Party
430 South Capitol St. SE.
Washington, DC 20003
Ronald H. Brown, chairman

DeMornay, Rebecca
9830 Wilshire Blvd.
Beverly Hills, CA 90212
Actress

Dempsey, Patrick
10100 Santa Monica Blvd.
(#1600)
Los Angeles, CA 90067
Actor

**Deneuve, Catherine
(Dorleac)**
c/o Artmedia
10 Ave. George V
75008 Paris, France
Actress

Deng Xiaoping
c/o People's Republic of China
2300 Connecticut Ave. NW.
Washington, DC 20008
Government official

De Niro, Robert
c/o Jay Julien
1501 Broadway
New York, NY 10036
Actor

Dennehy, Brian
121 N. San Vicente Blvd.
Los Angeles, CA 90211
Actor

Denver, Bob
P.O. Box 426
Pacific Palisades, CA 90272
"Gilligan's Island" actor

Denver, John (Henry John Deutschendorf, Jr.)
P.O. Box 1587
Aspen, CO 10019
Pop singer

Denver Broncos
5700 Logan St.
Denver, CO 80216
Patrick Bowen, president

Denver Nuggets
McNichols Arena
1635 Clay St.
Denver, CO 80204
Vince Boryla, president

De Palma, Brian Russell
25 5th Ave. (#4A)
New York, NY 10003
Film director

Depardieu, Gerard
c/o Artmedia
10 Ave. George V
75008 Paris, France
Actor

DePasse, Suzanne
10202 W. Washington Blvd.
Culver City, CA 90230
Entertainment executive

Depeche Mode
429 Harrow Rd.
London W10 4RE England
Rock group

Depp, Johnny
1901 Ave. of the Stars (#840)
Los Angeles, CA 90067
Actor

Der Spiegel
c/o German Language
    Publications
560 Sylvan Ave.
Englewood Cliffs, NJ 07632
Rudolf Augstein, editor

**Derek, Bo
(Cathleen Collins)**
9830 Wilshire Blvd.
Beverly Hills, CA 90212
Actress

Dern, Bruce Macleish
9830 Wilshire Blvd.
Beverly Hills, CA 90212
Actor

Dern, Laura
760 N. La Cienega Blvd.
Los Angeles, CA 90069
Actress

Dershowitz, Alan Morton
c/o Harvard Law School
Cambridge, MA 02138
Attorney

Derwinski, Edward J.
810 Vermont Ave. NW.
Washington, DC 20420
Secretary of Veterans Affairs

Des Barres, Michael
P.O. Box 4160
Hollywood, CA 90078
Rock star/actor

Des Barres, Pamela
3575 Cahuenga Blvd. (#470)
Los Angeles, CA 90068
Famous ex-groupie

**Descendants of the Signers
of the Declaration of
Independence**
1300 Locust St.
Philadelphia, PA 19107

Details Magazine
611 Broadway (#711)
New York, NY 10012
Annie Flanders, editor

Detroit Lions
1200 Featherstone Rd.
Pontiac, MI 48507
William Clay Ford, president

Detroit Pistons
The Palace at Auburn Hills
3777 Lapeer Rd.
Auburn Hills, MI 48057
Jack McCloskey, general
   manager

Detroit Red Wings
600 Civic Center Dr.
Detroit, MI 48226
Jim Devellano, general manager

Detroit Tigers
Tiger Stadium
Detroit, MI 48216
Glenn "Bo" Schembechler,
   president

Devane, William
8899 Beverly Blvd.
Los Angeles, CA 90048
Actor

DeVito, Danny Michael
P.O. Box 27365
Los Angeles, CA 90027
Comic actor

DeVrees, William C., Dr.
Humana Heart Institute
One Audubon Plaza Dr.
Louisville, KY 40202
Heart surgeon

Dewhurst, Colleen
9301 Wilshire Blvd. (#312)
Beverly Hills, CA 90210
Actress

Dey, Susan
151 El Camino Dr.
Beverly Hills, CA 90212
Actress

DiBiaggio, John, Dr.
Michigan State University
East Lansing, MI 48824
University president

Diamond, Neil
P.O. Box 3357
Hollywood, CA 90028
Pop singer

**Princess Diana
(Spencer)**
Kensington Palace
London W8 England
Princess of Wales

Dickerson, Eric Demetric
P.O. Box 535000
Indianapolis, IN 46253
Football star

**Dickinson, Angie
(Angeline Brown)**
2121 Ave. of the Stars (#410)
Los Angeles, CA 90067
Actress

Diddley, Bo
(Ellas McDaniel)
P.O. Box 659
Hawthorne, FL 32640
Blues rock guitarist

Dietrich, Marlene
(Maria Magdalena von
   Losch)
12 Avenue Montaigne
75008 Paris 8th Arr., France
Actress

Digital Equipment Corp.
111 Powdermill Rd.
Maynard, MA 01754
Kenneth H. Olsen, cofounder

Diller, Barry
10201 W. Pico Blvd.
Los Angeles, CA 90035
20th Century Fox chairman

Diller, Phyllis
(Driver)
151 El Camino Dr.
Beverly Hills, CA 90212
Comedienne

Dillon, Matt
151 El Camino Dr.
Beverly Hills, CA 90212
Actor

Dine, Jim
c/o Pace Gallery
32 E. 57th St.
New York, NY 10022
Painter

Dingell, John D.
2221 Rayburn House Office Bldg.
Washington, DC 20515
Congressman from Michigan

Dinkins, David
City Hall
New York, NY 10007
Mayor of New York City

Dinosaur Catalog
P.O. Box 546
Tallman, NY 10982
Sells everything about dinosaurs

Dionne Quintuplets
St. Bruno
Quebec, QU Canada

Directors Guild of America
7920 Sunset Blvd.
Hollywood, CA 90046
Glenn Gumpel, executive director

Disney Channel
John F. Cooke, president
3800 W. Alameda Ave.
Burbank CA 91505
Family cable network

District 925, Service
   Employees Union
Karen Nussbaum, president
1313 S St. NW.
Washington, DC 20005
National union of office workers

Ditka, Mike
(Michael Keller)
c/o Chicago Bears
250 North Washington, Halas
   Hall
Lake Forest, IL 60045
Football coach

Dixon, Willie James
2700 Cahuenga Blvd. (#4206)
Los Angeles, CA 90068
Blues singer

83

Do-Right, Dudley (also Rocky, Bullwinkle, Boris, and Natasha)
8218 Sunset Blvd.
Hollywood, CA 90046
Cartoon characters

Doctorow, E.L. (Edgar Lawrence)
c/o Random House
210 E. 50th St.
New York, NY 10022
Author

Doda, Carol
c/o Condor Club
300 Columbus Ave.
San Francisco, CA 94133
Ecdysiast

Dodd, Christopher J.
444 Senate Russell Bldg.
Washington, DC 20510
Senator from Connecticut

Doe, John
c/o Geffen Records
9130 Sunset Blvd.
Los Angeles, CA 90069
Singer/songwriter

Dolby, Ray
100 Potrero Ave.
San Francisco, CA 94103
Creator of Dolby Stereo

Dole, Elizabeth Hanford
200 Constitution Ave. NW.
Washington, DC 20210
Secretary of Labor

Dole, Robert J.
141 Senate Hart Bldg.
Washington, DC 20510
Senator from Kansas

Dolenz, Mickey
Seifert, 8-A Brunswick Gardens
London, W8 England
Ex-Monkee

Domingo, Placido
c/o Eric Semon
111 W. 57th St.
New York, NY 10019
Opera tenor

Donahue, Phil
300 Central Park West
New York, NY 10024
Talk show host

Donaldson, Sam (Samuel Andrew)
c/o ABC News
1717 DeSales St. NW.
Washington, DC 20036
Television journalist

Donnelly & Sons
J.R. Walter, CEO
2223 Martin Luther King Dr.
Chicago, IL 60616
Prints telephone books

Dornan, Robert K.
301 Cannon House Office Bldg.
Washington, DC 20515
Congressman from California

Doubleday Books
666 5th Ave.
New York, NY 10103
Nancy Evans, president

Douglas, Kirk
(Issur Danielovitch Demsky)
141 El Camino Dr.
Beverly Hills, CA 90212
Actor

Douglas, Michael Kirk
P.O. Box 49054
Los Angeles, CA 90049
Actor

Dow Chemical
2030 Willard H. Dow Center
Midland, MI 48640
P.F. Oreffice, president

Down Beat Magazine
180 W. Park Ave.
Elmhurst, IL 60126
John Ephland, editor

Downey, Robert, Jr.
9830 Wilshire Blvd.
Beverly Hills, CA 90212
Actor

Downey, Thomas J.
2232 Rayburn House Office Bldg.
Washington, DC 20515
Congressman from New York

Downs, Hugh Malcolm
P.O. Box 1132
Carefree, AZ 85331
Television journalist

Dr. Demento
(Barry Hansen)
P.O. Box 884
Culver City, CA 90203
Comic radio expert

**Dr. Leonard's Health Care
    Products Catalog**
74 Twentieth St.
Brooklyn, NY 11232
Newsletter

Drake, Lynn, Dr.
Harvard Medical School
Boston, MA 02215
Aging-skin specialist

Dramatists Guild
David E. LeVine, executive
    director
234 West 44th St.
New York, NY 10036
Playwrights group

Dream Guys Magazine
Grace Catalano, editor
250 W. 5th Ave. (#2012)
New York, NY 10019
Magazine for teenage girls

Drexler, Clyde
c/o Portland Trailblazers
700 N.E. Multnomah St. (#600)
Portland, OR 97232
Basketball's "Clyde the Glide"

Dreyfuss, Richard Stephan
151 El Camino Dr.
Beverly Hills, CA 90212
Actor

**Drinkers Against Mad
    Mothers**
1355 Joliet Pl.
Detroit, MI 48207
James T. Van Velzor, president

Driver, David
c/o Noble Press
213 W. Institute Place (#508)
Chicago, IL 60610
Volunteerism advocate

Drucker, Mort
c/o MAD Magazine
485 Madison Ave.
New York, NY 10022
Cartoonist

Dryden, Robert, Dr.
1241 N. Wilmot Rd.
Tucson, AZ 85711
Reconstructive eye surgeon

Dryer, Fred
8721 Sunset Blvd. (#101)
Los Angeles, CA 90069
Actor/former football star

Du Pont de Nemours & Co.
1007 Market St.
Wilmington, DE 19898
Edgar S. Woolard, Jr., CEO

Dubcek, Alexander
c/o Forestry Enterprise
Bratislava, Czechoslovakia
Politician

Dubinin, Yuri
1125 16th St. NW.
Washington, DC 20036
Soviet Ambassador to U.S.

Duderstadt, James J.
University of Michigan
Ann Arbor, MI 48109
University president

Duffy, Julia
10100 Santa Monica Blvd. (#700)
Los Angeles, CA 90067
Actress

Duffy, Patrick
P.O. Box "D"
Tarzana, CA 91356
Actor

Dukakis, Olympia
10100 Santa Monica Blvd.
  (#1600)
Los Angeles, CA 90067
Actress

**Duke, Patty
(Anna Marie)**
10351 Santa Monica Blvd. (#211)
Los Angeles, CA 90025
Actress

Dummar, Melvin
Dummar's Cafe
Gabbs, NV 89409
*Howard Hughes' fortune
  claimant*

Dun & Bradstreet
C.W. Moritz, CEO
299 Park Ave.
New York, NY 10171
Business information services

Dunaway, (Dorothy) Faye
8899 Beverly Blvd.
Los Angeles, CA 90048
Actress

Duncan, Sandy
8899 Beverly Blvd.
Los Angeles, CA 90048
Actress

Dunham, Katherine
Performing Arts Training Center
East St. Louis, IL 62201
Dancer/choreographer

Dunne, Griffin
10100 Santa Monica Blvd.
(#1600)
Los Angeles, CA 90067
Actor

Duracell Rabbit
Berkshire Industrial Park
Bethel, CT 06801
Keeps going and going

Duran, Roberto
P.O. Box 157, Arena Colon
Panama City, PAN
"Hands Of Stone" boxer

Durang, Christopher
555 W. 57th St. (#1230)
New York, NY 10019
Playwright

Duvalier, Jean-Claude
Villa Mohamedia, Cote d'Azur
Mongans, France
Exiled Haitian dictator

Duvall, Robert Selden
8899 Beverly Blvd.
Los Angeles, CA 90048
Actor

Duvall, Shelley
12725 Ventura Blvd. (#J)
Studio City, CA 91604
Actress/television producer

Dylan, Bob
(Robert Allen Zimmerman)
P.O. Box 264, Cooper Station
New York, NY 90028
Rock star

Dymally, Mervyn M.
1717 Longworth House Office
Bldg.
Washington, DC 20515
Congressman from California

Dyslexia Correction Center
1799 Old Bayshore (#248)
Burlingame, CA 94010
Ronald D. Davis, director

E

Eagleburger, Lawrence S.
2201 C St. NW.
Washington, DC 20520
Deputy Secretary of State

Eaglestein, William, Dr.
University of Pittsburgh
Pittsburgh, PA 15261
Dermatology specialist

Earnhardt, Dale (Ralph)
Rt. 8, Box 463
Mooresville, NC 28115
Stock car driver

Earth, Wind & Fire
4323 W. Verdugo Ave.
Burbank, CA 91505
Rock band

Earth First!
c/o John Davis
P.O. Box 5871
Tucson, AZ 85703
Militant environmental group

Earthwatch
Brian A. Rosborough, president
680 Mt. Auburn St.
Watertown, MA 02172
Amateurs join science research

Eastern Airlines
Miami International Airport
Miami, FL 33148
Frank Lorenzo, chairman

Eastman Kodak Co.
343 State St.
Rochester, NY 14650
Colby H. Chandler, chairman

Easton, Robert
9169 Sunset Blvd.
Los Angeles, CA 90069
Actor/dialect specialist

**Easton, Sheena
(Sheena Shirley Orr)**
151 El Camino Dr.
Beverly Hills, CA 90212
Singer

**Eastwood, Clint
(Clinton, Jr.)**
c/o Malpaso Productions
4000 Warner Blvd.
Burbank, CA 91522
Actor

Ebert, Roger
c/o N.Y. Daily News
220 E. 42nd St.
New York, NY 10017
Film critic

Ebony Magazine
820 S. Michigan Ave.
Chicago, IL 60605
John H. Johnson, publisher

Ebsen, Buddy
(Christian Rudolf)
P.O. Box 356
Agoura, CA 91301
"Beverly Hillbillies" actor

Eckersley, Dennis
c/o Oakland Athletics
Oakland-Alameda County
　Coliseum
Oakland, CA 94621
Baseball reliever

Eden, Barbara
(Barbara Jean Huffman)
151 El Camino Dr.
Beverly Hills, CA 90212
"I Dream of Jeannie" actress

Edmonton Oilers
Northlands Coliseum
Edmonton, AL Canada
T5B 4M9
Glen Sather, general manager

Edmunds, Dave
119–121 Freston Rd.
London W11 4DB England
Rock musician

Edwards, Anthony
211 S. Beverly Dr. (#201)
Beverly Hills, CA 90212
Actor

Edwards, Blake
(William Blake McEdwards)
11777 San Vicente Blvd. (#501)
Los Angeles, CA 90049
Film director/writer

Egghead, Inc.
14784 N.E. 95th St.
Redmond, VA 98052
Victor D. Alhadeff, president

Ehrlichman, John Daniel
P.O. Box 5559
Santa Fe, NM 87502
Watergate conspirator

Eikenberry, Jill
P.O. Box 900
Beverly Hills, CA 90213
Actress

Einstein, Bob
8955 Beverly Blvd.
Los Angeles, CA 90048
"Super Dave" stuntman

Eisenstaedt, Alfred
c/o Time, Inc.
Time/Life Bldg. (#2850)
New York, NY 10020
Photographer

Eisner, Michael Dammann
c/o Walt Disney Co.
500 S. Buena Vista St.
Burbank, CA 91521
Entertainment executive

Elder Hostel, Inc.
William D. Berkeley, president
80 Boylston St. (#400)
Boston, MA 02116
Low-cost travelling for seniors

Eli Lilly & Co.
Richard D. Wood, CEO
Lilly Corp. Center
Indianapolis, IN 46285
Drug manufacturer

Elion, Gertrude Belle, Dr.
3030 Cornwallis Rd.
Research Triangle Pk, NC 27709
Nobel Prize pharmacologist

Elite Models
150 E. 58th St.
New York, NY 10155
John Casablancas, president

Queen Elizabeth II
(Alexander Mary
Mountbatten-Windsor)
Buckingham Palace
London SW1 England
Queen of England

Elle Magazine
551 5th Ave.
New York, NY 10176
Catherine Ettlinger, editor

Ellery Queen's Mystery
Magazine
380 Lexington Ave.
New York, NY 10017
Eleanor Sullivan, editor

Elliott, Bill
c/o NASCAR
1811 Volusia Ave.
Daytona Beach, FL 32015
Stock car driver

Elliott, Denholm
75 Albert St., Regents Park
London NW1 England
Actor

Ellison, Ralph Waldo
730 Riverside Dr.
New York, NY 10031
Author

Elway, John
c/o Denver Broncos
5700 Logan St.
Denver, CO 80216
Football quarterback

Elwes, Cary
9830 Wilshire Blvd.
Beverly Hills, CA 90212
Actor

Embry, Joan
c/o San Diego Zoo
Park Blvd.
San Diego, CA 92104
Animal trainer

Encouragement of Correct
Punctuation, Spelling and
Usage
88 Garfield Ave.
Madison, NJ 07940
Verdenal H. Johnson, president

Encyclopaedia Britannica
310 S. Michigan Ave.
Chicago, IL 60604
Robert P. Gwinn, chairman

End Hunger Network
Jerry Michaud, executive
   director
222 N. Beverly Dr.
Beverly Hills, CA 90210
Hunger relief organization

End Violence Against the
   Next Generation
977 Keeler Ave.
Berkeley, CA 94708
Anti-spanking organization

Engel, Albert J.
U.S. Court of Appeal
Sixth Circuit
Cincinnati, OH 45202
Chief Judge

English, Alex
c/o Denver Nuggets
1635 Clay Street
Denver, CO 80204
Basketball star

English First
George Tryfiates, director
8001 Forbes Place (#102)
Springfield, VA 22151
*Seeks English as official
language*

Englund, Robert
9200 Sunset Blvd. (#625)
Los Angeles, CA 90069
"Freddy Krueger" actor

Eno, Brian
330 Harrow Rd.
London W9 2HP England
Rock musician

**Entertainers Against
Hunger**
P.O. Box 150934
Nashville, TN 37215

**Environmental Defense
Fund**
257 Park Ave. S.
New York, NY 10010
Frederic D. Krupp, executive
administrator

**Environmental Protection
Agency
(EPA)**
401 M Street SW.
Washington, DC 20460
William K. Reilly, administrator

Ephron, Nora
c/o Janklow and Assoc.
598 Madison Ave.
New York, NY 10022
Author

Episcopal Church
P.O. Box 6120
Little Rock, AR 72216
Rev. Edmond I. Browning,
president

**Equal Employment
Opportunity Comm.**
1801 L Street NW.
Washington, DC 20507
Clarence Thomas, chairman

Ertegun, Ahmet
c/o Atlantic Records
75 Rockefeller Plaza
New York, NY 10019
Music executive

Ervin, Sam J., III
U.S. Court of Appeal
Fourth Circuit
Richmond, VA 23219
Chief Judge

**Erving, Julius Winfield, III
("Dr. J")**
P.O. Box 25040, Southpark
Station
Philadelphia, PA 19147
Ex-basketball great

Esiason, Boomer (Norman)
200 Riverfront Stadium
Cincinnati, OH 45202
Football quarterback

ESPN (Entertainment Sports Programming Network)
ESPN Plaza
Bristol, CT 06010

Esquire Magazine
1790 Broadway
New York, NY 10019
Lee Eisenberg, editor

Essel, David
3530 Pine Valley Dr.
Sarasota, FL 34239
Fitness expert

Essence Magazine
1500 Broadway
New York, NY 10036
Stephanie Stokes Oliver, editor

Estefan, Gloria (and Miami Sound Machine)
8390 S.W. 4th St.
Miami, FL 33144
Pop group

Estevez, Emilio
9830 Wilshire Blvd.
Beverly Hills, CA 90212
Actor

Etheridge, Melissa
c/o Island Records
14 E. 4th St.
New York, NY 10012
Singer/songwriter

Ethics Resource Center
Gary Edwards, executive director
600 New Hampshire Ave. NW. (#400)
Washington, DC 20037
Studies ethics

Eurythmics (Annie Lennox/ Dave Stewart)
P.O. Box 245
London N8 90G England
Rock musicians

Evans, Dwight
c/o Boston Red Sox, Fenway Park
24 Yawkey Way
Boston, MA 02215
Baseball star

Evans, Harold J., Dr.
Lab for Nitrogen Fixation Research
Oregon State University
Corvallis, OR 97331
Plant physiologist

Evans, Linda
9000 Sunset Blvd. (#1112)
Los Angeles, CA 90069
Actress

Eveready Battery Co.
Checkerboard Sq.
St. Louis, MO 63164
J.P. Mulcahy, CEO

Everett, Jim
c/o Los Angeles Rams
2327 W. Lincoln Ave.
Anaheim, CA 92801
Football quarterback

Everett, Rupert
c/o Duncan Heath
162 Wardour St.
London W1 4AB England
Actor

Everhart, Thomas E., Dr.
California Institute of Technology
Pasadena, CA 91125
University president

Evert, Chris
(Christine Marie)
c/o Int. Management Group
One Erieview Plaza
Cleveland, OH 44114
Former tennis great

Ewing, Patrick
c/o New York Knickerbockers
4 Pennsylvania Plaza
New York, NY 10001
Basketball star

Expose
8370 Wilshire Blvd. (#300)
Beverly Hills, CA 90211
Pop singers

Exxon
200 Park Ave.
Florham Park, NJ 07932
Lawrence G. Rawl, CEO

F

F.A.O. Schwarz
767 5th Ave.
New York, NY 10153
Peter Harris, president

Fahd, Ibn Abdul Aziz
Royal Diwan
Riyadh, Saudi Arabia
King of Saudi Arabia

Fair, William, Dr.
Sloan-Kettering Cancer Center
New York, NY 10021
Urology specialist

Fairbairn, Bruce
2744 W. 33rd Ave.
Vancouver, BC Canada
V6N 2G1
Record producer

Fairbanks, Douglas Elton, Jr.
c/o Inverness Corporation
545 Madison Ave.
New York, NY 10022
Actor

Fairchild, Morgan (Patsy McClenny)
P.O. Box 8170
Universal City, CA 91608
Actress

Falk, Peter
9200 Sunset Blvd. (#428)
Los Angeles, CA 90069
Actor

Falwell, Jerry, Rev.
P.O. Box 1111
Lynchburg, VA 24505
Religious leader

Family Circle Magazine
110 5th Ave.
New York, NY 10011
Arthur Hettich, editor

Fan Club Directory
2730 Baltimore Ave.
Pueblo, CO 81003

Fans of General Hospital
7623 Thames Ct.
Westchester, OH 45069
Sue Corbett, president

Farm Aid
21 Erie St. (#20)
Cambridge, MA 02139
Janet M. Corpus, executive
   director

Farr, Jamie
9000 Sunset Blvd. (12th floor)
Los Angeles, CA 90069
Actor

Farrakhan, Louis, Rev.
(Louis Eugene Walcott)
734 W. 79th St.
Chicago, IL 60620
Nation of Islam leader

Farrar, Straus & Giroux
19 Union Sq. West
New York, NY 10003
Roger Straus, president

Farrell, Mike
P.O. Box 5961-306
Sherman Oaks, CA 91413
Actor

Farrow, Mia (Maria de
Lourdes Villiers)
c/o Lionel Larner
850 7th Ave.
New York, NY 10019
Actress

Fascell, Dante B.
2354 Rayburn House Office Bldg.
Washington, DC 20515
Congressman from Florida

Fast, Howard
c/o Houghton Mifflin
2 Park St.
Boston, MA 02107
Author

Fat Boys, The
250 W. 57th St. (#1723)
New York, NY 10107
Rap group

Father Flanagan's Boys
Home
Boys Town, NE 68010
Valentine J. Peter, executive
   director

Fauntroy, Walter E.
2135 Rayburn House Office Bldg.
Washington, DC 20515
District of Columbia delegate

Fawcett, Farrah Leni
9830 Wilshire Blvd.
Beverly Hills, CA 90212
Actress

Fazio, Victor W., Dr.
Cleveland Clinic Foundation
Cleveland, OH 44106
Colon and rectal surgeon

Feather, Leonard
c/o Los Angeles Times
Times Mirror Square
Los Angeles, CA 90053
Jazz critic

Federal Aviation
   Administration
(FAA)
400 Seventh St. SW.
Washington, DC 20590
James Busey, chairman

Federal Bureau of
   Investigation
(FBI)
Ninth St. and Pennsylvania Ave.
Washington, DC 20535
William Steele Sessions, director

Federal Communications
   Commission
(FCC)
1919 M St. N.
Washington, DC 20554
Al Sikes, director

Federal Express Corp.
2990 Airway
Memphis, TN 38194
Frederick W. Smith, chairman

Federal Trade Commission (FTC)
Pennsylvania Ave. at 6th St. NW.
Washington, DC 20580
Daniel Oliver, chairman

Feiffer, Jules
c/o Dramatists Guild
234 West 44th St.
New York, NY 10036
Playwright/cartoonist

Feighan, Edward F.
1124 Longworth House Office Bldg.
Washington, DC 20515
Congressman from Ohio

Feinberg, Wilfred
U.S. Court of Appeal
Second Circuit
New York, NY 10007
Chief Judge

Feinstein, Diane
909 Montgomery St.
San Francisco, CA 94133
Former mayor of San Francisco

Feld, Kenneth
c/o Ringling Brothers
P.O. Box 2366, L'Enfant Plaza St.
Washington, DC 20026
Circus executive

Feldman, Corey
1917 1/2 Westwood Blvd. (#2)
Los Angeles, CA 90025
Actor

Feliciano, Jose
8961 Sunset Blvd. (#2B)
Los Angeles, CA 90069
Musician

Feminist Karate Union
5429 Russell Ave. NW.
Seattle, WA 98107
Teaches self-protection to women

Fenn, Sherilyn
1901 Ave. of the Stars (#840)
Los Angeles, CA 90067
Actress

Ferguson, Sarah Margaret
Buckingham Palace
London SW1 England
Duchess of York

Field, Sally
9830 Wilshire Blvd.
Beverly Hills, CA 90212
Actress

Field, Ted (Frederick)
c/o Interscope
10900 Wilshire Blvd. (#1400)
Los Angeles, CA 90024
Entertainment executive

Field and Stream Magazine
380 Madison Ave.
New York, NY 10017
Duncan Barnes, editor

Field Museum of Natural History
Roosevelt Rd. at Lake Shore Dr.
Chicago, IL 60605
Dr. Willard L. Boyd, CEO

Fields, Debbie, Mrs.
P.O. Box 680370
Park City, UT 84068
Cookie entrepreneur

Fine, Sally
3530 Pine Valley Dr.
Sarasota, FL 34239
Food and wine columnist

Fine, Stuart L., Dr.
Wilmer Eye Institute
Johns Hopkins Hospital
Baltimore, MD 21205
Retina specialist

Fine Young Cannibals
c/o AGM Mgmt.
1312 N. La Brea Ave.
Los Angeles, CA 90028
Rock group

Finks, Jim
c/o New Orleans Saints
1500 Poydras St.
New Orleans, LA 70112
Football executive

Finney, Albert
8899 Beverly Blvd.
Los Angeles, CA 90048
Actor

Firestone, Laurie
Office of the First Lady
1600 Pennsylvania Ave.
Washington, DC 20500
Social secretary

Firestone Tire and Rubber Co.
1200 Firestone Pkwy.
Akron, OH 44317
John J. Nevin, chairman

Fisher, Carrie
151 El Camino Dr.
Beverly Hills, CA 90212
Actress

Fisher, Paul
c/o Fisher Space Pen Company
711 Yucca St.
Boulder City, NV 89005
Scientist/economist/inventor

Fisk, Carlton
c/o Chicago White Sox
35th and Shields Ave.
Chicago, IL 60616
Baseball's "Pudge"

Fitzgerald, Ella
c/o Norman Granz
451 N. Canon Dr.
Beverly Hills, CA 90210
Jazz singer

Fitzwater, Max Marlin
c/o The White House
1600 Pennsylvania Ave. NW.
Washington, DC 20500
Presidential press secretary

Flanagan, Fionnula Manon
9220 Sunset Blvd. (#625)
Los Angeles, CA 90069
Actress

97

Fleetwood Mac
(Mick Fleetwood)
c/o Warner Bros.
3300 Warner Blvd.
Burbank, CA 91510
Rock group

Fleischer, Charles
c/o Walt Disney Pictures
500 S. Buena Vista St.
Burbank, CA 91521
Voice of Roger Rabbit

Fleming, Peggy Gale
P.O. Box 173
Los Gatos, CA 95030
Former ice skating star

Flex Magazine
21100 Erwin St.
Woodland Hills, CA 91367
Joe Weider, publisher

Flintstones, The (Fred,
Wilma, Pebbles and Dino)
3400 Cahuenga Blvd. West
Hollywood, CA 90068
Prehistoric family

Florio, James J.
2162 Rayburn House Office Bldg.
Washington, DC 20515
Congressman from New Jersey

Flynn, Raymond Leo
City Hall, Government Center
Boston, MA 02201
Mayor of Boston

FM-2030
(F.M. Esfandiary)
P.O. Box 24421
Los Angeles, CA 90024
Futurist

FOCUS
c/o Carol Giambalvo
2567 Columbus Ave.
Oceanside, NY 11572
Support group for former cult members

Fogerty, John
P.O. Box 9245
Berkeley, CA 94709
Singer/songwriter

Foley, Thomas
House Office Bldg.
Washington, DC 20515
Speaker of the House from Washington

Folger Shakespeare Library
201 Capitol St. SE.
Washington, DC 20003
Dr. Werner Gundersheimer, director

Follett, Ken
P.O. Box 708
London, England SW10 ODH
Author

Fonda, Bridget
Rt. #38, Box 2024
Livingston, MT 59047
Actress

Fonda, Jane
P.O. Box 491355
Los Angeles, CA 90049
Actress

Fonda, Peter
RR #38, Box 2024
Livingston, MT 59047
Actor

**Food & Drug Administration
(FDA)**
5600 Fishers Lane
Rockville, MD 20857
Frank E. Young, commissioner

Foote, Horton
c/o Kroll
390 West End Ave.
New York, NY 10024
Theater/film writer

Foray, June
1717 Highland Ave. (#414)
Hollywood, CA 90028
Voice of Olive Oyl

Forbes Magazine
60 5th Ave.
New York, NY 10011
James W. Michaels, editor

**Ford, Betty Bloomer
(Elizabeth)**
P.O. Box 927
Rancho Mirage, CA 92262
Former First Lady

**Ford, Ernie
(Tennessee)**
P.O. Box 31-552
San Francisco, CA 94131
Country singer

Ford, Faith
9229 Sunset Blvd. (#306)
Los Angeles, CA 90069
Actress

Ford, Gerald Rudolph, Jr.
P.O. Box 927
Rancho Mirage, CA 92270
Former President

Ford, Harrison
P.O. Box 5617
Beverly Hills, CA 90210
Actor

Ford, William D.
239 Cannon House Office Bldg.
Washington, DC 20515
Congressman from Michigan

Ford Motor Company
The American Road
Dearborn, MI 48121
Donald E. Petersen, chairman

Foreign Affairs
58 E. 68th St.
New York, NY 10021
William G. Hyland, editor

Forman, Milos
c/o Robert Lantz
888 7th Ave.
New York, NY 10106
Film director

Forsyth, Bill
c/o Lake Film Prods.
20 Winton Dr.
G-12 Glasgow, Scotland
Film director

**Forsythe, John
(Freund)**
9000 Sunset Blvd. (#1112)
Los Angeles, CA 90069
Actor

Foster, Jodie
(Alicia Christian)
8899 Beverly Blvd.
Los Angeles, CA 90048
Actress

Foster Parents Plan
156 Plan Way
Warwick, RI 02886
Kenneth Phillips, president

Four-H (4-H) Clubs
Extension Service
U.S. Dept. of Agriculture
Washington, DC 20250

Fowler, William Alfred, Dr.
California Institute of Technology
Pasadena, CA 91125
Nobel Prize physicist

Fox, Michael J.
9255 Sunset Blvd. (#710)
Los Angeles, CA 90069
Actor

Fox, Samantha
P.O. Box 159
Colchester CO3 5RD England
Pop singer

Fox, Tracy Pollan
10100 Santa Monica Blvd.
(#1600)
Los Angeles, CA 90067
Actress

Foxx, Redd
(John Elroy Sanford, Jr.)
c/o Eddie Murphy Prods.
Melrose Ave.
Los Angeles, CA 90038
Comedian

Foyt, A.J.
(Anthony Joseph, Jr.)
c/o NASCAR
1811 Volusia Ave.
Daytona Beach, FL 32015
Racecar driver

Franchise of Americans
Needing Sports
2213 Middlebury Rd.
Sacramento, CA 95815
Promotes a fan's Bill of Rights

Francis, Dick
c/o G.P. Putnam's Sons
200 Madison Ave.
New York, NY 10016
Mystery novelist

Francis, Genie
15301 Ventura Blvd. (#345)
Sherman Oaks, CA 91403
Actress

Frankenthaler, Helen
173 E. 94th St.
New York, NY 10028
Painter

Franklin, Aretha
P.O. Box 12137
Birmingham, MI 48102
Queen of Soul

Franklin, Joe
c/o WOR-TV
1440 Broadway
New York, NY 10019
Talk show host

Franklin Institute
Science Museum and Planetarium
20th & Benjamin Franklin Pkwy.
Philadelphia, PA 19103
Joel N. Bloom, president

Frazier, Joe
6290 Sunset Blvd. (#326)
Hollywood, CA 90028
Boxing's "Smokin' Joe"

Freed, Donald
8955 Beverly Blvd.
Los Angeles, CA 90048
Playwright

**Freedom of Information
   Center**
U. of Missouri
20 Walter Williams Hall
Columbia, MO 65211

Freeman, Morgan
10100 Santa Monica Blvd.
   (#1600)
Los Angeles, CA 90210
Actor

Frewer, Matt
9200 Sunset Blvd. (#625)
Los Angeles, CA 90069
"Max Headroom" actor

Frey, Glenn
7250 Beverly Blvd. (#200)
Los Angeles, CA 90036
Singer/songwriter

Friedan, Betty
One Lincoln Place (#40K)
New York, NY 10023
Feminist author

Friedman, Bruce Jay
8955 Beverly Blvd.
Los Angeles, CA 90048
Writer

Friedman, Budd
8162 Melrose Ave.
Los Angeles, CA 90046
Co-owner, Improv comedy clubs

**Friedman, Kinky
(Richard)**
511 Cozzens Ln.
North Brunswick, NJ 08902
Singer/author

Friedman, Milton
Hoover Institute, Stanford U.
Quadrangle Office
Palo Alto, CA 94305
Economist

Friel, Brian
Drumaweir House
Greencastle
County Donegal, Ireland
Playwright

Friends of the Earth
530 7th St. SE.
Washington, DC 20003

Friends United Meeting
Paul Enyart, presiding clerk
101 Quaker Hill Dr.
Richmond, IN 47374
Quaker organization

Fries, Chuck
6922 Hollywood Blvd.
Hollywood, CA 90028
Film/television producer

Frito-Lay
7701 Legacy Dr.
Plano, TX 75024
Michael H. Jordan, president

Frost, David Paradine
115-123 Bayham St.
London NW1 England
Television personality

Fruit of the Loom
6300 Sears Tower
Chicago, IL 60606
William F. Farley, CEO

Fry, Art
Minnesota Mining &
   Manufacturing
3M Center
St. Paul, MN 55101
Inventor of the Post-It

Frye Shoe
P.O. Box 888, Union Station
Union, NY 13760
Donald Coleman, CEO

Fuchs, Michael J.
1100 6th Ave.
New York, NY 10036
Home Box Office, president

Fuentes, Carlos
c/o Brandt and Brandt
1501 Broadway
New York, NY 10036
Author

Fugard, Athol
P.O. Box 50909, Walmer
Port Elizabeth, Republic of South
   Africa
Playwright

Fuji Photo
26-30 Nishiazabu
2-Chome, Minato-Ku
Tokyo 106 Japan
Minoru Ohnishi, president

Fulbright Scholars
3400 International Dr. NW. (#M-
   500)
Washington, DC 20008
Dr. M. Carlota Baca, executive
   director

Fulghum, Robert
c/o Random House
201 E. 50th St.
New York, NY 10022
Author/social critic

Fuller, Charles Henry, Jr.
1350 6th Ave.
New York, NY 10019
Playwright

Fuller Brush Co.
Westport Addition, P.O. Box 729
Great Bend, KS 67530
Leonard Dunlap, president

Funk and Wagnalls
70 Hilltop Rd.
Ramsey, NJ 07446
Edward Volkwein, president

Fuster, Valentin, Dr.
Mount Sinai Medical Center
New York, NY 10029
Cardiology specialist

Future Farmers of America
5632 Mt. Vernon Memorial Hwy.
Alexandria, VA 22309
C. Coleman Harris, executive
   secretary

G

Gable, Dan
RR 2, P.O. Box 55
Iowa City, IA 52240
Wrestling coach

Gabor, Zsa Zsa (Sari)
8721 Melrose Ave. (#108)
Los Angeles, CA 90069
Miss Hungary of 1936

Gabriel, Peter
25 Ives St.
London SW3 England
Rock musician

Galbraith, John Kenneth
Harvard University
207 Littauer Center
Cambridge, MA 02138
Economist

Gale, Robert Peter, Dr.
c/o UCLA Medical Center
Center for Health Sciences (#42-121)
Los Angeles, CA 90024
Radiation physician

Gallagher
P.O. Box 657
N. Hollywood, CA 91603
Comedian

Gallagher, Peter
40 W. 57th St.
New York, NY 10019
Actor

Gallaudet University
King Jordan, president
800 Florida Ave. NE.
Washington, DC 20002
University for the deaf

Gallo, Ernest and Julio
600 Yosemite Blvd.
Modesto, CA 95354
Vintners

Gallup, George Horace, III
P.O. Box 628
Princeton, NJ 08540
Research executive

Galway, James
c/o London Artists
73 Baker St.
London W1M 1AH England
Flutist

Gamblers Anonymous Fellowship
P.O. Box 17173
Los Angeles, CA 90017
Jim Z., national executive secretary

Gann, Dianne
5 School St.
Methuen, MA 01844
Created "Trump the Game"

Gannett Co.
P.O. Box 7858
Washington, DC 20044
John J. Curley, CEO

Gap
900 Cherry Ave. (#60)
San Bruno, CA 94066
Millard S. Drexler, president

Garcia, Andy
9301 Wilshire Blvd. (#312)
Beverly Hills, CA 90210
Actor

**Garcia, Jerry
(Jerome John)**
c/o Grateful Dead
1492 Pacific (#4)
San Francisco, CA 94109
Rock guitarist

Garcia Marquez, Gabriel
c/o Carmen Balcelos
Diagonal 580
Barcelona, Spain
Author

Garland, Judy
153 5th St.
Locke Haven, PA 17745
Late entertainer's fan club

**Garn, Jake
(Edward Jacob)**
4225 Federal Bldg.
Salt Lake City, UT 84138
Senator from Utah/astronaut

**Garner, James
(Baumgarner)**
8899 Beverly Blvd.
Los Angeles, CA 90048
Actor

Garr, Teri
9830 Wilshire Blvd.
Beverly Hills, CA 90212
Actress

Garrett, H. Lawrence, III
The Pentagon
Washington, DC 20350
Secretary of the Navy

Gay, William, Dr.
U. of Utah Medical Center
Salt Lake City, UT 84132
Heart transplant specialist

**Gayle, Crystal
(Brenda Webb)**
51 Music Square E.
Nashville, TN 37203
Country singer

Gaylord, Mitch
10000 Santa Monica Blvd. (#305)
Los Angeles, CA 90067
Gymnast/actor

**G.E. Stockholders Alliance
Against Nuclear Power &
Weapons**
P.O. Box 966
Columbia, MD 21044
Patricia T. Birnie, chairman

Geffen, David
9130 Sunset Blvd.
Los Angeles, CA 90069
Entertainment executive

Gehry, Frank
1520B Cloverfield Blvd.
Santa Monica, CA 90404
Architect

Gelberman, Richard, Dr.
Harvard Medical School
Boston, MA 02215
Hand surgeon

Geldof, Bob, Sir (Robert Frederick Xenon Geldof)
Davington Priory
London, England
Rock musician/founder of Live Aid

Geller, Uri
P.O. Box 5175
New York, NY 10150
Psychic

Genentech
R.A. Swanson, CEO
460 Pt. San Bruno Blvd.
S. San Francisco, CA 94080
World's largest biotechnology co.

General Electric (GE)
3135 Easton Turnpike
Fairfield, CT 06430
John F. Welch, Jr., chairman

General Foods
250 North St.
White Plains, NY 10625
Robert S. Morrison, president

General Mills (Wheaties, Cheerios, Betty Crocker)
9200 Wayzatta Blvd.
Minneapolis, MN 55440
H.B. Atwater, Jr., CEO

General Motors Corp. (GMC)
3044 W. Grand Blvd.
Detroit, MI 48202
Robert Stemple, CEO

Genesis
25 Ives St.
London SW3 England
Rock band

George (Brown), Phyllis
P.O. Box 4308
Lexington, KY 40503
Chicken manufacturer

George, Wally
P.O. Box 787
Los Angeles, CA 90078
Volatile talk show host

Georgia-Pacific Corp.
133 Peachtree St. NE
Atlanta, GA 30303
T. Marshall Hann, Jr., CEO

Gephardt, Richard Andrew
218 Cannon House Office Bldg.
Washington, DC 20515
Congressman from Missouri

Gere, Richard
c/o PMK
One Lincoln Plaza
New York, NY 10023
Actor

Gerrold, David
8955 Beverly Blvd.
Los Angeles, CA 90048
Science fiction writer

Gerry Baby Products
12520 Grant Dr.
Denver, CO 80241
Mary Snyder, CEO

Gertz, Jami
P.O. Box 5617
Beverly Hills, CA 90210
Actress

Getty, Gordon P.
17985 Pacific Coast Hwy.
Malibu, CA 90265
Composer/philanthropist

G.H. Bass Co.
218 Main St.
Wilton, ME 04294
Morris Tobaksplat, CEO

Ghirardelli Chocolate Co.
111 139th St.
San Leandro, CA 94578
Dennis DeDomenico, chairman

Gibbons, John J.
U.S. Court of Appeal
Third Circuit
Philadelphia, PA 19106
Chief Judge

Gibbs, Joe
c/o Washington Redskins
P.O. Box 17247, Dulles Airport
Washington, DC 20041
Football coach

Gibson, Debbie
P.O. Box 489
Merrick, NY 11566
Pop singer/songwriter

Gibson, Kirk
c/o Los Angeles Dodgers
1000 Elysian Park Ave.
Los Angeles, CA 90012
Baseball star

Gibson, Mel
P.O. Box 2156
Santa Monica, CA 90406
Actor

Gielgud, (Arthur) John, Sir
South Pavilion
Wotton Underwood
Aylesbury HP18 OSB England
Actor

Gifted Child Society
190 Rock Rd.
Glen Rock, NJ 07452
Gina Ginsberg Riggs, executive
director

Gifted Children Monthly
P.O. Box 7200
Bergenfield, NJ 08621
James Alverno, editor

Gilbert, Walter
c/o Biological Laboratories
Divinity Ave., Harvard U.
Cambridge, MA 02138
*Mapping human genetic
blueprint*

**Gillespie, Dizzy
(John Birks)**
1995 Broadway (#501)
New York, NY 10023
Jazz great

Gilley, Mickey Leroy
P.O. Box 1242
Pasadena, TX 77501
Country singer

Gilliam, Terry Vance
c/o The Old Hall
South Grove, Highgate
London N6 6BP England
Film director

Gingrich, Newt
2438 Rayburn House Office Bldg.
Washington, DC 20515
Congressman from Georgia

Ginsberg, Allen
c/o City Lights
261 Columbus Ave.
San Francisco, CA 94133
Poet

Girl Scouts of the U.S.A.
830 3rd Ave.
New York, NY 10022
Betty F. Pilsbury, president

Giscard d'Estaing, Valery
c/o Assemblee National
75355 Paris, France
Politician

Gish, Lillian
(de Guiche)
40 E. 57th St.
New York, NY 10022
Actress

Givenchy, Hubert James
Marcel Taffin
(De Givenchy)
3 Ave. George V
75008 Paris, France
Fashion designer

Givens, Bill
7510 Sunset Blvd. (#100)
Los Angeles, CA 90046
Movie blooper collector

Glamour Magazine
350 Madison Ave.
New York, NY 10015
Ruth Whitney, editor

Glanville, Jerry
c/o Atlanta Falcons
Suwanee Road at I-85
Suwanee, GA 30174
Football coach

Glass, Philip
853 Broadway (#2120)
New York, NY 10003
Composer

Glasser, Ira Saul
American Civil Liberties Union
132 W. 43rd St.
New York, NY 10036
ACLU head

Glauber, Roy Jay, Dr.
Harvard University
Lyman Lab of Physics
Cambridge, MA 02138
Theoretical physicist

Glenn, John Herschell, Jr.
503 Senate Hart Bldg.
Washington, DC 20510
Senator from Ohio/astronaut

Glenn, Scott
P.O. Box 1902
Santa Fe, NM 87504
Actor

**Glenn Miller Birthplace
Society**
P.O. Box 61
Clarinda, IA 51632
Wilda Martin, secretary

Glover, Danny
P.O. Box 885464
San Francisco, CA 94188
Actor

**Godard, Jean-Luc
(Hans Lucas)**
c/o Sonimage
99 Rue du Roule
92200 Neuilly, France
Film director

**Godden, Rumer
(Margaret)**
Ardnacloich, Moniaive, Thornhill
Dumfriesshire D63 4HZ Scotland
Children's author

Gold Fields of South Africa
75 Fox St.
Johannesburg 2001 Republic of
South Africa
R.A. Plumbridge, chairman

Gold Medal Bakery
1397 Bay St.
Fall River, MA 02724
L.S. LeConte, chairman

Goldberg, Gary David
4024 Radford St.
Studio City, CA 90049
Television producer

**Goldberg, Whoopi
(Caryn Johnson)**
9830 Wilshire Blvd.
Beverly Hills, CA 90212
Actress/comedian

Goldblum, Jeff
8225 Hollywood Blvd.
Los Angeles, CA 90069
Actor

Golden Gloves Association
1503 Linda Lane
Hutchinson, KS 67502
Jim Beasley, executive secretary

Golden State Warriors
Oakland Coliseum Arena
Oakland, CA 94621
James Fitzgerald, chairman

Golding, William
Ebble Thatch, Bowerchalke
Wilshire, England
Author

Goldstein, Joseph L., Dr.
5323 Harry Hines Blvd.
Dallas, TX 75235
Nobel Prize geneticist

Goldwater, Barry Morris
P.O. Box 1601
Scottsdale, AZ 85252
Politician

**Good Housekeeping
Magazine**
959 8th Ave.
New York, NY 10019
John Mack Carter, editor

Good Sam RV Owners Club
29901 Agoura Rd.
Agoura, CA 91301
Sue Bray, executive director

Goodall, Jane
P.O. Box 26846
Tucson, AZ 85726
Chimpanzee expert

Goode, Wilson
215 City Hall
Philadelphia, PA 19107
Mayor of Philadelphia

Gooden, Dwight Eugene
c/o New York Metropolitans
126th and Roosevelt Ave.
Flushing, NY 11368
Baseball's "Dr. K"

Goodman, John
P.O. Box 5617
Beverly Hills, CA 90210
Actor

Goodwill Industries of America
9200 Wisconsin Ave. NW.
Bethesda, MD 20814
David M. Cooney, CEO

Goodwin, Albert T.
U.S. Court of Appeal
Ninth Circuit
San Francisco, CA 94101
Chief Judge

Goodyear Tire and Rubber Co.
1144 E. Market St.
Akron, OH 44316
Tom H. Barrett, CEO

Gorbachev, Mikhail Sergeyevich
Gorbacheva, Raisa Maksimovna
Staraya pl 4
Moscow, U.S.S.R.
President of U.S.S.R./First Lady

Gordon, Irving
2B Summit St.
East Patchogue, NY 11772
Owns world's longest running Volvo

Gore, Albert, Jr.
393 Senate Russell Bldg.
Washington, DC 20510
Senator from Tennessee

Gorlin, Richard, Dr.
Mount Sinai Medical Center
New York, NY 10029
Medical leader

Gorshin, Frank
P.O. Box 48559
Los Angeles, CA 90048
Impressionist

Gossett, Louis, Jr.
P.O. Box 6187
Malibu, CA 90264
Actor

Gould, Elliott (Goldstein)
151 El Camino Dr.
Beverly Hills, CA 90212
Actor

Gould, Stephen Jay
c/o Museum of Comparative
  Zoology
Harvard University
Cambridge, MA 02138
Scientist/author

Gourmet Magazine
560 Lexington Ave.
New York, NY 10022
Jane Montant, editor

Grace, J. Peter
Grace Plaza
1114 6th Ave.
New York, NY 10036
Business leader

Graceland Mansion
P.O. Box 16508
Memphis, TN 38186
Shrine/home of Elvis Presley

Grade, Lord Lew
c/o Embassy
3 Audley Sq.
London W1Y 5DR England
Entertaiment executive

Grady, Mary
3575 Cahuenga Blvd. West
  (#320)
Los Angeles, CA 90068
Children's talent agent

**Graf, Steffi
(Stephanie Maria)**
12-D 6000 Frankfurt-am-Main
71, Germany
Tennis star

Graham, Bill
201 11th St.
San Francisco, CA 94103
Rock music promoter

**Graham, Billy
(William Franklin)**
1300 Harmon Place
Minneapolis, MN 55403
Religious leader

Graham, Katharine
c/o Washington Post
1150 15th St. NW.
Washington, DC 20071
Newspaper publisher

Graham, Martha
316 E. 63rd St.
New York, NY 10021
Dancer/choreographer

Graham, Robert
69 Windward Ave.
Venice, CA 90291
Sculptor

Gramm, Phil
370 Senate Russell Bldg.
Washington, DC 20510
Senator from Texas

Grammer, Kelsey
345 N. Maple Dr.
Beverly Hills, CA 90210
"Cheers" actor

Grand Ole Opry House
2804 Opryland Dr.
Nashville, TN 37214
Home of country music

Grandmother Clubs of America
203 N. Wabash Ave.
Chicago, IL 60601

Grant, Amy
Riverstone Farm, Moran Rd.
Franklin, TN 37064
Christian pop singer

Grant, Bob
c/o WABC
2 Penn Plaza
New York, NY 10121
Talk show host

Grant, Johnny
5800 Sunset Blvd.
Hollywood, CA 90028
"Mayor of Hollywood"

Grant, Lee (Lyova Rosenthal)
151 El Camino Dr.
Los Angeles, CA 90212
Actress/film director

Granta
William Buford, editor
40 W. 23rd St.
New York, NY 10010
Journal of new writing

Grateful Dead, The
P.O. Box 1566, Main Office St.
Montclair, NJ 07043
Rock band

Gray, Hanna Holborn
University of Chicago
Chicago, IL 60637
University president

Gray, Linda
P.O. Box 1370
Canyon Country, CA 91351
Actress

Gray, Paul E., Dr.
c/o Massachusetts Inst. of Tech.
Cambridge, MA 02139
University president

Gray, William H., III
2454 Rayburn House Office Bldg.
Washington, DC 20515
Congressman from Michigan

Gray Panthers
Karen Talbot, executive director
311 S. Juniper St. (#601)
Philadelphia, PA 19107
Seniors activist group

Great Expectations
Jeffrey Ullman, president
16830 Ventura Blvd. (Suite P)
Encino, CA 91436
Video dating service

Great Wallendas
138 Frog Hollow Rd.
Churchville, PA 18966
Circus high-wire artists

Great White
P.O. Box 67487
Los Angeles, CA 90067
Rock band

Greek Orthodox Archdiocese
8-10 E. 79th St.
New York, NY 10021
Archbishop Iakovos, president

Greeley, Andrew (Moran)
6030 S. Ellis
Chicago, IL 60637
Novelist

Green, Al, Rev.
9200 Sunset Blvd. (#823)
Los Angeles, CA 90069
Soul singer

Green Bay Packers
1265 Lombardi Ave.
Green Bay, WI 54303
Dominic Olejniczak, chairman

Greenburg, Dan
9000 Sunset Blvd. (#1200)
Los Angeles, CA 90069
Writer

Greene, Bob
c/o Chicago Tribune
435 N. Michigan Ave.
Chicago, IL 60611
Journalist

Greene, Graham
c/o Reinhardt Books
27 Wright's Lane
London W8 5T2 England
Novelist

Greene, Michele
c/o Kohner
9169 Sunset Blvd.
Los Angeles, CA 90069
Actress

Greene, Shecky
Charles Rapp Enterprises
1650 Broadway
New York, NY 10019
Comedian

Greenfield, John Charles, Dr.
c/o Upjohn Co.
Drug Metabolism Research
Kalamazoo, MI 49007
Bio-organic chemist

Greenpeace, USA
1436 U St. NW.
Washington, DC 20009
Peter Bahouth, executive director

Greenspan, Alan
20th St. & Constitution Ave. NW.
Washington, DC 20551
Federal Reserve System, chairman

Greenspan, Bud
33 E. 68th St.
New York, NY 10021
Sports film producer

Greer, Germaine
c/o Aitken and Stone
29 Fernshaw Road
London SW10 OTG England
Author

Greer Egg Farm
Rt. 1, Box 68
Muchie, TN 38357
Joe Greer, president

Gregory, Dick
P.O. Box 3266, Tower Hill Farm
Plymouth, MA 02361
Weight loss expert

Gretzky, Wayne
c/o Los Angeles Kings
P.O. Box 17013
Inglewood, CA 90308
Hockey's "Great One"

Grey, Jennifer
121 N. San Vicente Blvd.
Beverly Hills, CA 90211
Actress

Grieco, Richard
10201 W. Pico Blvd. (#761)
Los Angeles, CA 90035
Actor

Grier, Rosie
(Roosevelt)
c/o Are You Committed?
1977 St. Vermont Ave. (#200)
Los Angeles, CA 90007
Evangelist/former football star

Griffin, Merv
(Mervyn Edward)
1541 N. Vine St.
Los Angeles, CA 90028
Entertainer/executive

Griffith, Andy
151 El Camino Dr.
Beverly Hills, CA 90212
Actor

Griffith, Melanie
8899 Beverly Blvd.
Los Angeles, CA 90048
Actress

Griffith, Nanci
P.O. Box 121684
Nashville, TN 37212
Country singer

Gritz, Bo
Center for Action
Box 9
Boulder City, NV 89005
Most decorated Green Beret

Grizzard, Lewis
P.O. Box 4689
Atlanta, GA 30302
Humorist

Grodin, Charles
445 N. Bedford Dr. (PH)
Beverly Hills, CA 90210
Actor

Groening, Matt
10201 W. Pico Blvd.
Los Angeles, CA 90035
"The Simpsons" cartoonist

Gros Louis, Kenneth R.R.
Indiana University
Bloomington, IN 47405
University president

Gross, Michael
8899 Beverly Blvd.
Los Angeles, CA 90048
Actor

Grossman, Robert, Dr.
Hospital of U. of Pennsylvania
Philadelphia, PA 19104
Kidney transplant specialist

Grotoswki, Jerzy
Via Manzoni 22
56025 Pontedera, Italy
Actor/teacher

Grumman Corp.
1111 Stewart Ave.
Bethpage, NY 11714
John O'Brien, chairman

GTE Corporation
One Stamford Forum
Stamford, CT 06904
James L. Johnson, CEO

Guardian Angels
Curtis Sliwa, founder
982 E. 89th St.
Brooklyn, NY 11236
Citizens' crime prevention group

Guare, John
555 W. 57th St. (#1230)
New York, NY 10019
Playwright

Guber, Peter
Columbia Pictures
Columbia Plaza
Burbank, CA 91505
Entertainment executive

Guccione, Bob
1965 Broadway
New York, NY 10023
Penthouse magazine, publisher

Guest, Christopher
8899 Beverly Blvd.
Los Angeles, CA 90048
Actor

Guggenheim Foundation
90 Park Ave.
New York, NY 11016
William Clarke Wescoe, chairman

Guinness
The Earl of Iveagh, president
39 Portman Sq.
London W1H 9HB England
Brewery

Guisewite, Cathy Lee
c/o Universal Press Syndicate
4900 Main St.
Kansas City, MO 64112
"Cathy" *cartoonist*

Gumbel, Bryant
30 Rockefeller Plaza (#1508)
New York, NY 10112
Today Show *host*

Gumby Fan Club
P.O. Box 3905
Schaumburg, IL 60168
A.J. Marsiglia, director

Gun World
34249 Camino Capistrano
Capistrano Beach, CA 92624
Jack Lewis, editor

Guns and Ammo Magazine
8490 Sunset Blvd.
Los Angeles, CA 90069
E.G. Bell, editor

Guns N' Roses
1830 S. Robertson Blvd. (#201)
Los Angeles, CA 90035
Rock band

Gurney, A.R.
c/o Dramatists Guild
234 West 44th St.
New York, NY 10036
Playwright

Guthrie, Arlo
The Farm
Washington, MA 01223
Folk singer

Guttenberg, Steve
8444 Wilshire Blvd. (#500)
Beverly Hills, CA 90211
Actor

Guy, Jasmine
9113 Sunset Blvd.
Los Angeles, CA 90069
Actress

Gwynn, Tony
c/o San Diego Padres
9449 Friars Rd.
San Diego, CA 92120
Baseball star

Gwynne, Fred
888 7th Ave. (#1602)
New York, NY 10019
Actor

H

Haake, James
("Gypsy")
c/o La Cage Aux Folles
643 La Cienega Blvd.
W. Hollywood, CA 90069
Female impersonator

Habilitat, Inc.
Vinny Marino, founder
P.O. Box AF
Kaneohi, HI 96744
Drug treatment center

Hacker, Richard Carleton
P.O. Box 634
Beverly Hills, CA 90213
Pipe smoking expert

Hackett, Buddy
(Leonard Hacker)
151 El Camino Dr.
Beverly Hills, CA 90212
Comedian

Hackford, Taylor
5750 Wilshire Blvd. (#600)
Los Angeles, CA 90036
Film director

Hackman, Gene
(Eugene Alden)
8500 Wilshire Blvd. (#801)
Beverly Hills, CA 90211
Actor

Hagen, Uta Thyra
c/o Herbert Berghof Studio
120 Bank St.
New York, NY 10014
Actress/teacher

Haggar Apparel Co.
6113 Lemmon Ave.
Dallas,TX 75209
Joseph M. Haggar, Jr., president

Haggard, Merle Ronald
P.O. Box 536
Palo Cedro, CA 96073
Country singer

Hagler, Marvelous Marvin
c/o Marvelous Enterprises
28 Ward St.
Brockton, MA 02401
Boxer

Hahn, Jessica
P.O. Box 58672
Phoenix, AZ 85074
*Former church secretary/nude
model*

Hailey, Arthur
P.O. Box N7776 Lyford Cay
Nassau, Bahamas
Author

Haim, Corey
c/o Light
113 N. Robertson Blvd.
Los Angeles, CA 90048
Actor

Halberstam, David
c/o William Morrow & Co.
105 Madison Ave.
New York, NY 10016
Author

Haley, Alex Palmer
P.O. Box 3338
Beverly Hills, CA 90213
Roots *author*

Hall, Alton David Jr.
P.O. Box 260
Boulder, CO 80309
Geographer

**Hall, Anthony Michael
(Michael Anthony Thomas
 Charles Hall)**
9255 Sunset Blvd. (#710)
Los Angeles, CA 90069
Actor

Hall, Arsenio
c/o Paramount Television
Melrose Ave.
Los Angeles, CA 90038
Talk show host/comedian

Hall, Deidre
15301 Ventura Blvd. (#345)
Sherman Oaks, CA 91403
Actress

Hall, Peter, Sir
18 Exeter St.
London WC2E 7DU England
Theater director

Hall, Rich T.
P.O. Box 2350
Hollywood, CA 90078
"Sniglets" *creator*

Hall, Robert J., Dr.
Texas Heart Institute
Houston, TX 77025
Cardiology specialist

**Hall & Oates
(Darryl/John)**
130 W. 57th St. (#2A)
New York, NY 10019
Rock singers

Halliwell, Leslie
36 Golden Sq., Granada
London, W1 England
Film historian

**Hallman, Henry Theodore,
 Jr.**
P.O. Box 250
Ledrach, PA 19450
Textile designer/artist

Hallmark Cards
2501 McGee Trafficway (#419580)
Kansas City, MO 64141
Irvine O. Hockaday, Jr., CEO

Hamill, Dorothy Stuart
One Erieview Plaza
Cleveland, OH 44114
Ice skating star

Hamill, Mark
P.O. Box 55
Malibu, CA 90265
Actor

Hamill, Pete
555 W. 57th St. (#1230)
New York, NY 10019
Writer

Hamilton, Lee H.
2187 Rayburn House Office Bldg.
Washington, DC 20515
Congressman from Indiana

Hamilton, Linda
10100 Santa Monica Blvd.
 (#1600)
Los Angeles, CA 90067
Actress

Hamlin, Harry
151 El Camino Dr.
Beverly Hills, CA 90212
Actor

Hamlisch, Marvin
c/o Songwriters Guild
276 5th Ave.
New York, NY 10001
Songwriter

Hammer, Armand, Dr.
c/o Occidental Petroleum
 Corporation
10889 Wilshire Blvd.
Los Angeles, CA 90024
Billionaire oilman

Hammer, MC
2599 Stevenson Blvd.
Fremont, CA 94538
Rapper

Hammill, James F., Dr.
Neurological Institute
Columbia-Presbyterian Med.
 Center
New York, NY 10032
Neurology specialist

Hampton, Henry
c/o Blacksides, Inc.
486 Shawmut Ave.
Boston, MA 02118
Documentary producer

**Hancock, Herbie
(Herbert Jeffrey)**
1250 N. Doheny Dr.
Los Angeles, CA 90069
Jazz musician

Handgun Control, Inc.
1255 I St. NW (#1100)
Washington, DC 20005
Sarah Brady, spokesperson

Hanks, Tom
P.O. Box 1276
Los Angeles, CA 90049
Actor

**Hanna-Barbera Productions
(William Denby/Joseph)**
3400 Cahuenga Blvd. West
Hollywood, CA 90068
Cartoon producers

Hansen, James
Goddard Inst. for Space Studies
2880 Broadway
New York, NY 10025
Global warming expert

Happy Humpers
11510 Montgomery Rd.
Beltsville, MD 20705
Englebert Humperdinck fan club

Harcourt Brace Jovanovich
6277 Sea Harbor Dr.
Orlando, FL 32821
Ralph D. Caulo, president

Hard Rock Cafe
Peter Morton, founder
510 N. Robertson Blvd.
Los Angeles, CA 90048
Hip restaurant

Harlem Globetrotters
6121 Sunset Blvd.
Los Angeles, CA 90038
Basketball's court jesters

Harley Davidson Motor Co.
3700 W. Juneau Ave.
Milwaukee, WI 53208
Vaughn Le Roy Beals, Jr.,
   president

Harmon, Mark
P.O. Box 5617
Beverly Hills, CA 90210
Actor

Harper, Jessica
151 El Camino Dr.
Beverly Hills, CA 90069
Actress

Harper, Tess
151 El Camino Dr.
Beverly Hills, CA 90212
Actress

Harper, Valerie
445 N. Bedford Dr. (PH)
Beverly Hills, CA 90210
Actress

Harper & Row
10 E. 53rd St.
New York, NY 10022
George Craig, president

Harper's Bazaar Magazine
1700 Broadway
New York, NY 10019
Anthony Mazzola, president

Harper's Magazine
666 Broadway
New York, NY 10012
Lewis H. Lapham, editor

Harris, Emmylou
P.O. Box 1384
Brentwood, TN 37027
Country singer

Harris, Jean
Bedford Hills Correctional
   Facility
Westchester County
Bedford Hills, NY 10507
*Murderer of Scarsdale Diet
   creator*

Harris, Jimmy "Jam"
c/o Flyte Tyme
4330 Nicollet Ave.
Minneapolis, MN 55409
Music producer

Harris, Julie
151 El Camino Dr.
Beverly Hills, CA 90212
Actress

Harris, Richard
P.O. Box N-1812
Nassau, Bahamas
Actor

Harris, Susan
1438 N. Gower St. (4th floor)
Los Angeles, CA 90028
Television producer

Harrison, George
Friar Park Rd.
Henley-On-Thames, England
Film producer/ex-Beatle

Harrison, Gregory
8899 Beverly Blvd.
Los Angeles, CA 90048
Actor

Harrison, John
5929 College Ave.
Oakland, CA 94618
Ice cream taster

Harrold, Kathryn
P.O. Box 5617
Beverly Hills, CA 90210
Actress

Harry, Deborah
12 Price Drive
Edison, NJ 08817
Jill Partner, fan club president

Hart, Mary
c/o "Entertainment Tonight"
Melrose Ave.
Los Angeles, CA 90038
Television personality

Hartford Whalers
One Civic Center Plaza
Hartford, CT 06103
Emile Francis, general manager

Harth, Robert
c/o Music Associates of Aspen
P.O. Box AA
Aspen, CO 81612
Music executive

Hartman, Lisa
10100 Santa Monica Blvd.
(#1600)
Los Angeles, CA 90067
Actress/singer

Hartz Mountain Corp.
700 S. Fourth St.
Harrison, NJ 07029
Leonard Stern, CEO

Harvey, Paul
360 N. Michigan Ave.
Chicago, IL 60601
Radio commentator

Harvey Milk School
Joyce Hunter, director
401 West St.
New York, NY 10014
High school for homosexual teens

Hasbro
1027 Newport Ave.
Pawtucket, RI 02861
Alan G. Hassenfeld, president

Hassan, Steven
P.O. Box 686
Boston, MA 02258
Cult deprogrammer

Hassan II, King
Royal Palace
Rabat, Morocco
King of Morocco

Hatch, Orrin Grany
135 Senate Russell Bldg.
Washington, DC 20510
Senator from Utah

Hauer, Rutger
9255 Sunset Blvd. (#505)
Los Angeles, CA 90069
Actor

Hauptman, Herbert Aaron, Dr.
Medical Foundation of Buffalo
73 High St.
Buffalo, NY 14203
Nobel Prize mathematician

Havel, Vaclav
Udejvickeho Rybnicky 4
1600 Prague 6, Czechoslovakia
*Pres. of Czechoslovakia/
playwright*

Havers, Nigel
60 St. James's St.
London SW1 England
Actor

Hawke, Ethan
9830 Wilshire Blvd.
Beverly Hills, CA 90212
Actor

Hawking, Stephen William
5 West Road
Cambridge, England
Scientist

Hawkins, Screamin' Jay (Jalacy)
1833 N. Orange Grove Ave.
Los Angeles, CA 90046
R&B musician

Hawn, Goldie
c/o Hollywood Pictures
500 S. Buena Vista Ave.
Burbank, CA 91505
Actress

Hayden, Tom
2141 State Capitol
Sacramento, CA 95814
Politician

Hayes, Read
5471 Lake Howell Rd. (#236)
Winter Park, FL 32792
Shoplifting expert

Hayflick, Leonard, Dr.
University of California
VA Medical Center
San Francisco, CA 94121
Gerontologist

Hays, Robert
151 El Camino Dr.
Beverly Hills, CA 90212
Actor

Headache Institute
360 San Miguel Dr. (#603)
Newport Beach, CA 92660
Dr. C. Philip O'Carroll, director

Healy, Timothy S., Rev.
Georgetown University
Washington, DC 20052
University president

Hearn, Chick
c/o Los Angeles Lakers
P.O. Box 10
Inglewood, CA 90306
Sportscaster

Hearns, Thomas
c/o Emmanuel Steward
19600 W. McNichol St.
Detroit, MI 48219
Boxing's "Hit Man"

Hearst, Patricia
P.O. Box 491187
Los Angeles, CA 90049
Newspaper fortune heiress

Hearst, Randolph A.
959 8th Ave.
New York, NY 10019
Newspaper industry leader

Heart
219 1st Ave. N. (#333)
Seattle, WA 98109
Rock group's fan club

Hee Haw
P.O. Box 140400
Nashville, TN 37214
Country television show

Heflin, Howell Thomas
728 Senate Hart Bldg.
Washington, DC 20510
Senator from Alabama

Hefner, Christine
919 Michigan Ave.
Chicago, IL 60611
Playboy magazine, publisher

Hefner, Hugh Marston
10236 Charing Cross Rd.
Los Angeles, CA 90024
Playboy magazine, founder

Heilman, Ken, Dr.
U. of Florida Medical Center
Gainesville, FL 32610
Neurology specialist

Heineken Breweries
NV Postbox 28 1000 AA
Amsterdam, Netherlands
Alfred Henry Heineken, CEO

Heller, Joseph
c/o Simon & Schuster
630 5th Ave.
New York, NY 10020
Author

Helmond, Katharine
151 El Camino Dr.
Beverly Hills, CA 90212
Actress

Helms, Jesse
403 Senate Dirksen Bldg.
Washington, DC 20510
Senator from North Carolina

Heloise
235 E. 45th St.
New York, NY 10017
Domestic life advisor

Hemlock Society
Derek Humphrey, president
P.O. Box 11830
Eugene, OR 97440
Euthanasia advocates

Henderson, Rickey Henley
c/o Oakland Athletics
Oakland-Alameda County
　Stadium
Oakland, CA 94621
Baseball star

Henley, Beth
1350 6th Ave.
New York, NY 10019
Playwright

Henley, Don
10880 Wilshire Blvd. (#2110)
Los Angeles, CA 90024
Rock musician

Henner, Marilu
2400 Broadway (#100)
Santa Monica, CA 90404
Actress

Henning, Doug
11940 San Vicente Blvd. (#49032)
Los Angeles, CA 90049
Magician

Henry, Buck
(B. Zuckerman)
151 El Camino Dr.
Beverly Hills, CA 90212
Actor/writer/comedian

Hepburn, Audrey
c/o Kurt Frings
9440 Santa Monica Blvd.
Beverly Hills, CA 90210
Actress

Herbranson, Janice
McLeod, ND 58057
Lowest-paid teacher in America

Herman, Pee-wee
(Paul Reubens)
P.O. Box 48243
Los Angeles, CA 90048
Comic actor

Herrmann, Edward
8899 Beverly Blvd.
Los Angeles, CA 90048
Actor

Hersh, Dale
c/o Lefty's Corner
P.O. Box 615
Clarks Summit, PA 18411
Sells left-handed products

Hershey, Barbara
(Barbara Herzstine)
9830 Wilshire Blvd.
Beverly Hills, CA 90212
Actress

Hershey Foods
R.A. Zimmerman, CEO
100 Mansion Rd.
Hershey, PA 17033
Chocolate maker

Hershiser, Orel Leonard IV
c/o Los Angeles Dodgers
1000 Elysian Park Ave.
Los Angeles, CA 90012
Baseball pitcher

Hervey, Jason
c/o "The Wonder Years"
2040 Ave. of the Stars
Los Angeles, CA 90067
Actor

Herzog, Werner
Lichtinger Str. 9 D-8000
60 Munich, Germany
Film director

Herzog, Whitey
(Dorrel Norman Elvert)
250 Stadium Plaza
St. Louis, MO 63102
Baseball's "White Rat"

Hesseman, Howard
151 El Camino Dr.
Beverly Hills, CA 90212
Actor

Heston, Charlton
(John Charlton Carter)
8730 Sunset Blvd. (6th floor)
Los Angeles, CA 90069
Actor

Hetrick-Martin Institute for
Lesbian and Gay Youth
401 West St.
New York, NY 10014
Damon Martin, cofounder

Hewitt, Don
c/o CBS News
524 W. 57th St.
New York, NY 10019
"60 Minutes" producer

Hewlett-Packard Co.
3000 Hanover St.
Palo Alto, CA 94304
David Packard, chairman

Heyerdahl, Thor
Hulen Meadows
Ketchum, ID 83340
Adventurer/scientist

Heyman, Ira Michael
U. of California at Berkeley
Berkeley, CA 94720
University president

Hiatt, Arnold
c/o Stride Rite Corporation
5 Cambridge Center
Cambridge, MA 02141
Business Leader

Hicks, Catherine
10100 Santa Monica Blvd.
(#1600)
Los Angeles, CA 90067
Actress

Hier, Marvin, Rabbi
Simon Wiesenthal Center
9760 W. Pico Blvd.
Los Angeles, CA 90035
Holocaust expert

Higgins, Jack
(Henry Patterson)
c/o David Higham
5-8 Lower John St.
London WIR 4HA England
Thriller author

Higgins, Joel
10100 Santa Monica Blvd.
(#1600)
Los Angeles, CA 90067
Actor

Higham, Charles
c/o Barbara Lowenstein
250 W. 57th St.
New York, NY 10019
Biographer

Highlights for Children Magazine
2300 W. 5th Ave.
Columbus, OH 43272
Walter B. Barbe, editor

Hill, Benny
2 Queens Gate (#7)
London SW7 England
Comedian

Hill, George Roy
c/o Pan Arts Productions
75 Rockefeller Plaza
New York, NY 10019
Film director

Hillary, Edmund Percival, Sir
c/o High Commission of New Zealand
25 Golf Links
New Delhi, India
Second man to climb Mt. Everest

Hillegass, Clifton Keith
1701 P Street
Lincoln, NE 68508
Cliff's Notes founder

Hills, Carla
600 17th Street NW.
Washington, DC 20506
U.S. trade representative

Hills Bros. Coffee
2 Harrison St.
San Francisco, CA 94105
Norman E. Dear, chairman

Hilton Hotels Corp.
9336 Civic Center Dr.
Beverly Hills, CA 90209
Barron Hilton, CEO

Hinckley, John, Jr.
c/o St. Elizabeth's Hospital
2700 Martin Luther King Ave.
Washington, DC 20005
Attacker of President Reagan

Hinton, S.E. (Susan Eloise)
8955 Beverly Blvd.
Los Angeles, CA 90048
Author

Hirt, Al
P.O. Box 1574
Lutz, FL 33549
New Orleans jazz trumpeter

Hitachi, Ltd.
4-6 Kanda-Surugadai, Chiyoda-ku
Tokyo, Japan
Hirokichi Yoshiyama, chairman

Hitchings, George H., Dr.
303 Cornwallis Rd.
Research Triangle Pk, NC 27709
Nobel Prize biochemist

Hite, Shere
P.O. Box 5282
FDR Station
New York, NY 10022
Human sexuality author

Hockney, David
c/o Knoedler Gallery
22 Cork St.
London W2 England
Painter

Hodges, David Julian, Dr.
695 Park Ave.
New York, NY 10021
Anthropologist

Hoff, Julian T., Dr.
U. of Michigan Medical Center
Ann Arbor, MI 48109
Neurosurgeon

Hoffman, Dustin Lee
9830 Wilshire Blvd.
Beverly Hills, CA 90212
Actor

**Hoffman, Jane
("The Backyard Scientist")**
P.O. Box 16966
Irvine, CA 92713
Author of science books for kids

Hoffman, Roald, Dr.
4 Sugarbush Lane
Ithaca, NY 14850
Nobel Prize chemist

Hoffs, Susanna
c/o Columbia Records
51 W. 52nd St.
New York, NY 10019
Pop singer

**Hogan, Hulk
(Terry Gene Bollea)**
P.O. Box 3859
Stamford, CT 06905
Professional wrestler

**Hogan, James Carroll, Jr.,
Dr.**
10 Clinton St.
Hartford, CT 06473
Biologist

Hogan, Paul
TCN 9 Artarmon Rd.
Willoughby 2068, NSW,
   Australia
"Crocodile Dundee" actor

Holbrook, Hal
151 El Camino Dr.
Beverly Hills, CA 90212
Actor

Holiday Hotel for Cats
2327 Cotner Ave.
Los Angeles, CA 90064
The Waldorf of the feline world

Holiday Inns
1023 Cherry Rd.
Memphis, TN 38117
Michael D. Rose, CEO

Holland, Jeffrey R., Dr.
Brigham Young University
Provo, UT 84602
University president

Hollander, Xaviera
c/o Penthouse
1965 Broadway
New York, NY 10023
Sex columnist

**Hollings, Ernest Frederick
("Fritz")**
115 Russell Senate Office Bldg.
Washington, DC 20510
Senator from South Carolina

Holloway, William J., Jr.
U.S. Court of Appeal
Tenth Circuit
Denver, CO 80294
Chief Judge

Hollywood Reporter
6715 Sunset Blvd.
Hollywood, CA 90028
Tichi Wilkerson Kassel, editor

Hollywood Studio Museum
2100 N. Highland Ave.
Hollywood, CA 90068
*Richard A. Adkins, executive
director*

Hollywood Walk of Fame
c/o Hollywood Chamber of
Commerce
6290 Sunset Blvd.
Hollywood, CA 90028

Holm, Ian
60 St. James's St.
London SW1 England
Actor

Holmes, Larry
704 Alpha Bldg.
Easton, PA 18042
*Former heavyweight boxing
champ*

Holmes, Sherlock
221B Baker Street
London W1 England
Master detective

**Holt, Victoria (Eleanor
Alice Burford Hibbert)**
c/o A.M. Heath
40 Williams IV St.
London WC2N 4DD England
Romance mystery author

Holtz, Lou
c/o Athletic Department
Notre Dame University
South Bend, IN 46556
Football coach

Home Depot
2727 Paces Ferry Rd.
Atlanta, GA 30339
Bernard Marcus, CEO

Home Savings of America
c/o H.F. Ahmanson & Co.
660 S. Figueroa St.
Los Angeles, CA 90017
Largest S&L in U.S.

**Homeopathic Educational
Services**
2124 Kittredge St.
Berkeley, CA 94704
Dana Ullman, director

Honda
2-6-20 Yaesu, Chu-ku
104, Tokyo Japan
Soichiro Honda, chairman

Honeywell
Honeywell Plaza
Minneapolis, MN 55408
J.J. Renier, CEO

Hooker, John Lee
P.O. Box 210103
San Francisco, CA 94121
Blues musician

Hoover Co.
101 E. Maple St.
North Canton, OH 44720
Robert J. Elsaesser, president

**Hoover Institution on War,
Revolution and Peace**
Stanford University
Stanford, CA 94305
Research institution

Hope, Bob
(Leslie Townes Hope)
3808 Riverside Dr.
Burbank, CA 91505
Comedian

Hopkins, Anthony
c/o Peggy Thompson
7 High Park Road, Kew,
Richmond
Surrey TW9 4BL England
Actor

Hopper, Dennis
P.O. Box 1889, Los Gallos
Taos, NM 87571
Actor

Hormel & Co.
501 16th Ave. NE
Austin, MI 55912
Richard L. Knowlton, CEO

Horne, Lena
1200 S. Arlington Ave.
Los Angeles, CA 90024
Singer

Horne, Marilyn
c/o Columbia Artists
   Management
165 W. 57th St.
New York, NY 10019
Opera soprano

Horner, James
3815 W. Olive Ave. (#202)
Burbank, CA 91505
Film composer

Horowitz, David Charles
P.O. Box 49740
Los Angeles, CA 90049
Consumer advocate

Horowitz, Paul
c/o Lyman Lab of Physics
Harvard University
Cambridge, MA 02138
Searches for extraterrestrial life

Horsley, Lee
9000 Sunset Blvd. (12th floor)
Los Angeles, CA 90069
Actor

Horton, Peter
8500 Wilshire Blvd. (#506)
Beverly Hills, CA 90210
Actor

Hoskins, Bob
(Robert William)
c/o Hope and Lyne
5 Milner Place
London N1 1TN England
Actor

Hotchner, A.E.
555 W. 57th St. (#1230)
New York, NY 10019
Writer

Houghton Mifflin Co.
One Beacon St.
Boston, MA 02108
Harold T. Miller, president

Hounsfield, Godfrey
EMI Central Research
  Laboratories
Trevor Rd., Hayes
Middlesex, England
Inventor of the CAT scan

House of Guitars
645 Titus Ave.
Rochester, NY 14617
Armand P. Schaubroeck,
  president

Houston, Whitney
410 E. 50th St.
New York, NY 10022
Pop singer

Houston Astros
The Astrodome
Houston, TX 77001
John McMullen, owner

Houston Oilers
P.O. Box 1516
Houston, TX 77521
K.S. "Bud" Adams, Jr., owner

Houston Rockets
The Summit
10 Greenway Plaza
Houston, TX 77277
Ray Patterson, general manager

Howard, Ron
P.O. Box 299
Cos Cob, CT 06807
Actor/film director

Howell, C. Thomas
P.O. Box 5356
New York, NY 10150
Actor

Hubel, David Hunter, Dr.
25 Shattuck St.
Boston, MA 02115
Nobel Prize physiologist

Hughes, Finola
c/o "General Hospital"
1438 N. Gower St.
Los Angeles, CA 90025
Actress

Hughes, John
100 Universal City Plaza (#507)
Universal City, CA 91608
Film director/writer

**Hughes, Ted (Edward
  James)**
c/o Faber and Faber
3 Queen Square
London WC1 England
Poet

Hughes Aircraft Co.
P.O. Box 45066
Los Angeles, CA 90045
Malcolm R. Currie, CEO

Hulce, Thomas
c/o Smith-Freedman
121 N. San Vicente Blvd.
Beverly Hills, CA 90211
Actor

Hull, Brett
c/o St. Louis Blues
5700 Oakland Ave.
St. Louis, MO 63110
Hockey star

Humana, Inc.
500 W. Main St.
Louisville, KY 40201
David A. Jones, CEO

Humane Society
2100 L St. NW.
Washington, DC 20037
John A. Hoyt, president

Humbard, Rex, Rev.
c/o Cathedral of Tomorrow
2700 State Rd.
Cuyahoga Falls, OH 44421
Evangelist

Hundertwasser, Friedrich
Muhle Odissenbach
Rapottenstein, Austria 3911
Painter

Hung Jury
Jim Boyd, president
P.O. Box 417
Los Angeles, CA 90078
Dating service for well-equipped men

Hunt, Lamar
1 Arrowhead Dr.
Kansas City, MO 64129
Kansas City Chiefs owner

Hunter, Catfish (James)
RR 1, Box 895
Hertsford, NC 27944
Former baseball star

Hunter, Holly
8899 Beverly Blvd.
Los Angeles, CA 90048
Actress

Hunter, Tab
P.O. Box 11167
Beverly Hills, CA 90213
Actor

Huppert, Isabelle
c/o Artmedia
10 Ave. George V
75008 Paris, France
Actress

Hurt, John
60 St. James's St.
London SW1 England
Actor

Hurt, William
RD # 1, Box 251A
Palisades, NY 10964
Actor

Hussein, Saddam
Office of the President
Baghdad, Iraq
President of Iraq

Hussein I, King
P.O. Box 1055
Amman, Jordan
King of Jordan

Hustler
9171 Wilshire Blvd. (#300)
Beverly Hills, CA 90210
Larry Claxton Flynt, publisher

Huston, Anjelica
151 El Camino Dr.
Beverly Hills, CA 90212
Actress

Hwang, David Henry
c/o Writers & Artists
70 W. 36th St.
New York, NY 10018
Playwright

Hutton, Timothy
P.O. Box 4306, Pt. Dume
Malibu, CA 90265
Actor

Hyde, Henry J.
2104 Rayburn House Office Bldg.
Washington, DC 20515
Congressman from Illinois

I

**Iacocca, Lee
(Lido Anthony)**
12000 Chrysler Dr.
Highland Park, MI 48288
Chrysler Motors, chairman

**IBM (International Business
Machines)**
Old Orchard Rd.
Amorak, NY 10504
John Fellow Akers, president

Ice-T
c/o Sire Records
75 Rockefeller Plaza
New York, NY 10019
Rapper

**Idol, Billy
(William Broad)**
c/o Eastend
8209 Melrose Ave.
Los Angeles, CA 90046
Rock singer

Iger, Bob
c/o ABC
2040 Ave. of the Stars
Los Angeles, CA 90067
Entertainment executive

**Iglesias, Julio (Julio Jose
Iglesias de la Cueva)**
4500 Biscayne Blvd.
Miami, FL 33137
Singer

Iliescu, Ion
R. 71341, Piata
Scinteis 1
Bucharest, Romania
Romanian leader

I Magnin
7 W. 7th St.
Cincinnati, OH 45202
Howard Goldfeder, chairman

Indiana Pacers
300 East Market
Indianapolis, IN 46204
Melvin and Herbert Simon,
owners

Indianapolis Colts
P.O. Box 53500
Indianapolis, IN 46253
Robert Irsay, president

**Indianapolis Motor
Speedway**
Hall of Fame and Museum
4790 W. 16th St.
Indianapolis, IN 46222

**Industrial Workers of the
World (IWW)**
3435 N. Sheffield (#202)
Chicago, IL 60657
Paul Poules, general secretary

Ingersoll-Rand Co.
200 Chestnut Ridge Rd.
Woodcliff Lake, NJ 07675
Theodore H. Black, CEO

Innovation Center
Sid Brotman, president
5130 MacArthur Blvd. NW.
Washington, DC 20016
New product development

Inouye, Daniel Ken
722 Senate Hart Bldg.
Washington, DC 20510
Senator from Hawaii

Insight Magazine
3600 New York Ave. NE.
Washington, DC 20002
Arnaud de Boerchgrave, editor

Interferon Sciences, Inc.
Samuel H. Ronel, president
783 Jersey Ave.
New Brunswick, NJ 08901
Manufactures Interferon

**Internal Revenue Service
(IRS)**
1500 Pennsylvania Ave. NW.
Washington, DC 20220
Fred T. Goldberg, commissioner

**International Bocce
Association**
400 Rutger St.
Utica, NY 13501
Paul F. Vitagliano, president

**International Boxing
Federation**
134 Evergreen Pl. (9th floor)
East Orange, NJ 07018
Marian Muhammed, executive
secretary

**International Brotherhood
of Old Bastards**
2330 S. Brentwood Blvd.
St. Louis, MO 63144

**International Brotherhood
of Magicians**
103 N. Main St.
Bluffton, OH 45817

**International Church of the
Foursquare Gospel**
1100 Glendale Blvd.
Los Angeles, CA 90026
Dr. John R. Holland, president

**International Columbian
Quincentenary Alliance**
P.O. Box 1492
Columbus, NJ 08022
Joseph M. Laufer, president

**International Documentary
Assoc.**
1551 S. Robertson Blvd.
Los Angeles, CA 90035

**International Flat Earth
Research Society**
P.O. Box 2533
Lancaster, CA 93539
Believes Earth is flat

International Flavors and Fragrances
521 W. 57th St.
New York, NY 10019
Eugene P. Grisanti, CEO

International Frankenstein Society
Dr. Jeanne Keyes Youngson, president
29 Washington Square West (PH N)
New York, NY 10011
Fan club

International House of Pancakes (IHOP)
6837 Lankershim Blvd.
N. Hollywood, CA 91605
Richard K. Herzer, chairman

International Listening Assoc.
Dr. Charles Roberts, director
P.O. Box 90340
Lake Charles, LA 70609
Conducts research on listening

International Monetary Fund
700 19th St. NW.
Washington, DC 20431
Michael Candessus, managing director

International Paper
Two Manhallanville Rd.
Purchase, NY 10577
John A. Georges, CEO

International Physicians for the Prevention of Nuclear War
126 Rogers St.
Cambridge, MA 02142
Peter Zheutlin, spokesperson

International Security Council
Dr. Joseph Churba, president
818 Connecticut Ave. NW. (#600)
Washington, DC 20006
Foreign affairs experts

International Sinatra Society
Gary J. Doctor, president
P.O. Box 5195
Anderson, SC 29623
Fan club

International Star Registry
Phyllis Mosele, president
1821 Willow Rd.
Northfield, IL 60093
Names stars for people as gifts

International Twins Association
P.O. Box 773868, Station C
Atlanta, GA 30357
Elspeth Corley, spokesperson

Inventors Clubs of America
P.O. Box 450261
Atlanta, GA 30345
Alexander T. Marinaccio, chairman

In Vitro Care, Inc.
R. J. Epstein, chrmn.
P.O. Box 267
Cambridge, MA 02238
Infertility medical services

INXS
145 Brougham St., King's Cross
Sydney, NSW, Australia
Rock group

Ionesco, Eugene
c/o Editions Gallimard
5 Rue Sebastiene-Bottin
75007 Paris, France
Playwright

I Put a Spell on You
1551 Eaton Ave.
San Carlos, CA 94070
"Bewitched" fan club

Irish Northern Aid
Martin Galvin, spokesperson
4951 Broadway
New York, NY 10034
*Opposes British rule in Northern
  Ireland*

Iron Maiden
P.O. Box 1AP
London W1 L1P England
Hard rock band

Irons, Jeremy John
200 Fulham Rd.
London SW10 England
Actor

Irving, Amy
10100 Santa Monica Blvd.
  (#1600)
Los Angeles, CA 90067
Actress

Irving, John Winslow
c/o Random House
201 E. 50th St.
New York, NY 10022
Novelist

**Irwin, Bill
(William Mills)**
56 7th Ave. (#4E)
New York, NY 10011
Actor

**Isaac Asimov's Science
  Fiction Magazine**
380 Lexington Ave.
New York, NY 10017
Gardner Dozois, editor

**IT&T (International
  Telephone & Telegraph)**
320 Park Ave.
New York, NY 10022
Rand Araskog, chairman

Ivey, Judith
10100 Santa Monica Blvd.
  (#1600)
Los Angeles, CA 90067
Actress

Ivory, James
c/o Merchant Ivory Productions
250 W. 57th St.
New York, NY 10019
Film producer

Ivy League
70 Washington Rd.
Princeton, NJ 08540.
Jeffrey H. Orleans, executive
  director

J

Jack and Jill Magazine
1100 Waterway Blvd.
Indianapolis, IN 46206
Steve Charles, editor

Jack Daniel's Distillery
Main Street
Lynchburg, TN 37352
Martin S. Brown, chairman

Jack-in-the-Box Restaurants
9330 Balboa Ave.
San Diego, CA 92112
Jack W. Goodall, Jr., chairman

Jackee
(Harry)
c/o Kohner
9169 Sunset Blvd.
Los Angeles, CA 90069
Actress

Jackson, Bo
(Vincent)
P.O. Box 2517
Auburn, AL 36831
Baseball/football player

Jackson, Freddie
c/o Hush Productions
231 W. 58th St.
New York, NY 10019
Soul singer

Jackson, Glenda
c/o Crouch Associates
59 Frith St.
London W1 England
Actress

Jackson, Janet
c/o A&M Records
1416 N. La Brea Ave.
Hollywood, CA 90028
Pop singer

Jackson, Jesse Louis, Rev.
930 E. 50th St.
Chicago, IL 60615
Civil rights leader

Jackson, Joe
c/o Basement Music
6 Pembridge Rd., Trinity House
London W11 England
Rock musician

Jackson, Kate
9830 Wilshire Blvd.
Beverly Hills, CA 90212
Actress

Jackson, Michael Joseph
10960 Wilshire Blvd. (#2206)
Los Angeles, CA 90024
Pop singer

Jackson, Reggie
(Reginald Martinez Jackson)
P.O. Box 500
Los Angeles, CA 90078
Baseball's "Mr. October"

Jacobi, Derek George
c/o ICM
388-396 Oxford St.
London W1N 9HE England
Actor

Jagger, Mick
(Michael Phillip)
c/o Jim Wiatt
8899 Beverly Blvd.
Los Angeles, CA 90048
Rock singer

Jaglom, Henry
9165 Sunset Blvd. (PH 300)
Los Angeles, CA 90069
Film director

Jakes, John
P.O Box 3248, Harbourtown St.
Hilton Head Island, SC 29928
Author

James, P.D.
c/o Alfred A. Knopf, Inc.
201 E. 50th St.
New York, NY 10022
Mystery author

James, Sharpe
920 Broad St.
Newark, NJ 07102
Mayor of Newark

James Bond 007 Fan Club
P.O. Box 414
Bronxville, NY 10708
Richard Schenkman, president

Janklow, Morton
598 Madison Ave.
New York, NY 10022
Attorney

Janowitz, Tama
c/o Crown Publishers
225 Park Ave. South
New York, NY 10003
Humorist

Jantzen
P.O. Box 3001
Portland, OR 97208
Jerome M. Pool, CEO

Jarrett, Keith
c/o Vincent Ryan
135 W. 16th St.
New York, NY 10011
Jazz pianist

Jaruzelski, Wojciech, Gen.
Ministerstwo Obrony
Narodwej ul Klonowa 1
Warsaw 009909 Poland
Former leader of Poland

Jarvik, Robert Koffler, Dr.
c/o Department of Surgery
College of Medicine, U. of Utah
Salt Lake City, UT 84112
Developed first artificial heart

J.C. Penney Co.
14841 N. Dallas Park
Dallas, TX 75240
William R. Howell, chairman

Jehovah's Witnesses
25 Columbia Heights
Brooklyn, NY 11201
Frederick W. Franz, president

Jenner, Bruce
P.O. Box 655
Malibu, CA 90265
Former decathlon champ

Jennings, Edward, Dr.
Ohio State University
Columbus, OH 43210
University president

Jennings, Peter Charles
c/o ABC News
7 W. 66th St.
New York, NY 10023
Television journalist

Jennings, Waylon
c/o Mark Rothbaum
225 Main St.
Danbury, CT 06811
Country singer

Jet Magazine
820 S. Michigan Ave.
Chicago, IL 60605
Malcolm R. West, editor

Jetsons, The (George, Jane, Judy, Elroy, Astro)
3400 Cahuenga Blvd. West
Hollywood, CA 90068
Cartoon family of the future

Jett, Joan
P.O. Box 600
Long Beach, NY 11561
Rock singer

Jewish Defense Organization
134 W. 32nd St. (#602)
New York, NY 10001
Mordechai Levy, founder

Jewison, Norman Frederick
18 Gloucester St.
Toronto, ONT, Canada
M4Y 1L5
Film director

Jillian, Ann
151 El Camino Dr.
Beverly Hills, CA 90212
Actress/singer

Jim Beam Brands Co.
510 Lake Cook Rd.
Deerfield, IL 60611
Barry M. Berish, CEO

Jimbo's Jumbos, Inc.
J. Tilman Keel, Jr., CEO
185 Peanut Dr.
Edenton, NC 27932
Peanut company

Jimi Hendrix Information
Management Institute
P.O. Box 374
Des Plaines, IL 60016
Ken Voss, president

Jim's Neighbors
c/o Cheryl Yurcak
4201 Wichita Ave.
Cleveland, OH 44109
Jim Nabors fan club

Jockey Club
Hans J. Stahl, executive director
380 Madison Ave.
New York, NY 10017
Registry for thoroughbreds

Joel, Billy
(William Martin)
c/o CBS Records
51 W. 52nd St.
New York, NY 10019
Pop musician

John, Elton Hercules
(Reginald Kenneth Dwight)
125 Kensington High St.
London W8 5SN England
Pop singer

John Birch Society
395 Concord Ave.
Belmont, MA 02178
Charles J. Humphries, chairman

John Paul II, Pope
(Karol Wojtyla)
Palazzo Apostolico Vaticano
Vatican City, Italy
Head of the Catholic church

J. Paul Getty Museum
17985 Pacific Coast Highway
Malibu, CA 90406
John Walsh, director

Johns, Jasper
c/o Leo Castelli Gallery
420 W. Broadway
New York, NY 10012
Painter

Johnson, Beverly
10390 Santa Monica Blvd. (#310)
Los Angeles, CA 90025
Model

Johnson, Don
(Donald Wayne)
8899 Beverly Blvd.
Los Angeles, CA 90048
Actor

Johnson, Kevin
c/o Phoenix Suns
2910 N. Central Ave.
Phoenix, AZ 85012
Basketball star

Johnson, Lady Bird
(Claudia Alta Taylor)
LBJ Library, 2313 Red River
Austin, TX 78705
Former First Lady

Johnson, Magic
(Earvin)
P.O. Box 10
Inglewood, CA 90306
Basketball star

Johnson, Mark
9830 Wilshire Blvd.
Beverly Hills, CA 90212
Film producer

Johnson & Johnson
One Johnson & Johnson Plaza
New Brunswick, NJ 08933
Ralph S. Larsen, CEO

Jones, Grace
P.O. Box 82
Great Neck, NY 11021
Singer/actress

Jones, Howard
P.O. Box 185, High Wycom
Buckinghamshire HP11 2E2
    England
Pop singer

Jones, James Earl
9220 Sunset Blvd. (#202)
Los Angeles, CA 90069
Actor

Jones, Miles James, Dr.
Herrin Hospital
201 S. 14th St.
Herrin IL 62948
Pathologist

Jones, Quincy
7520 Beverly Blvd. (#207)
Los Angeles, CA 90036
Music producer

Jones, Shirley
9000 Sunset Blvd. (#1112)
Los Angeles, CA 90069
Actress/singer

**Jones, Tom
(Thomas Woodward)**
10100 Santa Monica Blvd. (#205)
Los Angeles, CA 90067
Pop singer

Jones, Tommy Lee
P.O. Box 966
San Saba, TX 76877
Actor

Jong, Erica Mann
P.O. Box 1034
Weston, CT 06883
Fear of Flying *author*

Jordan, Charles M.
c/o Technical Center
Mound Road and Twelve Mile
Warren, MI 48090
*Head of design for General
   Motors*

Jordan, Joey
P.O. Box 60122, Terminal Annex
Los Angeles, CA 90060
Chainsaw juggler

Jordan, Michael
c/o Chicago Bulls
980 N. Michigan Ave. (#1600)
Chicago, IL 60611
Basketball's "Air Jordan"

Jostens, Inc.
H. William Lurton, CEO
5501 Norman Center Dr.
Minneapolis, MN 55437
Class ring makers

**Journal of the American
   Medical Association
   (JAMA)**
535 N. Dearborn St.
Chicago, IL 60610
George D. Lundberg, editor

**Journal of the Institute of
   Scientific Santa Clausism**
P.O. Box 70829
New Orleans, LA 70172
Believes in Santa Claus

Joygerms Unlimited
Joan E. White, founder
P.O. Box 219, Eastwood Station
Syracuse, NY 13206
*Spreads smiles to cure
   depression*

Joyner, Florence Griffith
11444 W. Olympic Blvd. (10th
   floor)
Los Angeles, CA 90064
Fashion designer/track star

Joyner, Wally
c/o California Angels
State College Blvd.
Anaheim, CA 92806
Baseball star

Juan Carlos, King
Palacio de la Carcuela
Madrid, Spain
King of Spain

**Judds, The
(Wynonna/Naomi)**
P.O. Box 17087
Nashville, TN 37210
Country stars

**Julia, Raul
(Raul Rafael Carlos)**
10100 Santa Monica Blvd.
 (#1600)
Los Angeles, CA 90067
Actor

Junior Achievement
Karl Flemke, president
45 Clubhouse Dr.
Colorado Springs, CO 80906
Teaches students about business

K

Kael, Pauline
c/o New Yorker
25 W. 43rd St.
New York, NY 10036
Film critic

Kaiser Aluminum And Chemical
300 Lakeside Dr.
Oakland, CA 94612
Cornel C. Maier, chairman

Kal Kan Foods
3250 E. 44th St.
Vernon, CA 90058
John Barrow, president

Kalb, Marvin Leonard
c/o JFK School of Government
79 JFK Street
Cambridge, MA 02138
Journalist

Kamali, Norma
11 West 56th St.
New York, NY 10019
Fashion designer

Kaminsky, Stuart M.
Northwestern University
School of Speech
Evanston, IL 60201
Mystery author

Kane, Carol
8899 Beverly Blvd.
Los Angeles, CA 90048
Actress

Kansas City Chiefs
1 Arrowhead Dr.
Kansas City, MO 64129
John Malkovich, coach

Kansas City Royals
Royals Stadium
Kansas City, MO 64141
Ewing Kauffman, owner

Karan, Donna
550 7th Ave. (14th floor)
New York, NY 10108
Fashion designer

Karle, Jerome, Dr.
U.S. Naval Research Labs
Code 6030
Washington, DC 20375
Nobel Prize physicist

Karsh, Yousuf
Chateau Laurier
Ottawa, ON Canada
K1N 8S7
Photographer

Kasdan, Lawrence Edward
c/o DGA
7920 Sunset Blvd.
Los Angeles, CA 90046
Film director/writer

Kasem, Casey
c/o "America's Top Ten"
5800 Sunset Blvd.
Los Angeles, CA 90028
Disc jockey

**Kasparov, Gary
(Weinstein)**
c/o World Chess Federation
Abendweg 1
CH-6006 Lucerne, Switzerland
World chess champ

Kassebaum, Nancy Landon
302 Senate Russell Bldg.
Washington, DC 20510
Senator from Kansas

Kastenmeier, Robert W.
2328 Rayburn House Office Bldg.
Washington, DC 20515
Congressman from Wisconsin

Katz, Sol, Dr.
Georgetown University Hospital
Washington, DC 20007
Pulmonary specialist

Katzman, Robert, Dr.
U. of California, San Diego
La Jolla, CA 92093
Alzheimer's disease specialist

Kawasaki
2-1-18 Nakamachidori, Churo-ku
Kobe, Japan
Kenko Hasegawa, chairman

Keach, Stacy, Jr.
1875 Century Park E. (#1600)
Los Angeles, CA 90067
Actor

Kean, Thomas H.
State House
Trenton, NJ 08625
Governor of New Jersey

Keanan, Staci
c/o "My Two Dads"
1438 N. Gower St.
Los Angeles, CA 90028
Actress

**Keaton, Diane
(Hall)**
1350 6th Ave.
New York, NY 10019
Actress

Keaton, Michael
9830 Wilshire Blvd.
Beverly Hills, CA 90212
Batman actor

Keebler Co.
One Hollow Tree Ln.
Elmhurst, IL 60126
Thomas M. Garvin, president

Keeshan, Bob
555 W. 57th St.
New York, NY 10019
"Captain Kangaroo"

**Keillor, Garrison
(Gary Edward)**
c/o Viking Press
375 Hudson St.
New York, NY 10014
Humorist

Keith, David
151 El Camino Dr.
Beverly Hills, CA 90212
Actor

Keith, Louis Gerald
333 E. Superior St. (#476)
Chicago, IL 60611
Studies multiple births

Kellerman, Sally Claire
2400 Broadway (#100)
Santa Monica, CA 90404
Actress

Kelley, Kitty
c/o Bantam Books
666 5th Ave.
New York, NY 10103
Biographer

Kellogg Co.
P.O. Box 3599
Battle Creek, MI 49016
William E. LaMothe, chairman

Kelly, Ellsworth
c/o Leo Castelli Gallery
420 W. Broadway
New York, NY 10012
Painter

Kelly, Gene Curran
c/o DGA
7920 Sunset Blvd.
Los Angeles, CA 90046
Actor/dancer

Kelly, Jim
c/o Buffalo Bills
One Bills Dr.
Orchard Park, NY 14127
Football quarterback

Kelly Services
William R. Kelly, chairman
999 W. Big Beaver Rd.
Troy, MI 48084
Home of the Kelly Girl

Kemp, Jack F.
451 7th St. SW.
Washington, DC 20410
*Sec., Housing & Urban
Development*

Kennedy, Anthony M.
U. S. Supreme Court Bldg.
One 1st St. NE
Washington, DC 20543
Supreme Court Justice

Kennedy, Donald, Dr.
Stanford University
Stanford, CA 94305
University president

Kennedy, Edward Moore
315 Senate Russell Bldg.
Washington, DC 20510
Senator from Massachusetts

Kennedy, Joseph P., II
1208 Longworth House Office
Bldg.
Washington, DC 20515
*Congressman from
Massachusetts*

Kennedy, Kathleen
100 Universal City Plaza (#477)
Universal City, CA 91608
Film producer

Kennedy, Paul
Dept. of History, Yale U.
New Haven, CT 06520
Historian

Kennedy, Rose Fitzgerald
The Compound
Hyannis, MA 02647
*Matriarch of the Kennedy
Family*

Kenny G
(Gorelick)
648 N. Robertson Blvd.
Los Angeles, CA 90048
Jazz/pop saxophonist

Kentucky Fried Chicken
P.O. Box 32070
Louisville, KY 40232
Richard P. Mayer, chairman

Keohane, Nannerl, Dr.
Wellesley College
Wellesley, MA 02181
College president

Kercheval, Ken
P.O. Box 1350
Los Angeles, CA 90078
"Dallas" actor

Kermit the Frog
117 E. 69th St.
New York, NY 10021
Hardest working frog in show biz

Kerns, Joanna
10100 Santa Monica Blvd.
(#1600)
Los Angeles, CA 90067
Actress

Kerry, John Forbes
421 Senate Russell Bldg.
Washington, DC 20510
Senator from Massachusetts

Kesey, Ken
P.O. Box 477
Pleasant Hill, OR 97401
Author

Ketcham, Hank
(Henry King)
P.O. Box 800
Pebble Beach, CA 93953
"Dennis the Menace" cartoonist

Khashoggi, Adnan
P.O. Box 6
Riyadh, Saudi Arabia
Billionaire

Kiam, Victor
c/o New England Patriots
Sullivan Stadium, Rt. 1
Foxboro, MA 02035
Remington Shaver Co. owner

Killebrew, Harmon
P.O. Box 626
Ontario, OR 97914
Former baseball slugger

Kilmer, Val
Rt. 4, Box 23
Santa Fe, NM 87501
Actor

Kilpatrick, James J.
White Walnut Hill
Woodville, VA 22749
Political commentator

Kilroy
Mountlake Terrace, WA 98043
World's heaviest dog

King, B.B.
(Riley "Blues Boy" King)
P.O. Box 16707
Memphis, TN 38131
Blues guitarist

King, Billie Jean
1801 Century Park E. (#1400)
Los Angeles, CA 90067
Former tennis great

King, Carole
(Klein)
9255 Sunset Blvd. (#505)
Los Angeles, Ca 90069
Singer/songwriter

King, Coretta Scott
449 Auburn Ave. NE.
Atlanta, GA 30312
Widow of Martin Luther King,
Jr.

King, Don
32 E. 69th St.
New York, NY 10021
Flamboyant boxing promoter

King, Larry
c/o Mutual Broadcasting
1755 S. Jefferson Davis Hwy.
Arlington, VA 22202
Talk show host

King, Perry
9830 Wilshire Blvd.
Beverly Hills, CA 90212
Actor

King, Spencer B., III, Dr.
Emory University Hospital
Atlanta, Ga 30322
Cardiovascular specialist

King, Stephen
c/o G.P. Putnam's Sons
200 Madison Ave.
New York, NY 10016
Scary author

Kingsley, Ben
(Krishna Banji) c/o ICM Ltd.
388/396 Oxford St.
London W1 England
"Gandhi" actor

Kinison, Sam
c/o Warner Bros. Records
3300 Warner Blvd.
Burbank, CA 91510
Comedian

Kinnock, Neil Gordon
House of Commons
London SW1 England
Head of Labour Party

Kinski, Klaus
c/o Artmedia
10 Ave. George V
75008 Paris, France
Actor

Kinski, Nastassja
888 7th Ave.
New York, NY 10106
Actress

Kiplinger Washington
Editors
Austin H. Kiplinger, chairman
1729 H St. NW.
Washington, DC 20006
Newsletter

Kirby, Thomas J., Dr.
Columbia-Presbyterian Med.
Center
New York, NY 10032
Lung surgeon

Kirkland, Sally
1800 N. Highland Ave. (#316)
Los Angeles, CA 90028
Actress

Kirkpatrick, Jeane Duane Jordan
c/o American Enterprise Inst.
1150 7th St. NW.
Washington, DC 20036
Foreign affairs commentator

KISS
P.O. Box 77505
San Francisco, CA 94107
Rock group

Kissinger, Henry Alfred
350 Park Ave.
New York, NY 10022
Foreign affairs expert

Kitaen, Tawny
445 N. Bedford Dr. (PH)
Beverly Hills, CA 90210
Actress/music video star

Kitaro
(Masanori Takahashi)
c/o Geffen Records
9130 Sunset Blvd.
Los Angeles, CA 90069
Japanese musician

Kiwanis International
3636 Woodview
Indianapolis, IN 46268
Kevin Krepinevich, secretary

Klanwatch
P.O. Box 548
Montgomery, AL 36195
Pat Clark, executive officer

Klarsfeld, Beate
515 Madison Ave.
New York, NY 10022
Nazi hunter

Klein, Calvin Richard
205 W. 39th St.
New York, NY 10018
Fashion designer

Klein, Lawrence Robert, Dr.
University of Pennsylvania
Dept. of Economics/Finance
Philadelphia, PA 19104
Nobel Prize economist

Klein, Robert
1350 6th Ave.
New York, NY 90028
Comedian

Kliban, B.
(Bernard)
c/o Workman Pub.
708 Broadway (6th floor)
New York, NY 10003
Cartoonist

Kline, Kevin Delaney
9830 Wilshire Blvd.
Beverly Hills, CA 90212
Actor

Kluge, John Werner
c/o Metromedia
One Harmon Plaza
Secaucus, NJ 07094
Wealthiest man in America

K-Mart Corp.
3100 W. Big Beaver
Troy, MI 48084
Joseph E. Antonini, CEO

Knapp, Charles B., Dr.
University of Georgia
Athens, GA 30602
University president

Knight, Bobby
c/o Indiana University
Assembly Hall
Bloomington, IN 47405
Basketball coach

Knight, Gladys
P.O. Box 42942
Las Vegas, NV 89104
R&B singer

Knight-Ridder
J.K. Batten, CEO
One Herald Plaza
Miami, FL 33132
Newspaper publisher

Knights of Columbus
One Columbus Plaza
New Haven, CT 06507
Catholic service organization

Knights of the Ku Klux Klan
P.O. Box 700
Five Points, Al 36855
Jim Blair, spokesperson

Knopf, Inc., Alfred A.
201 E. 50th St.
New York, NY 10022
A.S. Mehta, president

Knopfler, Mark
10 Southwick Mews
London SW2 England
Rock musician

Knotts, Don
6404 Wilshire Blvd. (#800)
Los Angeles, CA 90048
Comic actor

Kohl, Helmut
6700 Ludwigshafen/Rhein
Marbacher Strasse 11, Germany
Chancellor of Germany

Koontz, Dean R.
c/o G.P. Putnam's Sons
200 Madison Ave.
New York, NY 10016
Novelist

Kopit, Arthur
555 W. 57th St. (#1230)
New York, NY 10019
Playwright

Koppel, Ted
1717 DeSales St. NW.
Washington, DC 20036
Journalist/"Nightline" host

Korbut, Olga
(Bortkevich)
Young Communist League St.
Minsk, U.S.S.R.
Ex-gymnastics star

Korda, Michael
555 W. 57th St. (#1230)
New York, NY 10019
Author

Kosar, Bernie
c/o Cleveland Browns
Cleveland Stadium
Cleveland, OH 44114
Football quarterback

Kostabi, Mark
c/o Ronald Feldman
31 Mercer St.
New York, NY 10013
Painter

Kostelanetz, Richard
P.O. Box 444
Prince St. Station
New York, NY 10012
Video artist/writer

Kosugi, Sho
6605 Hollywood Blvd. (#220)
Hollywood, CA 90028
Martial arts star

Kotler, Robert, Dr.
2080 Century Park E.
Los Angeles, CA 90067
Plastic surgeon

Koufax, Sandy
P.O. Box BB
Carpinteria, CA 93013
Baseball great

Kowalski, Robert E.
c/o Harper & Row
10 E. 53rd St.
New York, NY 10022
Health author

Kozlowski, Linda
151 El Camino Dr.
Beverly Hills, CA 90212
"Crocodile Dundee" actress

Kozol, Jonathan
P.O. Box 145
Byfield, MA 01922
author

Kraft
Kraft Court
Glenview, IL 60025
Michael A. Miles, CEO

Kragen, Ken
1112 N. Sherbourne Dr.
Los Angeles, CA 90069
Show biz manager

Krane, Jonathan
1888 Century Park E. (#1616)
Los Angeles, CA 90067
Film producer

Krantz, Judith Tarcher
9601 Wilshire Blvd. (#343)
Beverly Hills, CA 90210
Novelist

Krassner, Paul
P.O. Box 1230
Venice, CA 90294
Political satirist

Krauthammer, Charles
c/o New Republic
1200 19th St.
Washington, DC 10030
Political commentator

Krens, Thomas
1071 5th Ave.
New York, NY 10128
*Solomon R. Guggenheim
   Museum, director*

Krim, Mathilde, Dr.
Amer. Foundation for AIDS
   Research
40 West 57th St.
New York, NY 10019
Geneticist

Kristiansen, Kjeld Kirk
555 Taylor Rd.
Enfield, CT 06082
Lego Toy Co. president

Kristofferson, Kris
8899 Beverly Blvd.
Los Angeles, CA 90048
Actor/singer

Krone, Julie
c/o Monmouth Park Racetrack
Oceanport Ave.
Oceanport, NJ 07757
Jockey

Kubrick, Stanley
P.O. Box 123, Borenamwood
Hertsford, England
Film director

Kundera, Milan
Ecole des Hautes Etudes
54 Blvd. Raspail
75006 Paris, France
Author

Kunin, Madeline May
State House
Montpelier, VT 05602
Governor of Vermont

Kuralt, Charles Bishop
c/o CBS News
51 W. 52nd St.
New York, NY 10019
"On the Road" journalist

Kurosawa, Akira
21-6 Seijo 2 chome
Matsubara-cho, Setagaya-ku
157 Tokyo, Japan
Film director

Kurtz, Swoozie
10100 Santa Monica Blvd.
 (#1600)
Los Angeles, CA 90067
Actress

Kushner, Harold
c/o Temple Israel
145 Hartford St.
Natick, MA 01760
Rabbi

Kuti, Fela Anikulapo
c/o The Shrine
Kalaskuta
Lagos, Nigeria
Nigerian musician

L

Labatt Brewing Co.
150 Simcoe St.
London, ON Canada
N6A 4MS
S.M. Oland, president

LaBelle, Patti
8730 Sunset Blvd. (PH W)
Los Angeles, CA 90069
R&B singer

LaBruzzo, John
3530 Pine Valley Dr.
Sarasota, FL 34239
Hotelier

La Costa Hotel and Spa
Costa Del Mar Rd.
Carlsbad, CA 92009
Health spa

Lacroix, Christian Marie Marc
73 Faubourg Saint Honoré
75008 Paris, France
Fashion designer

Ladd, Cheryl
(Cheryl Jean Stoppelmoor)
8899 Beverly Blvd.
Los Angeles, CA 90048
Actress

Ladies Garment Workers Union
1710 Broadway
New York, NY 10019
Jay Mazur, president

Ladies' Home Journal
100 Park Ave.
New York, NY 10017
Myrna Blyth, editor

Ladies Professional Golf Assoc.
(LPGA)
4675 Sweetwater Blvd.
Sugar Land, TX 77479
William A. Blue, commissioner

Laffer, Arthur
P.O. Box 1167
Rancho Santa Fe, CA 92067
Supply side economist

Lagasse, Leo D., Dr.
Cedars-Sinai Medical Center
Los Angeles, CA 90024
Gynecological cancer specialist

La-Z-Boy Chair Co.
1284 N. Telegraph Rd.
Monroe, MI 48161
C.T. Knabusch, chairman

Lahti, Christine
10100 Santa Monica Blvd.
(#1600)
Los Angeles, CA 90067
Actress

**Laine, Cleo (Clementina
Dinah Dankworth)**
c/o Int. Artists
235 Regent St.
London W1 England
Jazz singer

LaLanne, Jack
P.O. Box 1249
Burbank, CA 91507
Fitness expert

Lamas, Lorenzo
9000 Sunset Blvd. (#115)
Los Angeles, CA 90069
Actor

**Lancaster, Burt
(Burton Stephen)**
P.O. Box 67838
Los Angeles, CA 90067
Actor

Landau, Martin
10000 Santa Monica Blvd. (#305)
Los Angeles, CA 90067
Actor

**Landers, Ann
(Esther P. Lederer)**
c/o Chicago Tribune
435 N. Michigan Ave.
Chicago, IL 60611
Advice columnist

Landis, John David
c/o Universal Studios
100 Universal City Plaza (#423)
Universal City, CA 91608
Film director

**Landon, Michael
(Eugene Maurice Orowitz)**
10351 Santa Monica Blvd. (#402)
Los Angeles, CA 90025
Actor

Lane, Diane
8899 Beverly Blvd.
Los Angeles, CA 90048
Actress

Lang, K.D.
41 Britain St. (#200)
Toronto, ON Canada
M5A 1R7
Country/pop singer

Langberg, Barry
10000 Santa Monica Blvd. (#450)
Los Angeles, CA 90067
Entertainment attorney

Lange, Ed
c/o Elysium Institute
814 Robinson Rd.
Topanga, CA 90290
Nudist leader

Lange, Jessica
100 Universal City Plaza
(Bungalow 72)
Universal City, CA 91608
Actress

Langella, Frank
c/o ICM
40 W. 57th St.
New York, NY 10019
Actor

Langston, Mark
c/o California Angels
State College Blvd.
Anaheim, CA 92806
Baseball pitcher

Lansbury, Angela
31 Soho Square
London W1 England
Actress

Lansing, Sherry
c/o Paramount Pictures
5555 Melrose Ave.
Los Angeles, CA 90038
Film producer

Lantos, Tom
1526 Longworth House Office
   Bldg.
Washington, DC 20515
Congressman from California

Lantz, Walter
4444 Lakeside Dr. (# 310)
Hollywood, CA 91505
"Woody Woodpecker" cartoonist

**LaRouche, Lyndon
   Hermyle, Jr.**
Rt. 3, Box 91
Leesburg, VA 22075
Controversial politician

Larroquette, John Bernard
P.O. Box 6303
Malibu, CA 90265
Actor

**Lasorda, Tommy
(Thomas Charles)**
1000 Elysian Park Ave.
Los Angeles, CA 90012
Dodgers baseball manager

Lauda, Niki
Can Costa de Baix, Santa Eulalia
Ibiza, Spain
Racecar driver

Lauder, Estee
767 5th Ave.
New York, NY 10153
Cosmetics queen

Lauper, Cyndi
65 W. 55th St. (#4G)
New York, NY 10019
Rock singer

**Lauren, Ralph
(Lifschitz)**
550 7th Ave.
New York, NY 10021
Fashion designer

Laurents, Arthur
P.O. Box 582
Quoque, NY 11959
Playwright

**Laurie, Piper
(Rosetta Jacobs)**
10100 Santa Monica Blvd.
   (#1600)
Los Angeles, CA 90067
Actress

**Laver, Rod
(Rodney George)**
P.O. Box 4798
Hilton Head Island, SC 29928
Former tennis great

Lavin, Linda
Columbia Pictures Television
Columbia Plaza E. (#15)
Burbank, CA 91505
Actress

Lawrence, Vicki Ann
151 El Camino Dr.
Beverly Hills, CA 90212
Actress

Laxalt, Paul
1455 Pennsylvania Ave. NW.
Washington, DC 20004
Former Senator

Lay, Donald P.
U.S. Court of Appeal
Eighth Circuit
St. Louis, MO 63101
Chief Judge

Leach, Robin
c/o TPE
1014 N. Sycamore
Los Angeles, CA 90038
"Lifestyles of Rich and Famous"

Leachman, Cloris
10390 Santa Monica Blvd. (#310)
Los Angeles, CA 90025
Actress

Leahy, Patrick Joseph
433 Senate Russell Bldg.
Washington, DC 20510
Senator from Vermont

Lean, David, Sir
c/o Film Producer's Association
162 Wardour St.
London W1 England
Film director

Lear, Frances
c/o Lear's Magazine
505 Park Ave.
New York, NY 10022
Magazine publisher

Lear, Norman
1800 Century Park E. (#200)
Los Angeles, CA 90067
Entertainment executive

Lear Jet Corp.
8220 W. Harry
Wichita, KS 67277
B.N. Lancaster, CEO

Leary, Timothy, Dr.
P.O. Box 69886
Los Angeles, CA 90069
Drug cult figure

Leavitt, David Keene
9454 Wilshire Blvd. (#200)
Beverly Hills, CA 90212
Private adoption attorney

LeBrock, Kelly
c/o Ford Models
344 E. 59th St.
New York, NY 10022
Actress/model

Le Carre, John (David John Moore Cornwell)
Tregiffian, St. Buryan, Penzance
Cornwall, England
Spy thriller author

Lederman, Leon Max, Dr.
34 Overlook Rd.
Dobbs Ferry, NY 10522
Nobel Prize physicist

Lee, Christopher
9000 Sunset Blvd. (#315)
Los Angeles, CA 90069
Actor

Lee, Edward L., III
3530 Pine Valley Dr.
Sarasota, FL 34239
Terrorism expert

Lee, Hyapatha
P.O. Box 1924
Los Angeles, CA 90069
Porno film star

**Lee, Michele
(Michelle Dusiak)**
151 El Camino Dr.
Beverly Hills, CA 90212
Actress

**Lee, Spike
(Shelton Jackson)**
124 DeKalb Ave.
Brooklyn, NY 11217
Film director

Lefebvre, Marcel
Séminaire Saint Pie X
1908 Econe
Valais, Switzerland
Ultraconservative Catholic leader

Le Figaro
Max Close, editor
25 Ave. Matignon
Paris, France
Leading French newspaper

Lefthanders International
P.O. Box 8249, N. Topeka
Topeka, KS 66608
Dean R. Campbell, president

Le Guin, Ursula K.
8955 Beverly Blvd.
Los Angeles, CA 90048
Writer

Lehrer, Jim
P.O. Box 2626
Washington, DC 20013
Television journalist

Leibowitz, Howard M., Dr.
Boston U. School of Medicine
Boston, MA 02118
Ophthalmology specialist

Leifer, Neil
c/o Time Magazine
Time/Life Bldg.
New York, NY 10020
Photographer

**Leigh, Janet
(Jeanette Helen Morrison)**
6310 San Vicente Blvd. (#407)
Los Angeles, CA 90048
Actress

**Leigh, Jennifer Jason
(Morrow)**
10100 Santa Monica Blvd.
 (#1600)
Los Angeles, CA 90067
Actress

Leisure, David
9000 Sunset Blvd. (#801)
Los Angeles, CA 90069
"Joe Isuzu" actor

Lemieux, Mario
c/o Pittsburgh Penguins
Civic Arena
Pittsburgh, PA 15219
Hockey star

Lemmon, Jack
141 El Camino Dr. (#201)
Beverly Hills, CA 90212
Actor

Lemon, Meadowlark
P.O. Box 398
Sierra Vista, AZ 85635
Former Harlem Globetrotter

LeMond, Greg
c/o ProServ
1101 Wilson Blvd. (#1800)
Arlington, VA 22209
1989 Tour de France winner

Le Monde
5 Rue des Italiens
Paris, France
French magazine

Lemper, Ute
Marek Liederberg-
  Konzertagentur
Hansalee 19
6000 Frankfurt 1, Germany
Torch singer/actress

Lendl, Ivan
c/o U.S. Tennis Association
51 E. 42nd St.
New York, NY 10017
Tennis star

Lennon, Julian
200 W. 57th St. (#1403)
New York, NY 10019
Pop singer/son of John Lennon

Leno, Jay
9000 Sunset Blvd. (#400)
Los Angeles, CA 90069
Comedian

Lenox Hill Hospital
Institute of Sports
Medicine
130 E. 77th Street
New York, NY 10021
Dr. James A. Nicholas, director

Leonard, Elmore John
c/o Bantam Books
666 5th Ave.
New York, NY 10010
Mystery author

Leonard, Gloria
801 2nd Ave.
New York, NY 10017
Sex magazine publisher

Leonard, Sugar Ray
(Ray Charles)
c/o Mike Trainer
4922 Fairmount Ave.
Bethesda, MA 20814
Boxing champ

LePen, Jean-Marie
6 Rue de Beaune
75007 Paris, France
Politician

Lessing, Doris (May)
c/o Jonathan Clowes Ltd.
22 Prince Albert Rd.
London NW1 7ST England
Novelist

Lester, Richard
River Lane, Petersham
Surrey, England
Film director

Let's Face It
Betsy Wilson, director
P.O. Box 711
Concord, MA 01742
Group for facially disfigured

Letter Exchange
P.O. Box 6218
Albany, CA 94706
Magazine for letter writers

Letterman, David
30 Rockefeller Plaza (#1400)
New York, NY 10020
"Late Night" comedian

Leveille, Gilbert, Dr.
c/o Amer. Institute of Nutrition
9650 Rockville Pike
Bethesda, MD 20814
Nutritionist

Levi Strauss
1155 Battery St.
San Francisco, CA 94111
Robert D. Haas, president

Levi-Strauss, Claude
52 Rue du Cardinal
College du France, Lemoine
75005 Paris, France
Social anthropologist

Levine, Arthur O.
8217 Beverly Blvd.
Los Angeles, CA 90048
*Newsletter on newsmaker
interviews*

Levine, Mel
132 Cannon House Office Bldg.
Washington, DC 20515
Congressman from California

Levine, Michael
8730 Sunset Blvd. (6th floor)
Los Angeles, CA 90069
Author, The Address Book

Levinson, Barry
10800 Wilshire Blvd. (#2110)
Los Angeles, CA 90024
Film director/writer

Levitz Furniture
6111 Broken Sand Pkwy. NW
Boca Raton, FL 33487
Robert M. Elliot, CEO

Lewis, Carl
1801 Ocean Park Blvd. (#112)
Santa Monica, CA 90405
World's fastest human

Lewis, Huey (and the News)
P.O. Box 819
Mill Valley, CA 94942
Rock singer

**Lewis, Jerry
(Joseph Levitch)**
3305 W. Spring Mountain Rd.
  (#1)
Las Vegas, NV 89102
Comedian/actor

Lewis, Jerry Lee
P.O. Box 3864
Memphis, TN 38173
"The Killer" rock 'n' roller

Lewis, Reginald F.
c/o TLC Group
99 Wall St. (16th floor)
New York, NY 10005
Business executive

Lewis, Richard
10100 Santa Monica Blvd.
(#1600)
Los Angeles, CA 90067
Comedian

Li Peng
c/o People's Republic of China
2300 Connecticut Ave. NW.
Washington, DC 20008
Premier of China

Liberace Club of Las Vegas
c/o Pauline Lachance
2994 Talbot St.
Las Vegas, NV 89109
Fan club

Libertarian Party
1528 Pennsylvania Ave. SE.
Washington, DC 20003
David Walter, chairman

Liberty Bell
Independence Nat. Historical
Park
313 Walnut St.
Philadelphia, PA 19106
Hobart G. Cawood,
superintendent

Liberty Mutual Insurance
175 Berkeley St.
Boston, MA 02117
Gary L. Countryman, CEO

Library of Congress
101 Independence Ave. SE.
Washington, DC 20540
James Hadley Billington,
librarian

Lichtenstein, Roy
P.O. Box 1369
Southampton, NY 11968
Painter

Lichter, Paul R., Dr.
c/o Kellogg Eye Center
U. of Michigan Medical Center
Ann Arbor, MI 48105
Glaucoma specialist

Light Living Library
Bert Davis, coordinator
P.O. Box 190
Philomath, OR 97370
For people living in RVs or tents

Liman, Arthur Lawrence
c/o Paul, Weiss, Rifkind, et al.
1285 6th Ave.
New York, NY 10019
Attorney

Limbaugh, Rush
c/o WMCA
Two Penn Plaza
New York, NY 10121
Radio talk show host

**Linden, Hal
(Harold Lipshitz)**
9200 Sunset Blvd. (#808)
Los Angeles, CA 90069
Actor

Linney, Romulus
555 W. 57th St. (#1230)
New York, NY 10019
Playwright

Linson, Art
c/o Paramount Pictures
5555 Melrose Ave.
Los Angeles, CA 90038
Film producer

Lions Clubs
300 22nd St.
Oak Brook, IL 60570
*Mark C. Lukas, executive
administrator*

Liotta, Ray
8730 Sunset Blvd. (6th floor)
Los Angeles, CA 90069
Actor

**Liposuction Institute of
America**
Dr. Leon Tcheupdjian, director
1700 W. Central (#100)
Arlington Heights, IL 60005
Fat reduction

Lipschultz, Larry, Dr.
Baylor College of Medicine
Houston, TX 77025
Male infertility specialist

Lithgow, John Arthur
9830 Wilshire Blvd.
Beverly Hills, CA 90212
Actor

Little, Brown & Co.
34 Beacon St.
Boston, MA 02108
Kevin L. Dolan, president

Little, Rich
10100 Santa Monica Blvd.
  (#1600)
Los Angeles, CA 90067
Impressionist

Little League Baseball
P.O. Box 3485
Williamsport, PA 17701
Beverly J. Gray, secretary

Little People of America
P.O. Box 9897
Washington, DC 20016
Organization for midgets/dwarves

**Little Richard
(Penniman)**
9200 Sunset Blvd. (#415)
Los Angeles, CA 90069
Rock 'n' roller

Litton Industries
360 N. Crescent Dr.
Beverly Hills, CA 90210
Orion L. Hoch, CEO

Living Colour
c/o Epic Records
51 W. 52nd St.
New York, NY 10019
Rock group

L.L. Bean
Freeport, ME 04033
Leon A. Gorman, president

**LL Cool J
("Ladies Love Cool James")**
298 Elizabeth St.
New York, NY 10012
Rapper

Lloyd, Christopher
222 N. Canon Dr. (#202)
Beverly Hills, CA 90210
Actor

Locke, Sondra
P.O. Box 69865
Los Angeles, CA 90069
Film director/actress

Lockhart, June
9000 Sunset Blvd. (12th floor)
Los Angeles, CA 90069
"Lassie" actress

Lockheed Corp.
4500 Park Granada Blvd.
Calabasas, CA 91399
Daniel M. Tellep, CEO

Locklear, Heather
151 El Camino Dr.
Beverly Hills, CA 90212
Actress

Loggins, Kenny
P.O. Box 10905
Beverly Hills, CA 90213
Pop singer

London, Jerry
9830 Wilshire Blvd.
Beverly Hills, CA 90212
Television director/producer

London Times
One Pennington St.
London E1 9XW England
Charles Wilson, editor

Long, Shelley
c/o Walt Disney Pictures
500 S. Buena Vista St.
Burbank, CA 91521
Actress

Long Distance Love
Roxanne Black, founder
P.O. Box 2301
Ventnor, NJ 08406
For people with disabilities

Lopez, Nancy
c/o Mark H. McCormack Agency
One Erieview Plaza
Cleveland, OH 44114
Golfer

**Loren, Sophia
(Scicolone)**
6 Rue Charles Bonnet
Geneva, Switzerland
Actress

Los Angeles Clippers
3939 South Figueroa
Los Angeles, CA 90037
Elgin Baylor, general manager

**Los Angeles County
Museum of Art**
5905 Wilshire Blvd.
Los Angeles, CA 90036
Dr. Earl A. Powell, director

Los Angeles Dodgers
Dodger Stadium
1000 Elysian Park Ave.
Los Angeles, CA 90012
Peter O'Malley, owner

Los Angeles Kings
3900 W. Manchester Blvd.
Inglewood, CA 90306
Rogie Vachon, general manager

Los Angeles Lakers
3900 W. Manchester Blvd.
Inglewood, CA 90306
Jerry West, general manager

Los Angeles Rams
2327 W. Lincoln Ave.
Anaheim, Ca 92801
Georgia Frontiere, president

Los Lobos
P.O. Box 1304
Burbank, CA 91507
Music group

Lost in Space Fannish Alliance
Flint Mitchell, president
7331 Terri Robyn
St. Louis, MO 63129
Fan club

Lott, Ronni
711 Nevada St.
Redwood City, CA 94061
Football star

Lotus Development Corp.
55 Cambridge Pkwy.
Cambridge, MA 02142
Jim P. Manzi, CEO

Louganis, Greg E.
P.O. Box 4068
Malibu, CA 90265
Champion diver

Love Connection
8601 Beverly Blvd. (# 5)
Los Angeles, CA 90048
Matchmaking television series

Lovejoy, Tom
1000 Jefferson Ave. SW. (#230)
Washington, DC 20560
Environmental lobbyist

Lovett, Lyle
1514 South St.
Nashville, TN 37212
Country musician

Lovitz, Jon
9830 Wilshire Blvd.
Beverly Hills, CA 90212
"Saturday Night Live" comedian

Lowe, Rob
8899 Beverly Blvd.
Los Angeles, CA 90048
Actor

Loyal Order of Moose
Mooseheart, IL 60539
Donald Ross, supreme secretary

Lucas, George
P.O. Box 2009
San Rafael, CA 94912
"Star Wars" director

Lucci, Susan
c/o "All My Children"
101 W. 67th St.
New York, NY 10023
Actress

Luce, Henry, III
750 5th Ave. (#504)
New York, NY 10019
Time, Inc., director

Luckenbill, Greg
c/o Sacramento Kings
One Sports Parkway
Sacramento, CA 95834
Basketball team owner

Ludlum, Robert
c/o Dell Publishing
One Dag Hammarskjold Plaza
New York, NY 10017
Spy thriller author

Luedtke, Kurt M.
1033 Gayley Ave.
Los Angeles, CA 90024
Screenwriter

Lugar, Richard G.
306 Hart Office Bldg.
Washington, DC 20510
Senator from Indiana

Lujan, Manuel
18th and C Streets NW.
Washington, DC 20240
Secretary of the Interior

Luken, Charles J.
City Hall
801 Plum St.
Cincinnati, OH 45202
Mayor of Cincinnati

Luken, Thomas A.
2368 Rayburn House Office Bldg.
Washington, DC 20515
Congressman from Ohio

Lumet, Sidney
c/o LAH Film Corporation
1775 Broadway
New York, NY 10019
Film director

Lunden, Joan
c/o ABC
1330 6th Ave.
New York, NY 10019
"Good Morning America" cohost

Lundgren, Dolph
1875 Century Park E. (#2200)
Los Angeles, CA 90067
Actor

Lupone, Patti
8899 Beverly Blvd.
Los Angeles, CA 90048
"Evita" actress

M

Ma, Yo-Yo
c/o ICM
40 W. 57th St.
New York, NY 10019
Cellist

Maathai, Wangari
c/o Greenbelt Movement
P.O. Box 67545
Nairobi, Kenya
Environmental activist

MacDonald, Jeffrey, Dr.
Federal Correctional Institution
Bastrop, TX 78602
"Fatal Vision" murderer

MacDowell, Andie
151 El Camino Dr.
Beverly Hills, CA 90212
Actress/model

MacGraw, Ali
(Alice)
900 Sunset Blvd. (12th floor)
Los Angeles, CA 90069
Actress

Mack, Bill
6400 Barrie Rd.
Minneapolis, MN 55435
Sculptor

Mack, Connie
(Cornelius McGillicudy III)
517 Senate Hart Bldg.
Washington, DC 20510
Senator from Florida

Mack Trucks
2100 Mack Blvd.
Allentown, PA 18105
Ralph E. Reins, CEO

MacKenzie, Spuds
2300 6th Ave.
North Riverside, IL 60546
Original Party Animal

Mackie, Bob
8636 Melrose Ave.
Los Angeles, CA 90069
Fashion designer

MacLaine, Shirley
(Maclean Beaty)
c/o Chasin
9255 Sunset Blvd.
Los Angeles, CA 90069
Actress/author

MacLeod, Charlotte
(Matilda)
c/o Jed Mathes, ICM
40 W. 57th St.
New York, NY 10019
Mystery author

MacNeil, Robert
Breckenridge Ware
c/o WNET
356 W. 58th St.
New York, NY 10019
Television journalist

Macy's
(R.H. Macy & Co.)
151 W. 34th St.
New York, NY 10001
Edward S. Finklestein, chairman

Mad Magazine
Nick Meglin/John Ficarra, editors
485 Madison Ave.
New York, NY 10022
Home of Alfred E. Newman

Madden, John
c/o CBS Sports
51 W. 52nd St.
New York, NY 10019
Sports commentator

Mademoiselle Magazine
350 Madison Ave.
New York, NY 10017
Amy Levin Cooper, editor

Madigan, Amy
10100 Santa Monica Blvd.
(#1600)
Los Angeles, CA 90067
Actress

Madonna
(Madonna Louise Ciccone)
9200 Sunset Blvd. (#915)
Los Angeles, CA 90069
Pop singer/actress

Madruga, Lenor
3530 Pine Valley Dr.
Sarasota, FL 34239
Author who triumphed over cancer

Madsen, Virginia
9830 Wilshire Blvd.
Beverly Hills, CA 90212
Actress

Mahony, Ann
World Trade Center (#275M)
San Francisco, CA 94111
Handwriting analyst

Mahony, Roger Michael,
Archbishop
1531 W. 9th St.
Los Angeles, CA 90012
Catholic leader

Mahre, Phil
White Pass Dr.
Naches, WA 98937
Skier

Mailer, Norman
c/o Rembar
19 W. 44th St.
New York, NY 10036
Author

Maine Wild Blueberry Co.
Elm St.
Machias, ME 04654
Fred W. Kneeland, CEO

Majkowski, Don
c/o Green Bay Packers
1265 Lombardi Ave.
Green Bay, WI 54307
Football's "Magic"

**Major League Baseball
Players Association**
805 3rd Ave.
New York, NY 10002
Donald M. Fehr, executive
director

Makarova, Natalia
c/o American Ballet Theatre
888 7th Ave.
New York, NY 10019
Prima ballerina

Make a Wish Foundation
Jean K. Elder, executive director
2600 N. Central Ave. (#936)
Phoenix, AZ 85004
Grants wishes to ill children

Makeba, Miriam
c/o Jazz Singer
472 North Woodlawn St.
Englewood, NJ 07631
South African singer

Mako
6310 San Vicente Blvd. (#407)
Los Angeles, CA 90048
Actor

**Malden, Karl
(Malden Sekulovich)**
151 El Camino Dr.
Beverly Hills, CA 90212
Actor

Male Liberation Foundation
701 N.E. 67th St.
Miami, FL 33138
Frank Bertels, director

Malkovich, John
c/o Steppenwolf Theatre
2851 N. Halstead St.
Chicago, IL 60657
Actor

Malle, Louis
c/o Nouvelles Editions de Films
15 Rue du Louvre
75001 Paris, France
Film director

Malone, Karl
c/o Utah Jazz
5 Triad Center (#500)
Salt Lake City, UT 84160
Basketball's "The Mailman"

Malone, Moses
c/o Altantic Hawks
One CNN Center, South Tower
   (#405)
Atlanta, GA 30303
Basketball star

Mamet, David
555 W. 57th St. (#1230)
New York, NY 10019
Playwright/film director

**Manatt, Phelps, Rothenberg,
   & Phllips**
11355 W. Olympic Blvd.
Los Angeles, CA 90064
Attorneys

Manchester, Melissa
10100 Santa Monica Blvd.
   (#1600)
Los Angeles, CA 90067
Singer

Manchester, William
P.O. Box 329, Wesleyan Station
Middletown, CT 06457
Author/historian

Mancini, Henry
9200 Sunset Blvd. (#823)
Los Angeles, CA 90069
Film music composer

Mancini, Ray "Boom Boom"
151 El Camino Dr.
Beverly Hills, CA 90212
Boxer

Mancuso, Frank
c/o Paramount Pictures
5555 Melrose Ave.
Los Angeles, CA 90038
Entertainment executive

Mandel, Babaloo
9830 Wilshire Blvd.
Beverly Hills, CA 90212
Screenwriter

Mandel, Howie
10100 Santa Monica Blvd.
(#1600)
Los Angeles, CA 90067
Comedian

**Mandela, Nelson
(Rolihlahla)**
Orlando West
Soweto, Republic of South Africa
Anti-apartheid leader

**Mandela, Winnie (Knosikazi
Nobandle Nomzamo
Madikizela)**
Orlando West
Soweto, Republic of South Africa
South African civil rights leader

Mandelbaum, Ellen
39–49 46th St.
Long Island City, NY 11104
Stained glass artist

M&M/Mars
High St.
Hackettstown, NJ 07840
Howard Walker, president

Mandrell, Barbara
P.O. Box 332
Hendersonville, TN 37075
Country singer

Manilow, Barry
P.O. Box 4095
Beverly Hills, CA 10506
Pop singer

Mankiewicz, Joseph
RFD #2, Box 82
Bedford, NY 90213
Film director/writer/producer

Mankiller, Wilma P.
P.O. Box 948
Talequah, OK 74465
Chief of the Cherokees

Manley, Michael Norman
89 Old Hope Rd.
Kingston 6, Jamaica
President of Jamaica

Manning, Michael, Father
11316 Cypress Ave.
Riverside, CA 92505
Religious leader

Manoff, Dinah
222 N. Canon Dr. (#202)
Beverly Hills, CA 90210
Actress

Mansfield, Jayne
7985 Santa Monica Blvd. (#109)
Box 117
West Hollywood, CA 90046
Late actress's fan club

Manson, Charles
Corcoran Prison
San Joaquin, CA 93660
Mass murderer

Manufacturers Hanover
270 Park Ave.
New York, NY 10017
John F. McGillicuddy, chairman

Maples, Marla
c/o Chuck Jones
150 W. 51st St. (#802)
New York, NY 10019
Model

Maradona, Diego Armando
Maternidad 2
Barcelona 4, Spain
Soccer great

Marceau, Marcel
Compagnie de Mime Marcel
 Marceau
21 Rue Jean-Mermoz
75008 Paris, France
Mime

March of Dimes
1275 Mamaroneck Ave.
White Plains, NY 10605
Marcia Stein, spokesperson

Margaret, Princess (Rose)
10 Kensington Place
London, W8 4PV England

Marilyn Forever
Wendy Beeby, president
P.O. Box 7544
Northridge, CA 91327
Marilyn Monroe fan club

Marino, Dan (Daniel Constantine, Jr.)
4770 Biscayne Blvd. (#1440)
Miami, FL 33137
Football quarterback

Markey, Edward J.
2133 Rayburn House Office Bldg.
Washington, DC 20515
*Congressman from
 Massachusetts*

Markey, Howard T.
U.S. Court of Appeal
Federal Circuit
Washington, DC 20439
Chief Judge

Markle, Clarke Wilson
c/o Colorization, Inc.
26 Soho St.
Toronto, ON Canada
M5T 127
Invented colorization for movies

Marriott Corporation
10400 Fernwood Rd.
Bethesda, MD 20058
J.W. Marriott, Jr., CEO

Marsalis, Wynton
9000 Sunset Blvd. (#1200)
Los Angeles, CA 90069
Jazz and classical trumpeter

Marsh, Jean
222 N. Canon Dr. (#202)
Beverly Hills, CA 90210
Actress

Marsh, John O.
The Pentagon
Washington, DC 20350
Secretary of the Army

Marshall, Penny
9830 Wilshire Blvd.
Beverly Hills, CA 90212
Film director/former actress

Marshall, Thurgood
U.S. Supreme Court Bldg.
One 1st Street NE.
Washington, DC 20543
Supreme Court Justice

Martell, Alice
555 5th Ave. (#1900)
New York, NY 10017
Literary agent

Martika
(Marrero)
c/o CBS Records
1801 Century Park W.
Los Angeles, CA 90067
Pop singer

Martin, Dean
(Dino Crocetti)
c/o Mort Viner
8899 Beverly Blvd.
Los Angeles, CA 90048
Singer/actor

Martin, Pamela Sue
P.O. Box 25578
Los Angeles, CA 90025
Actress

Martin, Steve
P.O. Box 929
Beverly Hills, CA 90213
Comedian/actor

Martin Marietta Corp.
6801 Rockledge Dr.
Bethesda, MD 20817
Norman R. Augustine, CEO

Martinez, Bob
State Capitol
Tallahassee, FL 32301
Governor of Florida

Martins, Peter
c/o New York City Ballet
Lincoln Center
New York, NY 10023
Dancer/New York City Ballet,
director

Marvel Comics
387 Park Ave. S.
New York, NY 10016
Tom DeFalco, editor

Marx, Richard
2519 Carmen Crest Dr.
Los Angeles, CA 90068
Pop singer

Mason, Marsha
8899 Beverly Blvd.
Los Angeles, CA 90048
Actress

Masons, General Grand
Chapter
1084 New Circle Rd. NE.
Lexington, KY 40505

Mast, Gerald
c/o University of Chicago
5811 S. Ellis Ave.
Chicago, IL 60637
Historian

Mastrantonio, Mary Elizabeth
10100 Santa Monica Blvd.
(#1600)
Los Angeles, CA 90067
Actress

Mastroianni, Marcello
c/o A. Cav
8 Via Maria Adelaide
Rome, Italy
Actor

Matheson, Tim
9000 Sunset Blvd. (#1200)
Los Angeles, CA 90069
Actor/business executive

Mathis, Johnny
3500 W. Olive Ave. (#750)
Burbank, CA 91505
Singer

Mathison, Melissa
P.O. Box 49344
Los Angeles, CA 90049
"E.T." screenwriter

Matlin, Marlee
121 N. San Vicente Blvd.
Beverly Hills, CA 90211
Actress

Matlock, John F., Jr.
U.S. Embassy
Ulitsa Chaykovskogo 19/21/23
Moscow, U.S.S.R.
U.S. Ambassador to U.S.S.R.

Mattel
5150 Rosecrans Ave.
Hawthorne, CA 90250
Thomas J. Kalinske, president

Matthau, Walter (Matasschanskayasky)
10100 Santa Monica Blvd.
(#2200)
Los Angeles, CA 90067
Actor

Mattingly, Don
RR #5
P.O. Box 74
Evansville, IN 47711
Baseball star

Max, Peter
118 Riverside Dr.
New York, NY 10024
Pop art painter

Max Factor & Co.
700 Fairfield Ave.
Stamford, CT 06904
Paul Masturgo, president

May, John L., Archbishop
1312 Massachusetts Ave. NW.
Washington, DC 20005
President, National Council of Catholic Bishops

Mayer, Robert, Dr.
Dana Farber Cancer Institute
Boston, MA 02115
Leukemia specialist

Mayflower Descendants
4 Winslow St.
Plymouth, MA 02360

Mayron, Melanie
10100 Santa Monica Blvd.
(#1600)
Los Angeles, CA 90067
Actress

Maytag Corp.
403 W. 47th St. N.
Newton, IA 50108
D.J. Krumm, president

Mazda Motor Corp.
3-1 Sinchi, Fuchu-ocho, Akigun
Hiroshima 730-19 Japan
Kenichi Yamamoto, chairman

Mazursky, Paul
8899 Beverly Blvd.
Los Angeles, CA 90048
Film director

McAnuff, Des
1350 6th Ave.
New York, NY 10019
Theater director

**McBain, Ed
(Evan Hunter)**
c/o Farquarson
250 W. 57th St.
New York, NY 10107
Mystery author

McCall's Magazine
230 Park Ave.
New York, NY 10169
Elizabeth Sloan, editor

McCarthy, Andrew
151 El Camino Dr.
Beverly Hills, CA 90212
Actor

McCarthy, Eugene Joseph
P.O. Box 22
Woodville, VA 22749
Former senator

**McCartney, Paul
(James)**
c/o MPL Communications Ltd.
One Soho Square
London W1V 6BQ England
Pop musician/former Beatle

**McClanahan, Rue
(Eddi-Rue McClanahan)**
8899 Beverly Blvd.
Los Angeles, CA 90048
Actress

McClintock, Barbara, Dr.
Carnegie Institute
Cold Spring Harbor
New York, NY 11724
Nobel Prize geneticist

**McClure, Jessica
(Baby)**
P.O. Box 3901
Midland, TX 79701
Child rescued from well

McCormick, Mark
c/o Bantam Books
666 5th Ave.
New York, NY 10103
Business author

McCormick, Pat
1930 Century Park W. (#303)
Los Angeles, CA 90067
Actor/writer/comedian

McCovey, Willie
P.O. Box 620342
Woodside, CA 94062
Former baseball great

McDaniel, Xavier
c/o Seattle Supersonics
10 Queen Anne Ave. N.
Seattle, WA 98109
Bastketball's "X Man"

McDonald, Ronald
One McDonald Plaza
Oak Brook, IL 60521
Spokesclown

McDonald's Corp.
One McDonald Plaza
Oak Brook, IL 60521
Fred L. Turner, CEO

McDonnell Douglas Corp.
P.O. Box 516
St. Louis, MO 63166
John F. McDonnell, CEO

McDowall, Roddy
222 N. Canon Dr. (#202)
Beverly Hills, CA 90210
Actor/photographer

**McDowell, Malcolm
(Malcolm Taylor)**
8899 Beverly Blvd.
Los Angeles, CA 90048
Actor

McEnroe, John
c/o U.S. Tennis Association
51 E. 42nd St.
New York, NY 10017
Tennis star

McFerrin, Bobby
9000 Sunset Blvd. (#1200)
Los Angeles, CA 90069
Vocalist

McGovern, Elizabeth
11726 San Vicente Blvd. (#300)
Los Angeles, CA 90049
Actress

**McGrath, Marcos Gregorio,
Archbishop**
Apartado 6386
Panama 5, Panama
Archbishop of Panama

McGraw-Hill
1221 6th Ave.
New York, NY 10020
Joseph L. Dionne, president

McGuire, Al
c/o NBC Sports
30 Rockefeller Plaza
New York, NY 10112
Basketball broadcaster

McGwire, Mark
c/o Oakland Athletics
Oakland-Alameda County
Coliseum
Oakland, CA 94621
Baseball star

McHale, Kevin
c/o Boston Celtics
150 Causeway St.
Boston, MA 02114
Basketball star

McHenry, Donald F.
c/o School of Foreign Service
Georgetown University
Washington, DC 20057
Diplomat

MCI Communications Corp.
1133 19th St. NW.
Washington, DC 20036
William G. McGowan, chairman

McKay, Harvey
c/o Wm. Morrow & Co.
105 Madison Ave.
New York, NY 10016
Business author

McKean, Michael
10100 Santa Monica Blvd.
(#1600)
Los Angeles, CA 90067
Actor

McKechnie, Donna
151 El Camino Dr.
Beverly Hills, CA 90212
Actress/singer/dancer

McKellen, Ian
c/o James Sharkey
15 Golden Square (3rd floor)
London W1R 3AG England
Actor

McKuen, Rod
P.O. Box G
Beverly Hills, CA 90213
Poet

McMahon, Ed
c/o NBC-TV
3000 Alameda Ave.
Burbank, CA 91505
Television sidekick

McMurtry, Larry
8955 Beverly Blvd.
Los Angeles, CA 90048
Author

McNichol, Kristy
10100 Santa Monica Blvd.
(#1600)
Los Angeles, CA 90067
Actress

McRaney, Gerald
247 S. Beverly Dr. (#102)
Beverly Hills, CA 90212
Actor

McShane, Ian
P.O. Box 5617
Beverly Hills, CA 90210
Actor

McTaggart, David
c/o Temple House
25–26 High Street
Lewes BN1 2LV England
Greenpeace, chairman

Mead Corp.
Courthouse Plaza, NE.
Dayton, OH 45463
B.R. Roberts, CEO

Mears, Rick
P.O. Box 2183
Bakersfield, CA 93303
Racecar driver

Medoff, Mark
P.O. Box 3072
Las Cruces, NM 88003
Playwright

Meese, Edwin, III
c/o Heritage Foundation
214 Massachusetts Ave. NE.
Washington, DC 20002
Former attorney general

Megadeth
9145 Sunset Blvd. (#100)
Los Angeles, CA 90069
Heavy metal band

Mehta, Zubin
c/o N.Y. Philharmonic Orchestra
Avery Fisher Hall
New York, NY 10023
Conductor

Melby, James C., Dr.
University Hospital
Boston, MA 02118
Endocrinology specialist

Mellencamp, John Cougar
P.O. Box 361
Nashville, IN 47448
Rock singer

**Melman, Larry "Bud"
(Calvert DeForest)**
"Late Night with David
  Letterman"
30 Rockefeller Plaza
New York, NY 10020
Comedian

Melody Maker Magazine
King's Reach Tower, Stamford
  St.
London SE1 9LS England
Alan Jones, editor

Mennen Company
Hanover Ave.
Morristown, NJ 07960
L. Donald Horne, CEO

Mennonite Brethren
8000 W. 21st St.
Wichita, KS 67212
Herb Brandt, chairperson

Mensa
c/o Lisa Trombetta
2626 E. 14th St.
Brooklyn NY 11235
Genius IQ group

Menudo
Padosa Hato Rey
157 Ponce de Leon
San Juan 00901 Puerto Rico
Pop group

Menuhin, Yehudi, Sir
c/o Anglo Swiss Artists
4–5 Primrose Mews, Regents Pk.
  Rd.
London NW1 8YL England
Violinist

Mercedes-Benz
c/o Daimler-Benz A.G.
Mercedestrasse 136 (D-700)
Stuttgart 60, Germany
Werner Breitschwerdt, chairman

Merck & Co.
P.O. Box 2000
Rahway, NJ 07065
P. Roy Vagelos, CEO

Meredith, Don
P.O. Box 597
Santa Fe, NM 87504
Football's "Dandy Don"

Merrifield, Robert Bruce, Dr.
Rockefeller University
1230 York Ave.
New York, NY 10021
Nobel Prize biochemist

Merrill Lynch & Co.
165 Broadway
New York, NY 10006
William A. Schreyer, chairman

Metallica
P.O. Box 1347
Roslyn Heights, NY 10017
Heavy metal band

Metheny, Pat
c/o Kurland
173 Brighton Ave.
Boston, MA 02134
Jazz guitarist

Metropolitan Life
One Madison Ave.
New York, NY 10010
Robert G. Schwartz, CEO

Metropolitan Museum of Art
Fifth Ave. at 82nd St.
New York, NY 10028
William H. Luers, president

Metzenbaum, Howard Morton
140 Russell Senate Office Bldg.
Washington, DC 20510
Senator from Ohio

Meyer, Nicholas
2109 Stanley Hills Dr.
Los Angeles, CA 90046
Motion picture writer/director

Meyer, Russ
P.O. Box 3748
Hollywood, CA 90078
Porno film king

Miami Dolphins
2700 Biscayne Blvd.
Miami, FL 33137
Don Shula, coach

Miami Heat
Miami Arena
Miami, FL 33136
Ron Rothstein, coach

Miami Herald
One Herald Plaza
Miami, FL 33132
Janet Chusmir, editor

Michael, George (Michael Panayiotou)
c/o Columbia Records
1801 Century Park W.
Los Angeles, CA 90067
Pop singer

Michaels, Al (Alan)
c/o ABC Sports
1330 6th Ave.
New York, NY 10019
Sportscaster

Michaels, Barbara (Louise Gross Mertz)
c/o Abel
498 West End Ave.
New York, NY 10024
Romance mystery author

Michaels, Lorne
c/o Broadway Video
1619 Broadway
New York, NY 10019
"Saturday Night Live" producer

Michel, Robert H.
2112 Rayburn House Office Bldg.
Washington, DC 20515
Congressman from Illinois

Michener, James Albert
P.O. Box 125
Pipersville, PA 18947
Author

Midler, Bette
P.O. Box 46703
Los Angeles, CA 90046
Actress/singer

Midnight Oil
P.O. Box 186, Glebe
Sydney 2037, NSW Australia
Rock group

Mighty Clouds of Joy
9200 Sunset Blvd. (#823)
Los Angeles, CA 90069
Gospel singers

Mikulski, Barbara
320 Senate Hart Office Bldg.
Washington, DC 20510
Senator from Maryland

Milano, Alyssa
P.O. Box 3684
Hollywood, CA 90078
Actress

Miles, Sarah
147–149 Wardour St.
London W1V 3TB England
Actress

Milius, John
1440 S. Sepulveda Blvd.
Los Angeles, CA 90025
Film director/writer

Miller, Arthur
RR #1
P.O. Box 320
Roxbury, CT 06783
Playwright

Miller, Claire
3530 Pine Valley Dr.
Sarasota, FL 34239
Expert on business etiquette

Miller, Dennis
c/o "Saturday Night Live"
30 Rockefeller Plaza
New York, NY 10020
Comedian

Miller, Frank, Dr.
University Hospital of Arkansas
Little Rock, AR 72205
Obstetrics and gynecology

Miller, George
2228 Rayburn House Office Bldg.
Washington, DC 20515
Congressman from California

Miller Brewing Co.
3939 W. Highland Blvd.
Milwaukee, WI 53201
William K. Howell, president

Milli Vanilli (Rob Pilatus/ Fabrice Morvan)
Wapping Lane, Gun Place
London E1 England
Pop singers

Milligan, Spike (Terence Alan)
9 Orme Court
London W2 England
"Goon Show" comedian

Mills, Donna
10351 Santa Monica Blvd. (#211)
Los Angeles, CA 90025
Actress

Milwaukee Brewers
County Stadium
Milwaukee, WI 53214
Tom Trebelhorn, manager

Milwaukee Bucks
The Bradley Center
1001 N. 4th St.
Milwaukee, WI 53203
Del Harris, coach

Minnelli, Liza
c/o ICM
40 W. 57th St.
New York, NY 10022
Actress/singer

Minnesota Mining & Manufacturing
3M Center
St. Paul MN 55101
Allen F. Jacobson, CEO

Minnesota North Stars
7901 Cedar Ave. S.
Bloomington, MN 55420
Bob Gainey, coach

Minnesota Timberwolves
730 Hennepin Ave.
Minneapolis, MN 55403
Bill Musselman, coach

Minnesota Twins
The Metrodome
Minneapolis, MN 55415
Andy MacPhail, general manager

Minnesota Vikings
9520 Viking Dr.
Eden Prairie, MN 55344
Jerry Burns, coach

Miss America Pageant
211 E. Chicago Ave.
Chicago, IL 60611
Lisa Grady, spokesperson

Mister Ed Fan Club
P.O. Box 1009
Cedar Hill, TX 75104
James Burnett, president

Mitchell, Arthur
466 W. 152nd St.
New York, NY 10031
Dance Theater of Harlem, founder

Mitchell, George John
176 Russell Office Bldg.
Washington, DC 20510
Senator from Maine

Mitchell, Joni
(Roberta Joan Anderson)
644 N. Doheny Dr.
Los Angeles, CA 90069
Pop/jazz singer

Mitchell, Kevin
c/o San Francisco Giants
Candlestick Park, Bay Shore
San Francisco, CA 94124
Baseball star

Mitchelson, Marvin
1801 Century Park E. (#1900)
Los Angeles, CA 90067
Divorce attorney

Mitchum, Robert Charles
Duran
10100 Santa Monica Blvd.
(#1600)
Los Angeles, CA 90067.
Actor

Mitterrand, François
Maurice Marie
Palais de l'Elysee
55–57 Rue de Faubourg Saint-
Honore
75008 Paris, France
President of France

Mobil Corporation
150 E. 42nd St.
New York, NY 10017
Allen E. Murray, president

Mobilization Against AIDS
1540 Market St. (#60)
San Francisco, CA 94102
Paul Boneberg, executive
director

Moby Dick Academy
Mary Tufts, administrator
P.O. Box 236
Ocean Park, WA 98640
Promotes home schooling

Modern Bride Magazine
475 Park Ave. S.
New York, NY 10016
Cele Goldsmith Lalli, editor

Modigliani, Franco, Dr.
Massachusetts Inst. of
Technology
Sloan School of Management
Cambridge, MA 02139
Nobel Prize economist

Modine, Matthew
151 El Camino Dr.
Beverly Hills, CA 90212
Actor

Moe, Doug
c/o Denver Nuggets
1635 Clay St., McNichols Arena
Denver, CO 80204
Basketball coach

Mofford, Rose
State House
Phoenix, AZ 85007
Governor of Arizona

Moiseyev, Igor
Alexandrovich
20 Ploshchad Mayakovskogo
Moscow, U.S.S.R.
Folk dance company founder

Moll, Richard
6430 Sunset Blvd. (#1203)
Los Angeles, CA 90028
Bull on "Night Court"

Molyneaux, James Henry
House of Commons
London SW1 England
Ulster Unionist Party

Mom's Apple Pie
Maidi Nickele, editor
P.O. Box 21567
Seattle, WA 98111
Newsletter for lesbian mothers

Mona Lisas and Mad Hatters
Rt. 1, P.O. Box 200
Todd, NC 28684
Elton John fan club

Monaghan, Thomas
30 Frank Lloyd Wright Dr.
(#997)
Ann Arbor, MI 48106
Domino's Pizza president

Monarchist Alliance
Prof. G.D.V. Wiebe,
  spokesperson
730 Blossom Way (#29)
Hayward, CA 94541
Wants monarchy for U.S.

Mondejar, Marily
1255 Post St. (#606)
San Francisco, CA 94109
Image and fashion consultant

Mondino, Bartly, Dr.
Jules Stein Eye Institute
UCLA Medical Center
Los Angeles, CA 90024
Cornea specialist

Monkees, The
P.O. Box 1461, Radio City
  Station
New York, NY 10101
Pop group

Monsanto Company
800 N. Lindbergh Blvd.
St. Louis, MO 63167
Richard J. Mahoney, CEO

Montalban, Ricardo
151 El Camino Dr.
Beverly Hills, CA 90212
Actor

Montana, Joe
c/o San Francisco 49ers
711 Nevada Street
Redwood City, CA 94061
Football quarterback

Montgomery Ward & Co.
Montgomery Ward Plaza
Chicago, IL 60671
Bernard F. Brennan, chairman

Montreal Canadiens
2313 St. Catherine St. West
Montreal, QU Canada
H3H 1N2
Serge Sevard, general manager

Montreal Expos
Olympic Stadium
Montreal, QU Canada
Charles Bronfman, owner

Moon, Warren
c/o Houston Oilers
P.O. Box 1516
Houston, TX 77001
Football quarterback

Moore, Demi
(Guynes)
9830 Wilshire Blvd.
Beverly Hills, CA 90212
Actress

Moore, Dudley Stewart John
73 Market St.
Venice, CA 90291
Actor

Moore, Mary Tyler
P.O. Box 49032
Los Angeles, CA 90049
Actress

Moore, Michael
2025 Pennsylvania Ave. NW.
(#918)
Washington, DC 20006
Me of "Roger & Me"
documentary

Moore, Robin Lowell, Jr.
c/o Manor Books
45 E. 30th St.
New York, NY 10016
Author

Moore, Roger
c/o London Management
235–241 Regent Street
London W1 England
Actor

Moore, William L.
4219 W. Olive (#247)
Burbank, CA 91505
UFO expert

Moranis, Rick
9000 Sunset Blvd. (#1200)
Los Angeles, CA 90069
Actor

Morbidity & Mortality
Weekly Report
Michael B. Gregg, editor
U.S. Government Printing Office
Washington, DC 20402
National death statistics

Moreno, Rita
(Rosita Dolores Alverio)
151 El Camino Dr.
Beverly Hills, CA 90212
Actress

Morganna
P.O. Box 20281
Columbus, OH 43220
Sports' buxom "kissing bandit"

Morita, Akio
7-35 Kitashinagawa
6-chome, Shinagawa-ku
Tokyo 141, Japan
Sony Corp., chairman

Morrison, Margo
3650 Clark Ave. (PH E)
Burbank, CA 91505
Murder mystery weekends

Morrison, Van
12304 Santa Monica Blvd. (#300)
Los Angeles, CA 90025
Rock musician

Mosbacher, Robert
15th and Constitution Ave.
Washington, DC 20230
Secretary of Commerce

Moschitta, John
11726 San Vicente Blvd. (#300)
Los Angeles, CA 90049
Fast talker

Moses, Edwin Corley
P.O. Box 9887
Newport Beach, CA 92660
Track athlete

Mother Jones Magazine
1663 Mission St.
San Francisco, CA 94103
Douglas Foster, editor

Motherwell, Robert
c/o Knoedler
19 E. 70th St.
New York, NY 10022
Painter

Motley Crue
c/o Elektra Records
75 Rockefeller Plaza
New York, NY 10019
Rock group

Motor Trend Magazine
8490 Sunset Blvd.
Los Angeles, CA 90069
Mike Anson, editor

Motown Museum
2648 W. Grand Blvd.
Detroit, MI 48208
Birthplace of Motown Records

Mourelatos, Alexander Phoebus
University of Texas
Department of Philosophy
Austin, TX 78712
Humanities educator

Moyers, Bill
524 W. 57th St.
New York, NY 10019
Television journalist

Moynihan, Daniel Patrick
464 Senate Russell Bldg.
Washington, DC 20510
Senator from New York

Mr. Perfect
P.O. Box 3859
Stamford, CT 06905
Professional wrestler

Mr. Rogers (Fred)
c/o Family Communications
4802 5th Ave.
Pittsburgh, PA 15213
Kids' TV star fan club

Mr. V Fan Club
Ethel Jackson Price, chairman
P.O. Box 44268
Tucson, AZ 85733
Bodybuilding fan club

Mr. Wizard (Donald Jeffrey Herbert)
P.O. Box 83
Canoga Park, CA 91305
Television's science teacher

MTV (Music Television)
1775 Broadway
New York, NY 10019
Tom Freston, president

Mubarak, (Muhammad) Hosni
Presidential Palace, Abdeen
Cairo, Egypt
President of Egypt

181

Muda, Hassanal Bolkiah
Waddauliah, Bandar Seri
Begawan, Brunei
Sultan of Brunei

Mugabe, Robert Gabriel
Office of the President
Harare, Zimbabwe
President of Zimbabwe

Mull, Kayla
1394 Tally Ho Lane
Norco, CA 91760
Breeder of miniature pet pigs

Mull, Martin
9000 Sunset Blvd. (#1200)
Los Angeles, CA 90069
Comic actor

Mulligan, Richard
8899 Beverly Blvd.
Los Angeles, CA 90048
Actor

Mullin, Chris
c/o Golden State Warriors
Oakland Coliseum Arena
Oakland, CA 94621
Basketball star

**Mulroney, Brian
(Martin)**
Stornoway
Ottawa, ON Canada
Prime Minister of Canada

Murdoch, (Keith) Rupert
c/o News Corp. Ltd.
210 South St.
New York, NY 10002
Media tycoon

Murdock, David H.
10900 Wilshire Blvd. (#1500)
Los Angeles, CA 90024
Business leader

Murphy, Dale
P.O. Box 4064
Atlanta, GA 30302
Baseball star

**Murphy, Eddie
(Edward Regan)**
P.O. Box 1028
Englewood Cliffs, NJ 07632
Comedian/actor

Murphy, Gerald Patrick, Dr.
State U. of New York at Buffalo
139 Parker Hall, Dept. of
    Urology
Buffalo, NY 14214
Urologist

Murphy, Thomas Aquinas
3004 W. Grand Blvd.
Detroit, MI 48202
General Motors, director

Murray, Anne
4881 Yonge St. (#412)
Toronto, ON CAN M4S 2B9
Pop/country singer

Murray, Bill
P.O. Box 250A
Palisades, NY 10964
Comedian/actor

Murray, Jim
c/o Los Angeles Times
Times Mirror Square
Los Angeles, CA 90053
Pulitzer Prize sportswriter

Musburger, Brent
c/o ABC Sports
1330 6th Ave.
New York, NY 10019
Sportscaster

**Muscular Dystrophy
Association**
810 7th Ave.
New York, NY 10019
Jerry Lewis, national chairman

Museum of Broadcasting
One E. 53rd St.
New York, NY 10022
Dr. Robert M. Batscha,
president

**Museum of Contemporary
Art
(MOCA)**
250 S. Grand Ave.
Los Angeles, CA 90012
William Kieschnick, chairman

Museum of Fine Arts
465 Huntington Ave.
Boston, MA 02115
Allan Shestack, director

**Museum of Modern Art
(MOMA)**
11 W. 53rd St.
New York, NY 10019
Richard E. Oldenburg, director

**Museum of Neon Art
(MONA)**
704 Traction Ave.
Los Angeles, CA 90013
Lili Lakich, director

**Museum of Science and
Industry**
57th St. & Lake Shore Dr.
Chicago, IL 60637
Dr. James S. Kahn, president

Musician Magazine
33 Commercial St.
Gloucester, MA 01930
Jock Baird, editor

Muskie, Edmond Sixtus
1101 Vermont Ave. NW. (#900)
Washington, DC 20005
Former senator

Musser, Tharon
21 Cornelia St.
New York, NY 10014
Theatrical lighting designer

Mutter, Anne-Sophie
Rychenbergstrasse 199d
CH-8400 Winterthur, Switzerland
Violinist

N

NAACP (National Assoc. for the Advancement of Colored People)
4805 Mt. Hope Dr.
Baltimore, MD 21215
Benjamin L. Hooks, executive
director

Nabisco Brands
Nabisco Brands Plaza
East Hanover, NJ 07936
John H. Greeniaus, CEO

Nabors, Jim
151 El Camino Dr.
Beverly Hills, CA 90212
Singer/actor

Nader, Ralph
P.O. Box 19367
Washington, DC 20036
Consumer advocate

Nagel, Jeff
P.O. Box 415
Greenvale, NY 11548
Blind date expert

Naismith Memorial Basketball Hall of Fame
150 W. Columbus Ave.
Springfield, MA 01101

Najibullah, Mohammad, Maj. Gen.
People's Democratic Party of
Afghanistan
Kabul, Afghanistan
President of Afghanistan

Namath, Joe
9255 Sunset Blvd. (#505)
Los Angeles, CA 90069
Football's "Broadway Joe"

NASA (National Aeronautics & Space Administration)
600 Independence Ave. SW.
Washington, DC 20546
Richard Truly, director

Nash, Graham
P.O. Box 838
Hanaleo, HI 96714
Pop singer

Nation
P.O. Box 1953
Marion, OH 43305
Victor Navasky, editor

National Abortion Federation
1436 U St. NW. (#103)
Washington, DC 20009

National Abortion Rights Action League
1101 14th St. NW. (#500)
Washington, DC 20005
Kate Michaelman, executive director

National Academy of Nannies
Terri Erich, president
3300 E. 1st Ave. (#520)
Denver, CO 80206
Nanny school

National Academy of Recording Arts & Sciences (NARAS)
303 N. Glenoaks Blvd. (#140M)
Burbank, CA 91502
Awards the Grammys

National Air and Space Museum
Sixth St. & Independence Ave. SW.
Washington, DC 20560
Martin O. Harwit, director

National Air Traffic Controllers
444 N. Capitol St. NW. (#845)
Washington, DC 20001
R. Steve Bell, president

National Amputation Foundation
12–45 150th St.
Whitestone, NY 11357

National Anti-Vivisection Society
53 W. Jackson (#1550)
Chicago, IL 60604
George J. Trapp, president

National Archives
Pennsylvania Ave. and 8th St. NW.
Washington, DC 20408
Dr. Franklin G. Burke, archivist

National Association of Chiefs of Police
1000 Connecticut Ave. NW. (#9)
Washington, DC 20036
Gerald S. Arenberg, spokesperson

National Audubon Society
950 3rd Ave.
New York, NY 10022
Peter A.A. Berle, president

National Aviation Club
1745 Jefferson Davis Hwy. (#406)
Arlington, VA 22202
G. Moore Lindsay, executive vice president

National Baptist Convention
52 S. 6th Ave.
Mt. Vernon, NY 10550
Dr. T.J. Jemison, president

National Baseball Fan Association
P.O. Box 4192
Mt. Laurel, NJ 08054
Robert E. Godfrey, president

National Baseball Hall of Fame
P.O. Box 590
Cooperstown, NY 13326
Howard C. Talbot, director

National Basketball Association (NBA)
645 5th Ave.
New York, NY 10022
David J. Stern, commissioner

National Basketball Players Assoc.
1285 6th Ave.
New York, NY 10019
Charles Gratham, executive officer

National Boating Federation
1000 Thomas Jefferson St. NW.
Washington, DC 20007
Ron Stone, treasurer

National Captioning Institute
Don Thieme, spokesperson
5203 Leesburg Pike
Falls Church, VA 22041
Captions television for the deaf

National Center for Air Travel Safety
108–18 Queens Blvd.
Forest Hills, NY 11375
Peter Baron, executive director

National Center for Missing and Exploited Children
2101 Wilson Blvd.
Arlington, VA 22201
Julia C. Cartwright, director

National Chastity Association
Mary Meyer, president
P.O. Box 402
Oak Forest, IL 60452
Advocates pre-marital chastity

National Child Support Enforcement Assoc.
444 N. Capitol NW. (#613)
Washington, DC 20001
Patricia Vogeley, spokesperson

National Citizens Coalition for Nursing Home Reform
1424 16th St. NW. (Suite L2)
Washington, DC 20036
Cynna R. Heffter, spokesperson

National Clearinghouse for Alcohol Information
P.O. Box 2345
Rockville, MD 20852

National Coalition Against Pornography
800 Compton Rd. (#9224)
Cincinnati, OH 45231
Dr. Jerry Kirk, president

National Coalition on Televison Violence
P.O. Box 2157
Champaign, IL 61825
Dr. Thomas Radecki, spokesperson

National Coalition to Abolish The Death Penalty
1419 V St. NW.
Washington, DC 20009
Leigh Dingerson, director

National Collegiate Athletic Association (NCAA)
P.O. Box 190
Mission, KS 66201
Richard D. Schultz, executive director

**National Committee for
Sexual Liberties**
98 Olden Ln.
Princeton, NH 08540
Dr. Arthur C. Warner, chairman

**National Committee to
Reopen the Rosenberg
Case**
833 Broadway (#1120)
New York, NY 10003
Aaron Katz, director

National Council of La Raza
Raul Yzaguirre, president
810 1st St. NE. (3rd floor)
Washington, DC 20022
Hispanic organization

**National Dropout
Prevention Network**
1517 L St.
Sacramento, CA 95814
Dr. Raymond Eberhard,
executive director

National Enquirer
600 S. East Coast Ave.
Lantana, FL 33464
Iain Calder, editor

**National Football League
(NFL)**
410 Park Ave.
New York, NY 10022
Paul Tagliabue, commissioner

**National Football League
Players Association**
2021 L St. NW. (6th floor)
Washington, DC 20036
Eugene Upshaw, Jr., executive
director

**National Fox Hunters
Association**
P.O. Box 538
Richmond, KY 40475
Jim Million, secretary

National Gallery of Art
4th St. and Constitution Ave.
NW.
Washington, DC 20565
Dr. Franklin Murphy, chairman

**National Gay Pentecostal
Alliance**
P.O. Box 1391
Schenectady, NY 12301
Rev. William H. Carey,
president

**National Genealogical
Society**
4527 17th St. N.
Arlington, VA 22207
Helps trace family trees

**National Geographic
Magazine**
P.O. Box 2895
Washington, DC 20077
Wilbur E. Garrett, editor

National Guild of Hypnotists
P.O. Box 308
Merrimack, NH 03054
Dr. Dwight F. Damon, executive
director

National Hobo Association
World Way Center, P.O. Box
90430
Los Angeles, CA 90009
Bob Hopkins, founding director

National Hockey League (NHL)
1155 Metcalfe St. (#960)
Montreal, QU Canada
H3B 2W2
John A. Ziegler, Jr., president

National Hockey League Players Association
37 Maitland St.
Toronto, ON Canada
M4Y 1C8
R. Alan Eagleson, executive director

National Hot Rod Association (NHRA)
2035 Financial Way
Glendora, CA 91740
Dallas J. Gardner, president

National Institute for Dispute Resolution
1901 L St. NW. (#600)
Washington, DC 20036
Madeline Crohn, president

National Institute for the Study of Satanology
P.O. Box 1092
South Orange, NJ 07079
Dr. Alan H. Peterson, executive director

National Investigations Committee on Unidentified Flying Objects
Victory Blvd. (#4)
Van Nuys, CA 91411
Dr. Frank E. Sturges, director

National Labor Relations Board Union
915 2nd Ave. (#2948)
Seattle, WA 98174
Henrik M. Sortun, president

National Lampoon Magazine
155 6th Ave.
New York, NY 10013
Matty Simmons, editor

National Lawyers Guild
55 6th Ave.
New York, NY 10013
Barbara Dudley, executive director

National League of Families of American Prisoners and Missing in South East Asia
1001 Connecticut Ave. NW. (#219)
Washington, DC 20036
Ann Mills Griffiths, executive director

National Organization for Women (NOW)
1041 New York Ave. NW.
Washington, DC 20005
Molly Yard, president

National Organization Taunting Safety and Fairness Everywhere
P.O. Box 5743
Montecito, CA 93150
Dale Lowdermilk, president

National Public Radio (NPR)
2025 M St. NW.
Washington, DC 20036
Douglas Bennet, president

National Review
150 E. 35th St.
New York, NY 10016
William F. Buckley, Jr., editor

National Rifle Association (NRA)
1600 Rhode Island Ave. NW.
Washington, DC 20036
J. Warren Cassidy, president

National Right to Life Committee
419 7th St. NW. (#500)
Washington, DC 20004
John C. Willke, president

National Right to Work Committee
8001 Braddock Rd.
Springfield, VA 22160
Reed Larson, president

National Task Force on Prostitution
Priscilla Alexander, executive director
P.O. Box 6297
San Francisco, CA 94101
Prostitutes' rights organization

National Urban League
500 E. 62nd St.
New York, NY 10021
John E. Jacob, president

National Victim Center
Anne Seymour, director public affairs
307 W. 7th St. (#1001)
Fort Worth, TX 76102
Support of crime victims

National Wheelchair Basketball Association
110 Seaton Bldg., U. of Kentucky
Lexington, KY 40506

National Wildlife Federation
1400 16th St. NW.
Washington, DC 20036
Dr. Jay D. Hair, president

Nationwide Patrol
George Dewey III, president
P.O. Box 2629
Wilkes-Barre, PA 18703
Searches for missing children

Native American Rights Fund
1506 Broadway
Boulder, CO 80302
John E. Echohawk, director

Natural History Magazine
Central Park West and 79th St.
New York, NY 10024
Alan Feines, editor

Natural History Museum of Los Angeles County
900 Exposition Blvd.
Los Angeles, CA 90007
Dr. Craig R. Black, director

Nature Conservancy
1815 N. Lynn St.
Arlington, VA 22209
Environmentalists' retail stores

Nature Magazine
4 Little Essex St.
London WC2R 3LF England
John Maddox, editor

Navratilova, Martina
c/o Int. Management Group
One Erieview Plaza
Cleveland, OH 44199
Tennis great

NCR
(National Cash Register)
1700 S. Patterson Blvd.
Dayton, OH 45479
Charles E. Exley, Jr., CEO

Nederlander, James M./
   James L.
810 7th Ave.
New York, NY 10019
Theater producers

Neeson, Liam
2121 Ave. of the Stars (#950)
Los Angeles, CA 90067
Actor

Nehru, Braj Kumar
1 Western Ave., Maharani Bagh
New Delhi 110-065 India
Politician

Neiman, Leroy
One W. 67th St.
New York, NY 10023
Sports painter

Neiman Marcus
Main and Ervay Sts.
Dallas, TX 75201
Richard C. Marcus, chairman

Nelson, Craig
c/o Harper & Row
10 E. 53rd St.
New York, NY 10022
Book editor

Nelson, Craig T.
8899 Beverly Blvd.
Los Angeles, CA 90048
Actor

Nelson, Don
c/o Golden State Warriors
Oakland Coliseum Arena
Oakland, CA 94621
Basketball coach

Nelson, Judd
9830 Wilshire Blvd.
Beverly Hills, CA 90212
Actor

Nelson, Willie
P.O. Box 2689
Danbury, CT 06813
Country singer

Nemerov, Howard
c/o Library of Congress
101 Independence Ave. SE.
Washington, DC 20540
Poet laureate of the U.S.

Nestle Foods Corp.
100 Manhattanville Rd.
Purchase, NY 10577
C.A. MacDonald, president

Neutrogena Corp.
5755 W. 96th St.
Los Angeles, CA 90045
Lloyd E. Costen, CEO

**New Beginning Foundation
for Agoraphobia**
P.O. Box 55218
Sherman Oaks, CA 91413
Melvin D. Green, director

**New England Journal of
Medicine**
P.O. Box 803
Waltham, MA 02254
Arnold S. Pelman, editor

New England Patriots
Sullivan Stadium
Foxboro, MA 02305

New Jersey Devils
Meadowlands Arena
E. Rutherford, NJ 07073
Max McNab, general manager

New Jersey Nets
Meadowlands Arena
East Rutherford, NJ 07073
Bill Fitch, coach

New Kids on the Block
Six St. Gregory St. (#7001)
Dorchester, MA 02124
Pop group

New Musical Express
King's Reach Tower, Stamford
St.
London SE1 9LS England
British music magazine

New Orleans Saints
6928 Saints Dr.
Metairie, LA 70003
Tom Benson, Jr., owner

New Republic Magazine
1220 Ninth St. NW.
Washington, DC 20036
Michael Kinsley, editor

New York Aquarium
Boardwalk and W. 8th St.
Brooklyn, NY 11224
Dr. George D. Ruggieri, director

New York City Marathon
New York Road Runners Club
9 East 89th St.
New York, NY 10128

New York Giants
Giants Stadium
East Rutherford, NJ 07073
Wellington T. Mara, president

New York Islanders
Nassau Coliseum
Uniondale, NY 11553
Bill Torrey, general manager

New York Knickerbockers
Madison Square Garden
Four Pennsylvania Plaza
New York, NY 10001
Al Bianchi, general manager

New York Mets
Shea Stadium
126th and Roosevelt Ave.
Flushing, NY 11368
Fred Wilpon, president

New York Rangers
Four Pennsylvania Plaza
New York, NY 10001

New York Review of Books
250 W. 57th St.
New York, NY 10107
Robert Silvers/Barbara Epstein,
editors

New York Stock Exchange
11 Wall St.
New York, NY 10005
John J. Phelan, Jr., chairman

New York Times
229 W. 43rd St.
New York, NY 10036
Max Frankel, editor

New York Yacht Club
37 W. 44th St.
New York, NY 10036

New York Yankees
Yankee Stadium
Bronx, NY 10451
Former owner, George
  Steinbrenner

New Yorker Magazine
25 W. 43rd St.
New York, NY 10036
Robert Gottlieb, editor

Newcombe, John David
P.O. Box 1200, Crow's Nest
New South Wales, Australia 2065
Former tennis star

Newhart, Bob
315 S. Beverly Dr.
Beverly Hills, CA 90212
Comedian/actor

Newman, Paul
P.O. Box 3090
Saugatuck, CT 06880
Actor/foodmaker

Newman, Randy
644 N. Doheny Dr.
Los Angeles, CA 90069
Singer/songwriter

Newsweek Magazine
444 Madison Ave.
New York, NY 10022
Richard M. Smith, editor

Newton, Wayne
3180 S. Highland Dr. (#1)
Las Vegas, NV 89109
Las Vegas entertainer

Newton-John, Olivia
P.O. Box 2710
Malibu, CA 90265
Pop singer

**Nichols, Mike
(Michael Igor Peschkowsky)**
c/o ICM
40 W. 57th St.
New York, NY 10019
Film director

Nicholson, Jack
c/o Bresler Kelly
15760 Ventura Blvd. (#1730)
Encino, CA 91436
Actor

Nicklaus, Jack William
11760 U.S. Highway 1
Palm Beach, FL 33408
Golf's "Golden Bear"

Nicks, Stevie
c/o Warner Bros. Records
3300 Warner Blvd.
Burbank, CA 91510
Pop singer

Nielsen, Leslie
15760 Ventura Blvd. (#1730)
Encino, CA 91436
Actor

Nike
3900 SW Murray Blvd.
Beaverton, OR 97005
Philip H. Knight, chairman

Nimoy, Leonard
c/o Walt Disney Studios
500 S. Buena Vista St.
Burbank, CA 91521
"Mr. Spock" actor/film director

Nintendo
4820 150th Ave. NE.
Redmond, WA 98052
Video games company

**Nixon, Mojo
(and Skid Roper)**
611 Broadway (#526)
New York, NY 10012
Comic rock singer

Nixon, Richard Milhous
26 Federal Plaza
New York, NY 10278
Former President

Nolte, Nick
8899 Beverly Blvd.
Los Angeles, CA 90048
Actor

**Non-Violent Anarchist
Network**
P.O. Box 1385
Austin, TX 78767
Jim Cole, executive officer

Noonan, Peggy
c/o Random House
201 E. 50th St.
New York, NY 10022
Political speechwriter

**Noriega, Manuel Antonio,
Gen.**
c/o Federal Bureau of Prisons
301 1st St. NW.
Washington, DC 20534
Ex-ruler of Panama

**Norman, Greg
(Gregory John)**
One Erieview Plaza (#1300)
Cleveland, OH 44114
Golf's "Great White Shark"

Norman, Jessye
1900 Broadway
New York, NY 10023
Opera soprano

**NORML (Nat. Org. for the
Reform of Marijuana
Laws)**
2001 S St. (#640)
Washington, DC 20009
Jon Gettman, director

Norris, Chuck
(Carlos Ray)
6464 Sunset Blvd. (#1150)
Hollywood, CA 90028
Action film star

North, Oliver Lawrence
c/o Freedom Alliance
P.O. Box 96700
Washington, DC 20090
Iran-Contra figure

North American Man-Boy
   Love Association
(NAMBLA)
P.O. Box 174, Midtown Station
New York, NY 10018
Pedophile group

North American Soccer
   League Players
   Association
2021 L St. NW (6th floor)
Washington, DC 20036

Northrop Corp.
1840 Century Park E.
Los Angeles, CA 90067
Thomas V. Jones, chairman

Norton Simon Museum
411 W. Colorado Blvd.
Pasadena, CA 91105
Norton Simon, president

Norville, Deborah
c/o "The Today Show"
30 Rockefeller Plaza
New York, NY 10020
Television cohost

Norwood, William I., Dr.
Children's Hospital
Philadelphia, PA 19104
Pediatric heart surgeon

Noticias del Mundo
P. Lerezundi, ed.
401 5th Ave.
New York, NY 10016
Largest Spanish-language paper

Novak, Kim
(Marilyn)
P.O. Box 524
Carmel Highlands, CA 93921
Actress

Novak, Robert D.
c/o Evans-Novak Political Report
1750 Pennsylvania Ave. NW.
   (#1312)
Washington, DC 20006
Political columnist

Novello, Don
(Father Guido Sarducci)
8899 Beverly Blvd.
Los Angeles, CA 90048
Comedian

NRBQ & the Whole Wheat
   Horns
P.O. Box 210103
San Francisco, CA 94121
Music group

Nunn, Sam
303 Senate Dirksen Bldg.
Washington, DC 20510
Senator from Georgia

Nureyev, Rudolf Hametovich
c/o S.A. Gorlinsky Ltd.
33 Dover St.
London W1X 4NJ England
Former ballet dancer

Nutri/System
3901 Commerce Ave.
Willow Grove, PA 19090
A. Donald McCulloch, Jr., CEO

O

Oak Ridge Boys, The
329 Rockland Rd.
Hendersonville, TN 37075
Country singers

Oakland Athletics
Oakland-Alameda County
  Coliseum
Oakland, CA 94621
Roy Eisenhardt, owner

Oates, Joyce Carol
c/o Department of English
Princeton University
Princeton, NJ 08544
Author

Obando y Bravo, Miguel
Arzobispado, Apartado 3058
Managua, Nicaragua
Catholic cardinal

Ochs, Michael
520 Victoria Ave.
Venice, CA 90291
Pop music expert

O'Connor, Carroll
P.O. Box 49935
Los Angeles, CA 90049
Actor

**O'Connor, John Joseph,
  Cardinal**
1011 1st Ave.
New York, NY 10022
Archbishop of New York

O'Connor, Maureen
202 C St.
San Diego, CA 92101
Mayor of San Diego

O'Connor, Sandra Day
U.S. Supreme Court Bldg.
One 1st St. NE.
Washington, DC 20543
Supreme Court Justice

O'Connor, Sinead
13 Red Lion Sq., 10 Halsey
  House
London WC1 England
Rock singer

Oingo Boingo
8335 Sunset Blvd. (3rd floor)
Los Angeles, CA 90069
Rock group

Ojemann, Robert G., Dr.
Massachusetts General Hospital
Boston, MA 02114
Brain tumor surgeon

O'Keefe, Miles
P.O. Box 69365
Los Angeles, CA 90069
Actor

Okoye, Christian
c/o Kansas City Chiefs
1 Arrowhead Dr.
Kansas City, MO 64129
Football runningback

Olajuwon, Akeem
c/o Houston Rockets
10 Greenway Plaza, The Summit
Houston, TX 77046
Basketball's "Akeem the Dream"

Old Time Western Film Club
P.O. Box 142
Siler City, NC 27344
Milo Holt, president

Oldenburg, Claes Thure
556 Broome St.
New York, NY 10013
Sculptor

Olin, Ken
222 N. Canon Dr. (#202)
Beverly Hills, CA 90210
Actor

Oliphant, Patrick
4900 Main St. (9th floor)
Kansas City, MO 62114
Political cartoonist

Olmos, Edward James
10000 Santa Monica Blvd. (#305)
Los Angeles, CA 90067
Actor

Omni Magazine
1965 Broadway
New York, NY 10023
Patrice Adcroft, editor

**Onassis, Jacqueline Lee
   Bouvier Kennedy**
c/o Doubleday & Co.
245 Park Ave.
New York, NY 10028
Former First Lady/book editor

O'Neal, (Patrick) Ryan
9230 Wilshire Blvd.
Beverly Hills, CA 90212
Actor

O'Neal, Tatum
853 7th Ave. (#9A)
New York, NY 10019
Actress

O'Neil, Kitty
P.O. Box 604
Medina, OH 44256
Stuntwoman

**O'Neill, Tip
(Thomas Philip, Jr.)**
1310 19th St. NW.
Washington, DC 20036
Former Speaker of the House

**Only Official Peggy Lee Fan
   Club**
133 W. 72nd St. (#601)
New York, NY 10023
Ray Richards Allen, president

Ono, Yoko
c/o William Morris
1350 6th Ave.
New York, NY 10019
Widow of John Lennon/artist

**OPEC (Organization of
   Petroleum Exporting
   Countries)**
Obere-Donaustrasse 93
A-1020 Vienna, Austria
Fadhil Al-Chalabi, deputy
   secretary general

Opera News
1865 Broadway
New York, NY 10023
Patrick O'Connor, editor

Option of Adoption
7624 Langdon St.
Philadelphia, PA 19111
Places black children

Orange Bowl
P.O. Box 350748
Miami, FL 33135

Organization of American States (OAS)
17th & Constitution Aves. NW.
Washington, DC 20006
Joao Baena Soares, secretary general

Organogenesis
Eugene Bell, science officer
83 Rogers St.
Cambridge, MA 02142
Fabricates living skin

Orlando Magic
One Magic Place, Orlando Arena
Orlando, FL 32801
Pat Williams, president

O'Rourke, P.J.
P.O. Box 462
Jaffrey, NH 03452
Journalist/humor author

Orphan Foundation of America
14261 Ben Franklin Station NW.
Washington, DC 20044
Father Joseph Rivers, director

Orr, Kay
State Capitol
Lincoln, NE 68509
Governor of Nebraska

Orthodox Presbyterian Church
2345 Willow Brook Dr.
Huntingdon Valley, PA 19006
Mark T. Bube, president

Osborne, Tom
c/o U. of Nebraska
116 South Stadium
Lincoln, NE 68588
College football coach

Osbourne, Ozzy
34 Windmill St.
London W1 England
Heavy metal singer

Oscar Mayer
P.O. Box 7188
Madison, WI 53707
James W. McVey, CEO

Osgood, Charles
c/o CBS News
524 W. 57th St.
New York, NY 10019
Television journalist

Osmond, Donny
3 Corporate Plaza (#200)
Newport Beach, CA 92664
Pop singer

Osmond, Marie
P.O. Box 6000
Provo, UT 84603
Pop singer

Oster/Sunbeam Appliance Co.
5055 N. Lydell Ave.
Milwaukee, WI 53217
David T. McGoldrick, president

O'Toole, Peter
151 El Camino Dr.
Beverly Hills, CA 90212
Actor

Our Lady of Enchantment
c/o Lady Sabrina
P.O. Box 1366
Nashua, NH 03061
First witchcraft school in U.S.

Ovitz, Michael
c/o Creative Artists Agency
9830 Wilshire Blvd.
Beverly Hills, CA 90212
Talent agent

Owens, Gary
P.O. Box 76860
Los Angeles, CA 90076
Radio personality

Owens, Roger
5216 Onyx St.
Torrance, CA 90503
Baseball game's peanut thrower

Oz, Frank
117 E. 69th St.
New York, NY 10024
Voice of Miss Piggy

Ozawa, Seiji
c/o Ronald A. Wilford
165 W. 57th St.
New York, NY 10019
Conductor

P

Pace, Stanley Carter
Pierre Laclede Center
St. Louis, MO 63105
General Dynamics, chairman

Pacific 10 Athletic Conference
800 S. Broadway (#400)
Walnut Creek, CA 94596
Thomas C. Hansen, commissioner

Pacifica Foundation
David Salniker, executive director
3729 Cahuenga Blvd. W.
N. Hollywood, CA 91604
Radio station owner

**Pacino, Al
(Alfredo James)**
% Actors Studio
432 W. 44th St.
New York, NY 10036
Actor

Packwood, Robert
259 Senate Russell Bldg.
Washington, DC 20510
Senator from Oregon

Pacula, Joanna
P.O. Box 5617
Beverly Hills, CA 90210
Actress

**Page, Jimmy
(James Patrick)**
% Geffen Records
9130 Sunset Blvd.
Los Angeles, CA 90069
Rock guitarist

Pahlevi II, Reza
Kubbeh Palace, Heliopolis
Cairo, Egypt
Exiled Iranian Shah

PaineWebber
1285 6th Ave.
New York, NY 10019
Donald B. Marron, CEO

**Palance, Jack
(Walter Palanuik)**
P.O. Box 805
Tehachapi, CA 93561
Actor

Palestine Human Rights Campaign
220 S. State (#1308)
Chicago, IL 60604
Rev. Donald E. Wagner, director

Palestine Solidarity Committee
P.O. Box 27462
San Francisco, CA 94127
Ginny Kraus, director

Palmer, Arnold Daniel
P.O. Box 616
Latrobe, PA 15650
Golfing great

Palmer, Jim
(James Alvin)
P.O. Box 145
Brooklandville, MD 21022
Sportscaster/former baseball star

Palmer, Robert
10100 Santa Monica Blvd.
(#1600)
Los Angeles, CA 90067
Pop singer

Panasonic Co.
One Panasonic Way
Secaucus, NJ 07094
Akiya Imura, president

Panetta, Leon E.
339 Cannon House Office Bldg.
Washington, DC 20515
Congressman from California

Papandreou, Andreas
George
Office of the Prime Minister
Odos Zalokosta 3
Athens, Greece
Prime Minister of Greece

Papp, Joseph
% New York Shakespeare
Festival
425 Lafayette St.
New York, NY 10003
Theater producer

Paramount Pictures
Melrose Ave.
Hollywood, CA 90038
Martin Davis, Chairman

Parapsychology Institute
P.O. Box 252
Elmhurst, NY 11380
Dr. Stephen Kaplan,
spokesperson

Parents Anonymous
6733 S. Sepulveda Blvd. (#270)
Los Angeles, CA 90045
Supports parents of problem kids

Parents Magazine
685 3rd Ave.
New York, NY 10164
Ann Pleshette Murphy, editor

Parents Music Resource
Center, (PMRC)
Jennifer Norwood, executive
director
1500 Arlington Blvd.
Arlington, VA 22209
Music "decency" watchdog group

Parents Rights Organization
Mae Dugan, president
12571 Northwinds Dr.
St. Louis, MO 63146
Promotes parents rights

Parkening, Christopher
165 W. 57th St.
New York, NY 10019
Classical guitarist

Parker, Alan
Pinewood Studios, Iver Heath
Buckinghamshire, England
Film director

Parker, Graham
% Ernest Chapman
11 Old Lincoln's Inn
London WC2 England
Rock musician

Parks, Rosa
% 305 Federal Bldg.
231 W. Lafayette
Detroit, MI 48226
Civil rights pioneer

Parton, Dolly Rebecca
P.O. Box 1976
Nolensville, TN 37135
Singer/actress

Paterno, Joseph
% Pennsylvania State U.
Dept. of Athletics
University Park, PA 16802
Football coach

Patterson, Floyd
P.O. Box 336
New Paltz, NY 12561
Former boxing champ

Patti, Sandi
% Helvering
530 Grand Ave.
Anderson, IN 46012
Gospel singer

Pattiz, Norm
% Westwood One
9540 Washington Blvd.
Culver City, CA 90232
Radio executive

Pauling, Linus Carl
Institute of Science & Medicine
440 Page Mill Rd.
Palo Alto, CA 94306
Scientist

Pavarotti, Luciano
% Herbert Breslin
119 W. 57th St.
New York, NY 10019
Opera tenor

Pax World Fund, Inc.
William M. Prifti, counsel
224 State St.
Portsmouth, NH 03801
Socially responsible mutual fund

Paz, Octavio
% Revista Vuelta
Leonardo da Vinci 17
Mexico City DF, 03910 Mexico
Writer

**PBS (Public Broadcasting
   Service)**
609 5th Ave.
New York, NY 10017

Peace Corps
1990 K St. NW.
Washington, DC 20526
Paul D. Coverdell, director

Peale, Norman Vincent
1025 5th Ave.
New York, NY 10028
Philosopher

Pearson, Durk
P.O. Box 1067
Hollywood, FL 33022
Health author

Peck, Gregory
P. O. Box 837
Beverly Hills, CA 90213
Actor

Peck, M. Scott, Dr.
Bliss Road
New Preston, CT 06777
Psychiatrist/author

Pedraja, Rafael R.
% Kitchens of Sara Lee
500 Waukegan Rd.
Deerfield, IL 60015
Food scientist

Pei, I.M. (Ieoh Ming)
600 Madison Ave.
New York, NY 10022
Architect

Pekar, Harvey
P.O. Box 18471
Cleveland Heights, OH 44118
Underground cartoonist

Pele (Edson Arantes do Nascimento)
75 Rockefeller Plaza
New York, NY 10019
Former soccer great

Pell, Claiborne
335 Russell Office Bldg.
Washington, DC 20510
Senator from Rhode Island

PEN American Center
Karen Kennerly, executive
director
568 Broadway
New York, NY 10012
Writers' organization

Pena, Federico Fabian
City-County Bldg.
1437 Bannock St. (#350)
Denver, CO 80202
Mayor of Denver

Penguin USA
Peter Mayer, Chairman
275 Hudson St.
New York, NY 10014
Book publisher

Penn, Sean
9830 Wilshire Blvd.
Beverly Hills, CA 90212
Actor

Penn & Teller
(Penn Jillette/Arthur Teller)
P.O. Box 1196
New York, NY 10185
Magicians

Pentecostal Church of God
P.O. Box 850
Joplin, MO 64802
Dr. James D. Gee, general
superintendent

People for the American Way
2000 M St. NW (#400)
Washington, DC 20036
Arthur J. Kropp, executive
director

People Weekly Magazine
1221 6th Ave.
New York, NY 10020
Jason McManus, editor

Pepsico
Anderson Hill Road
Purchase, NY 10577
D. Wayne Calloway, CEO

Peres, Shimon
Ministry of Foreign Affairs
Jerusalem, Israel
Politician

Perez de Cuellar, Javier
One Dag Hammarskjold Plaza
New York, NY 10017
United Nations Secretary
General

Parfumerie Fragonard
20 Boulevard Fragonard
Grasse, France
Perfume factory open to public

Perkins, Anthony
P.O. Box 5617
Beverly Hills, CA 90210
Actor

Perkins, Elizabeth
151 El Camino Dr.
Beverly Hills, CA 90212
Actress

Perlman, Itzhak
% ICM
40 W. 57th St.
New York, NY 10019
Violinist

Perlman, Rhea
9830 Wilshire Blvd.
Beverly Hills, CA 90212
Actress

Perot, H. Ross
(Henry)
12377 Merit Dr.
Dallas, TX 75251
Billionaire

Perpich, Rudy George
State Capitol
St. Paul, MN 55155
Governor of Minnesota

Pet Shop Boys
478 Welbeck St.
London W1 England
Pop singers

Peter, Paul & Mary
(Yarrow, Stookey, and
Travers)
648 S. Robertson Blvd.
Los Angeles, CA 90069
Folk singers

Peters, Bernadette
(Lazzara)
9000 Sunset Blvd. (12th Floor)
Los Angeles, CA 90069
Actress/singer

Peters, Jon
% Columbia Studios
Columbia Plaza
Burbank, CA 90515
Entertainment executive

Peters, Tom
555 Hamilton Ave.
Palo Alto, CA 94301
Business expert

Petersen, Wolfgang
8022 Geiselgasteig
Bavaria Atelier
Munich, Germany
Film director

Petersmeyer, Gregg
The White House
1600 Pennsylvania Ave. (#100)
Washington, DC 20500
Dep. Assistant to the President

Peterson, Cassandra
P.O. Box 38246
Hollywood, CA 90038
"Elvira" the Horror Queen

Pettibon, Raymond
1240 21st St.
Hermosa Beach, CA 90254
Underground artist

Petty, Richard
P.O. Box 631
Randleman, NC 27317
Stock car king

Petty, Tom
% MCA Records
70 Universal City Plaza
Universal City, CA 91608
Rock musician

Pfeiffer, Michelle
8899 Beverly Blvd.
Los Angeles, CA 90048
Actress

Philadelphia 76ers
P.O. Box 25040
Philadelphia, PA 19147
Harold Katz, president

Philadelphia Eagles
Veterans Stadium
Philadelphia, PA 19148
Norman Braman, owner

Philadelphia Flyers
Pattison Place
Philadelphia, PA 19148

Philadelphia Phillies
Veterans Stadium
Broad St. and Pattison Ave.
Philadelphia, PA 19101
Bill Giles, president

Philip, A.G. Davis, Dr.
Van Vleck Observatory
Middletown, CT
Astronomer

**Philip, Prince
(Mountbatten-Windsor)**
Buckingham Palace
London SW1 England
Duke of Edinburgh

Phillip Morris Companies
120 Park Ave.
New York, NY 10017
Hamish Maxwell, chairman

**Phillips, Lou Diamond
(Lou Upchurch)**
2121 Ave. of the Stars (#950)
Los Angeles, CA 90067
Actor

Phillips, Michelle
8899 Beverly Blvd.
Los Angeles, CA 90048
Actress/singer

Phillips Petroleum
6A1 Phillips Bldg.
Bartlesville, OK 74004
C.J. Silas, CEO

Phoenix, River
P.O. Box 520
Royal Palm Beach, FL 33411
Actor

Phoenix Cardinals
51 W. 3rd
Tempe, AZ 85281
William V. Bidwill, owner

Phoenix Suns
2910 N. Central Ave.
Phoenix, AZ 85102
Jerry Colangelo, general
  manager

Phonemate, Inc.
20665 Manhattan Pl.
Torrance, CA 90501
Shun Yamaura, CEO

Picasso, Paloma
% Tiffany & Co.
727 5th Ave.
New York, NY 10022
Fashion designer

**Pickens, T. Boone
(Thomas)**
P.O. Box 2009
Amarillo, TX 79189
Corporate raider

Pickering, Thomas R.
799 United Nations Plaza
New York, NY 10017
*U.S. Ambassador to United
  Nations*

Piggy, Miss
117 E. 69th St.
New York, NY 10021
Porky diva

Pilcher, Rosamunde
Over Pilmore
Inqowrie by Dundee, Scotland
Novelist

Pillsbury Co.
200 S. 6th St.
Minneapolis, MN 55402
Ian Martin, CEO

Pillsbury Doughboy
200 S. 6th St.
Minneapolis, MN 55402
Chubby mascot

Pinals, Robert S., Dr.
Princeton Medical Center
Princeton, NJ 08540
Rheumatologist

Pinchot, Bronson
P.O. Box 2714
Malibu, CA 90265
Actor

Pinckus, Edward
360 Adams St. (#1180)
Brooklyn, NY 11201
*N.Y. State Supreme Court
  Justice*

Piniella, Lou (Louis Victor)
% Cincinnati Reds
Riverfront Stadium
Cincinnati, OH 45202
Baseball team manager

Pink Floyd
43 Portland Rd.
London W11 England
Rock group

Pinkerton's
6727 Odessa Ave.
Van Nys, CA 91407
Thomas W. Wathan, CEO

Pinter, Harold
% Judy Daish Assoc.
83 Eastbourne Mews
London W2 6LQ England
Playwright

Piper, Rowdy Roddy
P.O. Box 3859
Stamford, CT 06905
Professional wrestler

Pitchford, Dean
1888 Century Park E. (#900)
Los Angeles, CA 90067
Songwriter

Pitelka, Frank Alois, Dr.
P.O. Box 9278
Berkeley, CA 94709
Zoologist

Pitkin, Roy M., Dr.
UCLA Medical Center
Los Angeles, CA 90024
Obstetrics and gynecology

Pitney Bowes
World Headquarters
Stamford, CT 06926
George B. Harvey, CEO

Pittman, Bob
% QMI Music
75 Rockefeller Plaza
New York, NY 10019
Founder of MTV

Pittsburgh Penguins
Civic Arena
Pittsburgh, PA 15219
Ed Johnston, general manager

Pittsburgh Pirates
Three Rivers Stadium
600 Stadium Circle
Pittsburgh, PA 15212
Jim Leyland, manager

Pittsburgh Steelers
Three Rivers Stadium
Pittsburgh, PA 15212
Chuck Noll, coach

Pizza Hut
9111 E. Douglas
Wichita, KS 67207
Steven S. Reinemund, CEO

Planetary Society
65 N. Catalina
Pasadena, CA 91106
Searches for life on other planets

Plant, Robert
% Atlantic Records
75 Rockefeller Plaza
New York, NY 10019
Rock singer

Playbill Magazine
Joan Alleman, editor
71 Vanderbilt Ave.
New York, NY 10169
Theater magazine

Player, Gary
One Erieview Plaza (#1300)
Cleveland, OH 44114
Golfer

Playgirl Magazine
801 2nd Ave.
New York, NY 10017
Nancie Martin, editor

Pleasence, Donald
7 W. Eaton Place Mews
London SW1 8LY England
Actor

Plendl, Matt
9363 Wilshire Blvd. (#212)
Beverly Hills, CA 90210
Hula Hoop world champ

Pleshette, Suzanne
P.O. Box 1492
Beverly Hills, CA 90213
Actress

Plimpton, George
541 E. 72nd St.
New York, NY 10021
Sports author

Ploughshares Quarterly
P.O. Box 529
Cambridge, MA 02139
Journal of new fiction

Plummer, Amanda
15760 Ventura Blvd. (#1730)
Encino, CA 91436
Actress

Plummer, Christopher
8899 Beverly Blvd.
Los Angeles, CA 90048
Actor

Podratz, Karl C., Dr.
Mayo Clinic
Rochester, MN 55905
Gynecological cancer specialist

**Pointer Sisters
(Anita, June, and Ruth)**
10100 Santa Monica Blvd.
(#1600)
Los Angeles, CA 90067
Pop singers

Poison
P.O. Box 6668
San Francisco, CA 94101
Rock group

Poitier, Sidney
% Verdon Productions
9350 Wilshire Blvd.
Beverly Hills, CA 90212
Actor

Polanski, Roman
Bureau Georges Beaume
3 Quai Malaquais
75006 Paris, France
Film director

Polaroid
549 Technology Sq.
Cambridge, MA 02139
William J. McCune, Jr., chairman

Pollack, Sydney
9830 Wilshire Blvd.
Beverly Hills, CA 90212
Film director

Pons, B. Stanley, Dr.
University of Utah
Salt Lake City, UT 84112
Cold fusion scientist

Pop Warner Football
1315 Walnut St. (#1632)
Philadelphia, PA 19107
David Glenn Tomlin, president

Popular Mechanics Magazine
224 W. 57th St.
New York, NY 10019
Joe Oldham, editor

Porizkova, Paulina
% Elite Models
150 E. 58th St.
New York, NY 10155
Actress/model

Porter, Sylvia
4900 Main St. (9th floor)
Kansas City, MO 62114
Financial journalist

Portin, Bertram A., Dr.
1616 Kensington Ave.
Buffalo, NY 14215
Colon and rectal surgeon

Portland Trailblazers
Lloyd Building
700 N.E. Multnomah St. (#600)
Portland, OR 97232
Lawrence Weinberg, chairman

Posner, Vladimir
% Embassy of the U.S.S.R.
1125 16th St. NW.
Washington, DC 20036
Soviet spokesman to the U.S.

Post, Mike
3815 W. Olive Ave. (#202)
Burbank, CA 91505
Television music composer

Postal Service, U.S.
475 L'Enfant Plaza SW.
Washington, DC 20260
Anthony M. Frank, Postmaster General

Potts, Annie
10100 Santa Monica Blvd. (#1600)
Los Angeles, CA 90067
Actress

Poundstone, Paula
9000 Sunset Blvd. (#1200)
Los Angeles, CA 90069
Comedienne

Povich, Maury
% "A Current Affair"
5746 Sunset Blvd.
Los Angeles, CA 90028
Television journalist

POWARS (Pet Owners With AIDS/ARC)
P.O. Box 1116
Madison Sq. Garden Station
New York, NY 10159

Powell, Colin L., Gen.
The Pentagon
Washington, DC 20301
Joint Chiefs of Staff, chairman

Powers, Stephanie (Stefania Federkiewcz)
8899 Beverly Blvd.
Los Angeles, CA 90048
Actress

Prager, Dennis
6020 Washington Blvd. (#2)
Culver City, CA 90232
Commentator

Pravda
(English translation)
2233 University Ave. (#225)
St. Paul, MN 55114
Soviet newspaper

President's Council on
Physical Fitness and
Sports
Washington, DC 20001
Arnold Schwarzenegger,
chairman

Presley, Priscilla
151 El Camino Dr.
Beverly Hills, CA 90212
Actress

Pretenders, The
3 E. 54th St.
New York, NY 10022
Rock group

Prevention Magazine
33 E. Minor St.
Emmaus, PA 18098
Robert Rodale, editor

Previn, Andre George
(Andreas Ludwig Priwin)
12 Penzance Place
London W11 4PA England
Conductor/composer

Price, Leontyne
% Columbia Artists Management
165 W. 57th St.
New York, NY 10019
Opera singer

Price, Vincent
% Kohner
9169 Sunset Blvd.
Los Angeles, CA 90069
Actor

Pride, Charley
% Maxine P. Luster, president
P.O. Box 670507
Dallas, TX 75367
Fan club

Prime Computer
Prime Park
Natick, MA 01760
James F. McDonald, CEO

Prince
(Prince Rogers Nelson)
P.O. Box 10118
Minneapolis, MN 55401
Pop singer

Prince, Hal
(Harold)
1270 6th Ave.
New York, NY 10020
Theater director

Princess Kitty Fan Club
Mona Wrinkle, president
P.O. Box 430784
Miami, FL 33243
Fan club for performing cat

Principal, Victoria
10100 Santa Monica Blvd.(#1600)
Los Angeles, CA 90067
Actress

Prine, John
4121 Wilshire Blvd. (#215)
Los Angeles, CA 90010
Singer/songwriter

Pro Football Hall Of Fame
2121 George Halas Dr. NW.
Canton, OH 44708

Prochnow, Jurgen
8899 Beverly Blvd.
Los Angeles, CA 90048
Actor

Procrastinators' Club Of America
1405 Locust St. (11th floor)
Philadelphia, PA 19102
Les Waas, president

Procter & Gamble Co.
One Procter and Gamble Plaza
Cincinnati, OH 45202
John G. Smale, CEO

Professional Bowlers Association (PBA)
P.O. Box 5118
Akron, OH 44313
Joseph R. Antenora,
commissioner

Professional Golfers Association (PGA)
P.O. Box 109601
Palm Beach Gardens, FL 33418
Franklin J. Schaeffer, president

Professional Rodeo Cowboys Assoc.
101 Pro Rodeo Dr.
Colorado Springs, CO 80919

Prudential Insurance
763 Broad St.
Newark, NJ 07102
Robert A. Beck, chairman

Pryor, Richard
% Columbia Pictures
Columbia Plaza
Burbank, CA 91505
Comic actor

Psychology Today Magazine
1515 Broadway
New York, NY 10036
Patrice Horn, editor

PTA (Parent Teachers Association)
700 N. Rush St.
Chicago, IL 60611
Manya S. Ungar, president

Public Broadcasting Service (PBS)
1320 Braddock Pl.
Alexandria, VA 22314
Bruce L. Christensen, president

Public Enemy
298 Elizabeth St.
New York, NY 10012
Rappers

Publishers Weekly
249 W. 17th St.
New York, NY 10011
John Baker, editor

Puck, Wolfgang
8795 Sunset Blvd.
Los Angeles, CA 90069
Chef/owner, Spago

Puckett, Kirby
% Minnesota Twins
The Metrodome
Minneapolis, MN 55415
Baseball star

Pulati, Evalene
P.O. Box 1404
Santa Ana, CA 92702
Greeting card consultant

Pulitzer, Joseph, Jr.
1133 Franklin Ave.
St. Louis, MO 63101
St. Louis Post Dispatch,
publisher

Punch Magazine
23-27 Tudor St.
London EC4Y OHR England
Alan Coren, editor

Putnam Publishing
Phyllis Grann, president
200 Madison Ave.
New York, NY 10016

Puttnam, David Terence
% Enigma Productions
11/15 Queens Gate Place Mews
London SW7 5BG England
Film producer

Python, Monty
20 Fitzroy Sq.
London WIP 6B8 England
Comedy troupe

Q

Qaddafi, Muammar, Col.
Bab el Aziziya
Tripoli, Libya
Ruler of Libya

Quaid, Dennis
222 N. Canon Dr. (#202)
Beverly Hills, CA 90210
Actor

Quaid, Randy
15760 Ventura Blvd. (#1730)
Encino, CA 91436
Actor

Quaker Oats
321 N. Clark St., Quaker Tower
Chicago, IL 60610
William D. Smithburg, CEO

Quaker State
255 Elm St.
Oil City, PA 16301
Jack W. Corn, CEO

Quant, Mary
3 Ives St.
London SW3 England
Fashion designer

**Quayle, J. Danforth
(also Marilyn)**
Admiral House
34th and Massachusetts
Washington, DC 20005
Vice-president of the U.S.

Quebec Nordiques
2205 Ave. du Colisee
Quebec, QU Canada
G1L 4W7

Quinlan, Kathleen
P.O. Box 2465
Malibu, CA 90265
Actress

**Quinn, Anthony
(Anthony Rudolph Oaxaca)**
9200 Sunset Blvd. (#1009)
Los Angeles, CA 90069
Actor

Quinn, Martha
% MTV
1775 Broadway
New York, NY 10019
MTV star/actress

R

Rabbit, Roger
% Touchstone Pictures
500 S. Buena Vista St.
Burbank, CA 91521
Toon star

Rachins, Alan
10000 Santa Monica Blvd. (#305)
Los Angeles, CA 90067
Actor

Radiance
Alice Ansfield, editor
P.O. Box 31703
Oakland, CA 94604
Magazine for large women

Radical Force
Kenneth O. Lee, chairman
2428 Myrtle SW
Seattle, WA 98106
Anarchist group

Radio Free Europe
1201 Connecticut Ave. NW.
Washington, DC 20036
E. Eugene Pell, president

Radio Shack
% Tandy
1800 One Tandy Center
Fort Worth, TX 76102
J.W. Roach, CEO

Raffi
(Cavoukian)
% Jensen Communications
120 S. Victory Blvd. (#201)
Burbank, CA 91502
Singer of children's songs

Rafsanjani, Hojatolislam
 Hashemi Ali Akbar
The Majlis
Teheran, Iran
President of Iran

Ragghianti, Marie
3530 Pine Valley Dr.
Sarasota, FL 34239
Former Tennessee parole head

Raines, Tim
P.O. Box 500
Olympic Station M
Montreal, QU Canada
PQ HIV 3P2
Baseball star

Rainforest Foundation
1776 Broadway
New York, NY 10019
Activists to save the Amazon

Rainier III, Prince (Louis
 Henri Maxence Bertrand)
Palais de Monaco
Monte Carlo, Monaco
Prince of Monaco

Raitt, Bonnie
P.O. Box 626
Los Angeles, CA 90078
Singer/songwriter/guitarist

R.A.L.P.H. (Royal Assoc.
for the Longevity &
Preservation of the
Honeymooners)
% C. W. Post
Greenvale, NY 11548
Bob Columbe, president

Ralston Purina Co.
Checkerboard Sq.
St. Louis, MO 63164
William P. Stiritz, president

Ramada Inns
3838 E. Van Buren St.
Phoenix, AZ 85008
Richard Snell, CEO

Ramaphosa, Matamela Cyril
National Union of Mineworkers
P.O. Box 2424
Johannesburg 2000, Republic of
South Africa
Union leader

Rampal, Jean-Pierre Louis
% M.L. Falcone
155 W. 68th St. (#1114)
New York, NY 10023
Classical flutist

Ranawat, Chitranjan S., Dr.
Hospital for Special Surgery
New York, NY 10021
Joint replacement specialist

Rand Corporation
Donald B. Rice, CEO
1700 Main St.
Santa Monica, CA 90406
Research organization

Rand McNally & Co.
8255 Central Park Ave.
Skokie, IL 60076
Andrew McNally III, chairman

Randall, Tony
(Leonard Rosenberg)
9200 Sunset Blvd. (#909)
Los Angeles, CA 90069
Actor

Random House
201 E. 50th St.
New York, NY 10022
Robert L. Bernstein, chairman

Rangel, Charles B.
2252 Rayburn House Office Bldg.
Washington, DC 20515
Congressman from New York

Raoul Wallenberg
Committee
823 United Nations Plaza
New York, NY 10017
Missing, saved Jews in WW II

Raphael, Sally Jesse
510 W. 57th St.
New York, NY 10019
Talk show host

Rashad, Ahmad
(Bobby Moore)
30 Rockefeller Plaza (#1411)
New York, NY 10112
Sportscaster

Rashad, Phylicia Ayers
449 W. 44th St.
New York, NY 10036
Actress

Rather, Dan
% CBS News
524 W. 57th St.
New York, NY 10019
Television journalist

Ratzenberger, John
10351 Santa Monica Blvd. (#211)
Los Angeles, CA 90025
Postman Cliff on "Cheers"

Rauschenberg, Robert
% Leo Castelli Gallery
420 W. Broadway
New York, NY 10012
Painter

Rawls, Lou
9200 Sunset Blvd. (#823)
Los Angeles, CA 90069
R&B singer

Ray, James Earl
Station "A" West
Tennessee State Prison
Nashville, TN 37203
Assassin of Martin Luther King, Jr.

Rayovac Corp.
601 Rayovac Dr.
Madison, WI 53711
Thomas F. Pyle, chairman

Raytheon Co.
141 Spring St.
Lexington, MA 02173
Thomas L. Phillips, CEO

Re, Edward D.
U.S. Court of International Trade
New York, NY 10007
Chief Judge

Reader's Digest
Pleasantville, NY 10570
Kenneth O. Gilmore, editor

Reagan, Ronald Wilson (and Nancy Davis)
2121 Ave. of the Stars (34th floor)
Century City, CA 90061
Former President

Reasoner, Harry
524 W. 57th St.
New York, NY 10019
Television journalist

Redbook Magazine
959 8th Ave.
New York, NY 10019
Annette Capone, editor

Redford, Robert
P.O. Box 837
Provo, UT 84601
Actor/film director

Redgrave, Vanessa
% Marine Martin Management
7 Windmill St.
London W1P 1HF England
Actress/activist

Redstone, Sumner Murray
200 Elm St.
Dedham, MA 02026
Billionaire

Reebok
150 Royall St.
Canton, MA 02021
Paul Fireman, CEO

Reed, Lou
38 E. 68th St.
New York, NY 10021
Rock musician

Reed, Oliver
314 High St., Dorking
Surrey RH4 1QX England
Actor

Reeve, Christopher
8899 Beverly Blvd.
Los Angeles, CA 90048
"Superman" actor

Reeves, Keanu
9100 Sunset Blvd. (#300)
Los Angeles, CA 90069
Actor

Regan, Donald Thomas
11 Canal Center Plaza (#301)
Alexandria, VA 22314
Politician

Rehnquist, William Hubbs
U.S. Supreme Court Bldg.
One 1st St. NE.
Washington, DC 20543
Supreme Court Justice

Reid, Tim
(and Daphne Maxwell Reid)
6922 Hollywood Blvd.
Los Angeles, CA 90028
Actors

Reiner, Carl
% DGA
7920 Sunset Blvd.
Los Angeles, CA 90046
Comedian/film director

Reiner, Rob
335 N. Maple Dr. (#135)
Beverly Hills, CA 90210
Film director

Reiser, Paul
9255 Sunset Blvd. (#716)
Los Angeles, CA 90069
Actor

Reitman, Ivan
% Columbia Pictures
Columbia Plaza, Prod. Bldg. 7
Burbank, CA 91505
Film director

Reitz, Bruce A., Dr.
Johns Hopkins Hospital
Baltimore, MD 21205
Heart/lung transplant specialist

R.E.M.
P.O. Box 8032
Athens, GA 30603
Rock band

Replacements, Ltd.
302 Gallimore Dairy Rd.
Greensboro, NC 27409
Has discontinued china patterns

Retired Greyhounds As Pets
1306 Bunker Hill Rd.
Mororesville, IN 46158
Sally Allen, spokesperson

Reverend Ike
(Frederick Joseph
Eikerenkoetter)
4140 Broadway
New York, NY 10033
Evangelist

Revlon
767 5th Ave.
New York, NY 10022
Ronald Owen Perelman,
president

Reynolds, Burt
9830 Wilshire Blvd.
Beverly Hills, CA 90212
Actor

Reynolds, Debbie
(Mary Frances)
151 El Camino Dr.
Beverly Hills, CA 90212
Actress/singer

Reynolds, Morgan O., Dr.
Dept. of Economics
Texas A&M University
College Station, TX 77843
Labor expert

Rhodes, Frank H.T., Dr.
Cornell University
Ithaca, NY 14853
University president

Rice, Anne
% Simon & Schuster
1230 6th Ave.
New York, NY 10020
Vampire *author*

Rice, Donald B.
The Pentagon
Washington, DC 20350
Secretary of the Air Force

Rice, Jerry
% San Francisco 49ers
711 Nevada St.
Redwood City, CA 94061
Football star

Rice, Jim
(James Edward)
Anderson, SC 29621
Former baseball star

Rice, Tim
118 Wardour St.
London W1 England
Musical theater lyricist

Richards, Ann
P.O. Box 12404
Austin, TX 78711
Politician

Richards, Keith
(Keith Richard)
% "Redlands"
West Wittering, Chichester
Sussex, England
Rock guitarist

Richie, Lionel B., Jr.
P.O. Box 1862
Encino, CA 91426
Pop singer

Rickles, Don
% Shefrin Co.
800 S. Robertson Blvd.
Los Angeles, CA 90035
Comedian

Ride, Sally Kristen
% NASA Johnson Space Center
Houston, TX 77058
First American woman in space

Rigby, Cathy
P.O. Box 387
Blue Jay, CA 92317
Singer/former gymnast

Rigg, Diana Elizabeth (Enid)
% London Management
235 Regent St.
London W1A 2JT England
Actress

Riley, Pat (Patrick James)
% NBC Sports
30 Rockefeller Plaza
New York, NY 10112
Former basketball coach/ sportscaster

Riney, Hall Patrick
735 Battery St.
San Francisco, CA 94111
Advertising executive

Ringwald, Molly
120 El Camino Dr. (#104)
Beverly Hills, CA 90212
Actress

Ripken, Cal, Jr.
% Baltimore Orioles
Memorial Stadium
Baltimore, MD 21218
Baseball's "Iron Man"

Ritter, John (Jonathan Southworth Ritter)
10100 Santa Monica Blvd. (#1600)
Los Angeles, CA 90067
Actor

Rivera, Geraldo (Jerry Rivers)
% Investigative News Group
311 West 43rd St.
New York, NY 10036
Television journalist

Rivers, Joan (Joan Sandra Molinsky)
P.O. Box 49774
Los Angeles, CA 90049
Comedienne

RJR Nabisco
Reynolds Blvd.
Winston-Salem, NC 27102
Edward Horrigan, vice-chairman

Robards, Jason Nelson, Jr.
% STE Representation
888 7th Ave.
New York, NY 10019
Actor

Robbins, Harold (Francis Kane)
% New English Library
47 Bedford Sq.
London WC1B 3DP England
Novelist

Robbins, Hulda Dornblatt
16 S. Buffalo Ave.
Ventnor, NJ 08406
Printmaker

Robbins, Jerome
% New York City Ballet
N.Y. State Theater, Lincoln
Center
New York, NY 10023
Choreographer

Robbins, Tim
151 El Camino Dr.
Beverly Hills, CA 90212
Actor

Roberts, Doris Emma, Dr.
6111 Kennedy Dr.
Chevy Chase, MD 20815
Epidemiologist

Roberts, Eric
853 7th Ave. (#9A)
New York, NY 10019
Actor

Roberts, Julia
151 El Camino Dr.
Beverly Hills, CA 90212
Actress

Robertson, Pat, Rev.
(Marion Gordon Robertson)
CBN Centre
Virginia Beach, VA 23463
Evangelist

Robertson, Robbie
% Geffen Records
9130 Sunset Blvd.
Los Angeles, CA 90069
Rock musician

Robinson, David
% San Antonio Spurs
600 E. Market (#102)
San Antonio, TX 78205
Basketball's "Admiral"

Robinson, Eddie
(Edward Gay)
% Grambling State University
P.O. Box 868
Grambling, LA 71245
Legendary football coach

Robinson, Frank
% Baltimore Orioles
Memorial Stadium
Baltimore, MD 21218
Baseball manager/former star

Robinson, Holly
222 N. Canon Dr. (#202)
Beverly Hills, CA 90210
"21 Jump Street" actress

Robinson, John
% Los Angeles Rams
2327 W. Lincoln Ave.
Anaheim, CA 92801
Football coach

Robinson, Smokey
(William)
% Michael Roshkind
6255 Sunset Blvd.
Los Angeles, CA 90028
Pop singer

Rockefeller, Jay
(John Davison, IV)
724 Senate Hart Bldg.
Washington, DC 20510
Senator from West Virginia

Rockford Files
% Debbie Okoniewski
4951 Cherry Ave. (#83)
San Jose, CA 95118
Fan club

Rockwell International
2230 E. Imperial Highway
El Segundo, CA 90245
Donald R. Beall, CEO

Rocky Horror Film Club
% Bruce Cutter
204 W. 20th St.
New York, NY 10011
"Rocky Horror Picture Show"
fans

Roddick, Anita
% The Body Shop
Hawthorne Rd., Wick, Lt.
  Hampton
West Sussex BM1 7LR England
Sells all-natural cosmetics

Rodriguez, Paul
151 El Camino Dr.
Beverly Hills, CA 90212
Comedian

Roeg, Nicolas Jack
% Terence Baker
19 Jermyn St.
London W1 England
Film director

Rogers, Kenny
P.O. Box 100
Colbert, GA 30628
Country singer/actor

Rogers, Mimi
9830 Wilshire Blvd.
Beverly Hills, CA 90212
Actress

Rogers, Roy
(and Dale Evans)
(Leonard Slye/Francis
  Octavia Smith)
15650 Seneca Rd.
Victorville, CA 92392
Western stars

Rogers, Tristan
2121 Ave. of the Stars (#950)
Los Angeles, CA 90067
Actor

Roh Tae Woo
Office of the President
108-17 Yonhui-Dong, Sodaemun-
  Gu
Seoul, Korea
President of South Korea

Rohrabacher, Dana
1017 Longworth House Office
  Bldg.
Washington, DC 20515
Congressman from California

Role Models Unlimited
Wayne Perryman, president
P.O. Box 256
Mercer Island, WA 98040
Provides help for blacks in gangs

Rolling Stone Magazine
745 5th Ave.
New York, NY 10151
Jann S. Wenner, editor

Rolling Stones, The
1776 Broadway (#507)
New York, NY 10019
Rock group

Rollins, Jack
130 W. 57th St.
New York, NY 10019
Film producer/show biz manager

Romance on the Rails
% Lori Beatty
5233 Elkhorn
Greenwell Springs, LA 70739
"Wild Wild West" fan club

Roney, Paul R.
U.S. Court of Appeal
Eleventh Circuit
Atlanta, GA 30303
Chief Judge

Ronstadt, Linda
644 N. Doheny Dr.
Los Angeles, CA 90069
Pop singer

Rooney, Andy
(Andrew Aitkin Rooney)
51 W. 52nd St.
New York, NY 10019
Television commentator

Rooney, Mickey
(Joe Yule, Jr.)
P.O. Box 5028
Thousand Oaks, CA 91360
Entertainer

Rosaaen, Robin Christine
Elvis Special Photo Assoc.
P. O. Box 1457
Pacifica, CA 94044
Elvis Presley experts

Rose, Noel Richard, Dr.
John Hopkins U. School of Public
   Health, Dept. of Immunology
Baltimore, MD 21205
Immunologist

Rose, Pete
(Peter Edward)
P.O. Box 590
Cooperstown, NY 13326
Baseball's "Mr. Hustle"

Ross, Diana
P.O. Box 1683
New York, NY 10185
Pop singer/actress

Rostenkowski, Dan
2111 Rayburn House Office Bldg.
Washington, DC 20515
Congressman from Illinois

Rostropovich, Mstislav
   Leopoldovich
% National Symphony Orchestra
JFK Center for the Performing
   Arts
Washington, DC 20566
Cellist

Rotary International
1560 Sherman Ave.
Evanston, IL 60201
Philip H. Lindsey, general
   secretary

Roth, David Lee
3960 Laurel Canyon Blvd. (#430)
Studio City, CA 91604
Rock singer

Rotisserie League Baseball Assoc.
Daniel Okrent, cofounder
211 W. 92nd St. (Box #9)
New York, NY 10025
Fantasy baseball creators

Rourke, Mickey (Philip Andrew)
400 S. Beverly Dr. (#216)
Beverly Hills, CA 90212
Actor

Rowlands, Gena
8899 Beverly Blvd.
Los Angeles, CA 90048
Actress

Roxette (Per Gessle/ Marie Frederiksson)
% Capitol
1750 N. Vine St.
Hollywood, CA 90048
Pop stars

Roybal, Edward R.
2211 Rayburn House Office Bldg.
Washington, DC 20515
Congressman from California

Royko, Mike
% Chicago Tribune
435 N. Michigan Ave.
Chicago, IL 60611
Newspaper columnist

Rubik, Erno
Bimbo ut 210
1026 Budapest, Hungary
Rubik's Cube inventor

Rubin, Rick
% Def American Records
9157 Sunset Blvd.
Los Angeles, CA 90069
Record company executive

Rubinstein, John Arthur
21900 Ave. of the Stars (#1630)
Los Angeles, CA 90067
Actor/musician

Rudman, Warren Bruce
530 Senate Hart Bldg.
Washington, DC 20510
Senator from New Hampshire

Ruedy, Elizabeth
% Ivy Stone
19 W. 44th St.
New York, NY 10036
Math anxiety expert

Run-DMC (Jason Mizell/ Joseph Simmons/Darryl McDaniels)
298 Elizabeth St.
New York, NY 10012
Rappers

Runcie, Robert Alexander Kennedy
Lambeth Palace
London SE1 7JU England
Archbishop of Canterbury

Rundgren, Todd
% Panacea
2705 Glendower Rd.
Los Angeles, CA 90027
Rock musician

**Rushdie, Salman
(Ahmed)**
% Deborah Rogers Ltd.
49 Blenheim Crescent
London W11 England
Satanic Verses *author in hiding*

Russell, Bill
P.O. Box 58
Mercer Island, WA 98040
Former basketball great

Russell, Ken
8899 Beverly Blvd.
Los Angeles, CA 90048
Film director

Russell, Kurt Von Vogel
151 El Camino Dr.
Beverly Hills, CA 90212
Actor

Russell, Theresa
9255 Sunset Blvd. (#505)
Los Angeles, CA 90069
Actress

**Rutan, Dick
(and Jeana Yeager)**
Hangar 17
Mojave, CA 93501
Pilots of Voyager aircraft

Ruttan, Susan
3518 Cahuenga Blvd. W. (#304)
Los Angeles, CA 90068
"L.A. Law" actress

Ryan, Meg
8899 Beverly Blvd.
Los Angeles, CA 90048
Actress

Ryan, Nolan
P.O. Box 409
Alvin, TX 77511
Baseball's "Express"

Ryan White National Fund
Elise Kim, executive director
8961 Sunset Blvd.
Los Angeles, CA 90069
Charity for kids with AIDS

**Ryder, Winona
(Horowitz)**
8899 Beverly Blvd.
Los Angeles, CA 90048
Actress

Ryder Truck Rental
3600 NW. 82nd Ave.
Miami, FL 33166
M. Anthony Burns, CEO

Ryun, Jim
P.O. Box 62B
Lawrence, KS 66044
Former mile record holder

S

SAAB-Scania
P.O. Box 697
Orange, CT 06477
Robert J. Sinclair, president

Saberhagen, Bret
% Kansas City Royals
Royals Stadium
Kansas City, MO 64141
Baseball pitcher

Sacks, Stephen L., Dr.
1916 Pike Place (#620)
Seattle, WA 98101
Genital herpes expert

Sacramento Kings
One Sports Parkway
Sacramento, CA 95834
Jerry Reynolds, general manager

Sade
% I.B.C.
1–3 Mortimer St.
London W1 England
Jazz/pop vocalist

Safer, Morley
51 W. 52nd St.
New York, NY 10019
Television journalist

Safire, William
% New York Times
1627 I St. NW.
Washington, DC 20006
Newspaper journalist

Saga Furs of Scandinavia
Lili Glassman, spokesperson
156 5th Ave. (#308)
New York, NY 10010
Fur trade association

Sagan, Carl Edward
% Space Sciences Bldg.
Cornell University
Ithaca, NY 14853
Space scientist

Sagansky, Jeff
% CBS
7800 Beverly Blvd.
Los Angeles, CA 90036
Television executive

Saget, Bob (Robert)
8899 Beverly Blvd.
Los Angeles, CA 90048
"America's Funniest Home Videos"

Sahl, Mort (Morton Lyon)
% Stanley Weinstein
210 Rutgers Lane
Parsippany, NJ 07054
Comedian/satirist

Said, Edward
Columbia University
419 Hamilton Hall
New York, NY 10027
Palestinian spokesperson

Saint James, Susan
(Miller)
9830 Wilshire Blvd.
Beverly Hills, CA 90212
Actress

Saint Louis Blues
5700 Oakland Ave.
St. Louis, MO 63110
Ron Caron, general manager

Saint Louis Cardinals
Busch Memorial Stadium
250 Stadium Plaza
St. Louis, MO 63102
August A. Busch III, owner

Saint Martin's Press
175 5th Ave.
New York, NY 10010
*Thomas J. McCormack,
chairman*

Saks, Michael
P.O. Box 467
Rockville Centre, NY 11571
Autograph collector

Salerno-Sonnenberg, Nadja
155 W. 68th St. (#1114)
New York, NY 10023
Violinist

Salinas de Gortari, Carlos
Presidencia de la Republica
Palacio Nacional
Mexico City DF 06220 Mexico
President of Mexico

Salinger, J.D.
(Jerome David)
% Harold Ober Associates
40 E. 49th St.
New York, NY 10017
Catcher In The Rye *author*

Salinger, Pierre Emil
George
% ABC News
44 W. 66th St.
New York, NY 10023
Television journalist

Salk, Jonas Edward
Institute for Biological Studies
P.O. Box 85800
San Diego, CA 92138
Inventor of polio vaccine

Salvaggio, John E., Dr.
Tulane U. Medical School
New Orleans, LA 70112
Immunology specialist

Salvation Army
132 W. 14th St.
New York, NY 10011
Lt. Col. Paul Kelley,
spokesperson

Samaranch, Juan Antonio
Chateau de Viey
CH-1007 Lausanne, Switzerland
*Int. Olympic Committee,
president*

Samms, Emma
P.O. Box 339
Tujunga, CA 90028
Actress

Samsonite Corp.
11200 E. 45th Ave.
Denver, CO 80239
Thomas Leonard, president

Samuel French, Inc.
M. Abbott Van Nostrand,
director
45 W. 25th St.
New York, NY 10010
Play publisher

Samuels, Ron
120 El Camino Dr.
Beverly Hills, CA 90212
Film producer

San Antonio Spurs
600 East Market (#102)
San Antonio, TX 78205
Bob Bass, general manager

San Diego Chargers
P.O. Box 20666
San Diego, CA 92120
Alex Spanos, president

San Diego Padres
San Diego Stadium
9449 Friars Rd.
San Diego, CA 92120
Jack McKeon, manager

San Francisco 49ers
711 Nevada St.
Redwood City, CA 94061
Charlie Siefert, coach

San Francisco Giants
Candlestick Park
Bay Shore
San Francisco, CA 94124
Bob Lurie, owner

San Giacomo, Laura
121 N. San Vicente Blvd.
Beverly Hills, CA 90211
Actress

Sanborn, David
% Patrick Rains
8752 Holloway Dr.
Los Angeles, CA 90069
Jazz saxophonist

Sandberg, Ryne
% Chicago Cubs
Clark and Addison
Chicago, IL 60613
Baseball star

Sanders, Barry
% Detroit Lions
1200 Featherstone Rd.
Pontiac, MI 48057
Football star

Santana
P.O. Box 26671
San Francisco, CA 94126
Rock group

Sara Lee Corp.
3 First National Plaza
Chicago, IL 60602
John H. Bryan, Jr., CEO

Sarandon, Chris
121 N. San Vicente Blvd.
Beverly Hills, CA 90211
Actor

**Sarandon, Susan Abigail
(Tomaling)**
1350 6th Ave.
New York, NY 10019
Actress

227

Sassoon, Vidal
2049 Century Park E.
Los Angeles, CA 90067
Hairdresser

Saucer Technology
P.O. Box 132
Eureka Springs, AZ 72632
How to build a flying saucer

Sauter, Van Gordon
% CBS News
51 W. 52nd St.
New York, NY 10019
Television news executive

Savage, Fred
P.O. Box 893
Tarzana, CA 91357
"Wonder Years" actor

Savage, Gus
1121 Longworth House Office
Bldg.
Washington, DC 20515
Congressman from Illinois

Savage, Randy
P.O. Box 3859
Stamford, CT 06905
Wrestling's "Macho Man"

**Savalas, Telly
(Aristoteles)**
333 Universal City Plaza
Universal City, CA 91608
Actor

Savvy Magazine
3 Park Ave.
New York, NY 10016
Annalyn Swan, editor

Sawyer, Diane
% ABC News
1330 6th Ave.
New York, NY 10020
Television journalist

Sawyer, Forrest
% CBS News
51 W. 52nd St.
New York, NY 10019
Television journalist

Sayles, John T.
110 W. 57th St.
New York, NY 10019
Film director/writer

Scacchi, Greta
121 N. San Vicente Blvd.
Beverly Hills, CA 90211
Actress

Scalia, Antonin
U.S. Supreme Court Bldg.
One First Street NE.
Washington, DC 20543
Supreme Court Justice

Scalia, Jack
9830 Wilshire Blvd.
Beverly Hills, CA 90212
Actor

Schell, Maximilian
Kepplerstrasse 2
8 Munich 80, Germany
Actor

Scheuer, James H.
2466 Rayburn House Office Bldg.
Washington, DC 20515
Congressman from New York

**Schirra, Wally
(Walter M., Jr.)**
P.O. Box 73
Rancho Santa Fe, CA 92067
Former astronaut

Schmidt, Benno C., Jr.
Yale University
New Haven, CT 06520
University president

Schmoke, Kurt
100 N. Holiday St. (#250)
Baltimore, MD 21202
Mayor of Baltimore

Schnabel, Julian
% Pace Gallery
32 E. 57th St.
New York, NY 10022
Painter

Schneider, John
151 El Camino Dr.
Beverly Hills, CA 90212
Actor/country singer

Schoemehl, Vincent C., Jr.
200 City Hall
1206 Market St.
St. Louis, MO 63103
Mayor of St. Louis

**Schoenfeld, Gerald, and
Bernard Jacobs
Shubert Organization**
225 West 44th St.
New York, NY 10036
Theater producers

Schroeder, Patricia
2208 Rayburn House Office Bldg.
Washington, DC 20515
Congresswoman from Colorado

Schulz, Charles Monroe
One Snoopy Place
Santa Rosa, CA 95401
"Peanuts" cartoonist

Schwab, Charles
101 Montgomery St.
San Francisco, CA 94104
Discount stock broker

Schwab, James L.
1875 Century Park E. (#2532)
Los Angeles, CA 90067
Wardrobe consultant

Schwartz, David
% Rent-a-Wreck
1100 Glendon Ave. (#1250)
Los Angeles, CA 90024
Discount car rental company

Schwartz, Melvin, Dr.
Stanford University
Physics Department
Stanford, CA 94305
Nobel Prize physicist

**Schwarzenegger, Arnold
Alois**
P.O. Box 1234
Santa Monica, CA 90406
Actor

Schygulla, Hanna
3 Quai Malaquais
75008 Paris, France
Actress

Science News
1719 N. Street NW.
Washington, DC 20036
E.G. Sherburne, Jr., publisher

Scorsese, Martin
% Jay Julien and Associates
1501 Broadway
New York, NY 10036
Film director

Scott, Ridley
9830 Wilshire Blvd.
Beverly Hills, CA 90212
Film director

Scott, George Campbell
% Jane Deacy Agency
300 E. 7th St.
New York, NY 10021
Actor

Scott, Willard Herman
% "The Today Show"
30 Rockefeller Plaza (#304)
New York, NY 10012
Weatherman

Scowcroft, Brent, Lt. Gen.
% National Security Council
Executive Office Bldg.
Washington, DC 20506
Military adviser

Screen Actors Guild
7065 Hollywood Blvd.
Hollywood, CA 90028
Barry Gordon, president

Screen Extras Guild
3629 Cahuenga Blvd. W.
Los Angeles, CA 90068
Gene Poe, president

Screw
P.O. Box 432
Old Chelsea Station
New York, NY 10011
Sex newspaper

**Scully, Vin
(Vincent Edward)**
% NBC Sports
30 Rockefeller Plaza
New York, NY 10112
Sportscaster

Seagal, Steven
9830 Wilshire Blvd.
Beverly Hills, CA 90212
Action film star

Sealy Mattress
4802 W. Van Buren
Phoenix, AZ 85043
Earnest M. Wuliger, CEO

Sears, Roebuck & Co.
Sears Tower
Chicago, IL 60684
Edward A. Brennan, CEO

Seattle Mariners
The Kingdome
2nd Ave. at South King St.
Seattle, WA 98104
Jim Lefebvre, manager

Seattle Seahawks
11220 NE 53rd St.
Kirkland, WA 98033
Chuck Knox, coach

Seattle Supersonics
190 Queen Anne Ave N.
Seattle, WA 98109
Bernie Bickerstaff, coach

Sedaka, Neil
10 Columbus Circle
New York, NY 10019
Pop singer

Seeger, Pete
Duchess Junction (#431)
Beacon, NY 12508
Folk singer

Segal, George
% Wallin, Simon and Black
1350 6th Ave.
New York, NY 10019
Actor

Segal, George
Davidson's Mill Road
New Brunswick, NJ 08901
Sculptor

Selective Service System
Washington, DC 20435
Samuel K. Lessey, Jr., director

Self Magazine
350 Madison Ave.
New York, NY 10017
Alexandra Penney, editor

Selig, Bud
(Allan)
% Milwaukee Brewers
County Stadium
Milwaukee, WI 53214
Baseball team owner

Sellecca, Connie
P.O. Box 60257
Los Angeles, CA 90060
Actress

Selleck, Tom
10390 Santa Monica Blvd. (#310)
Los Angeles, CA 90025
Actor

Sendak, Maurice Bernard
% Harper & Row
10 E. 53rd St.
New York, NY 10022
Illustrator

Sensenbrenner, F. James,
Jr.
2444 Rayburn House Office Bldg.
Washington, DC 20515
Congressman from Wisconsin

Sesame Street
Children's Television Workshop
One Lincoln Plaza
New York, NY 10023
Children's television series

Seuss, Dr.
(Ted Geisel)
7301 Encelia Dr.
San Diego, CA 92037
"Grinch" cartoonist

Seven-Up Company
8144 Walnut Hill Lane
Dallas, TX 75231
John R. Albers, CEO

Seventeen Magazine
P.O. Box 100
Radnor, PA 19088
Sarah Crichton, editor

Seventh-Day Adventists
6840 Eastern NW.
Washington, DC 20012
Neal C. Wilson, president

Severance, Joan
P.O. Box 67492
Los Angeles, CA 90067
Actress

Severinsen, Doc
(Carl H.)
% "The Tonight Show"
3000 W. Alameda Ave.
Burbank, CA 91523
Trumpeter/bandleader

Sexaholics Anonymous
P.O. Box 300
Simi Valley, CA 93062

Seymour, Jane
(Joyce Frankenberg)
10390 Santa Monica Blvd. (#310)
Los Angeles, CA 90025
Actress

Sgt. Pepper's Lonely Hearts
  Club
% Jason M. Sebell
14 Belknap Dr.
Andover, MA 01810
Beatles fan club

Shaffer, Paul
"Late Night with David
  Letterman"
30 Rockefeller Plaza
New York, NY 10112
*Leads "World's Most Dangerous
  Band"*

Shagan, Steve
% William Morrow & Co.
105 Madison Ave.
New York, NY 10016
Novelist

Shalala, Donna E., Dr.
University of Wisconsin
Madison, WI 53706
University president

Shalit, Gene
% "The Today Show"
30 Rockefeller Plaza
New York, NY 10020
Film critic

Shamir, Yitzhak
(Jazernicki)
Kiriyat Ben Gurian
Jerusalem 91919 Israel
Politician

Shandling, Garry
151 El Camino Dr.
Beverly Hills, CA 90212
Comedian

Shannon, Dell
(Elizabeth Barbara
  Linnington)
2715 S. View Ave.
Arroyo Grande, CA 93420
Mystery author

Shapiro, Harold T.
Princeton University
Princeton, NJ 08544
University president

Share Your Birthday
  Foundation
Elizabeth D. Heller, president
14th and F Sts. NW.
Washington, DC 20045
*U.S. and foreign children
  program*

Sharif, Omar
(Michael Shalhoub)
% William Morris Agency
147 Wardour St.
London W1 England
Actor

Sharkey, Ray
8961 Sunset Blvd. (#2A)
Los Angeles, CA 90069
Actor

**Sharpe, Tom
(Thomas Ridley)**
% Richard Scott Simon Ltd.
43 Doughty St.
London WC1N 2LF England
Author

Shatner, William
1717 N. Highland Ave. (#414)
Hollywood, CA 90028
"Captain Kirk" actor

Shaver, Helen
10100 Santa Monica Blvd.
(#1600)
Los Angeles, CA 90067
Actress

Shaw, E. Clay, Jr.
440 Cannon House Office Bldg.
Washington, DC 20515
Congressman from Florida

Shearer, Harry
9000 Sunset Blvd. (#1200)
Los Angeles, CA 90069
Humorist/actor

Shearson Lehman Hutton
American Express Tower C
World Financial Center
New York, NY 10285
Jeffrey Lane, president

Sheedy, Ally
P.O. Box 6327
Malibu, CA 90265
Actress

Sheehan, Daniel P.
% Christic Institute
1324 N. Capitol St. NW
Washington, DC 20002
Activist

Sheehy, Gail
% William Morrow & Co.
105 Madison Ave.
New York, NY 10016
Author

**Sheen, Martin
(Ramon Estevez)**
P.O. Box 4293
Malibu, CA 90265
Actor/activist

Sheffer, Albert, Dr.
Brigham & Women's Hospital
110 Francis St.
Boston, MA 02215
Allergy specialist

Sheldon, Sidney
% William Morrow & Co.
105 Madison Ave.
New York, NY 10016
Novelist

Shell Oil Company
One Shell Plaza
Houston, TX 77001
L.C. van Wachem, chairman

Shepard, Chuck
% "News of the Weird"
P.O. Box 57141
Washington, DC 20037
Offbeat columnist

Shepard, Sam
(Samuel Shepard Rogers)
240 W. 44th St.
New York, NY 10036
Playwright/actor

Shepherd, Cybill
15301 Ventura Blvd. (#345)
Sherman Oaks, CA 91403
Actress

Sheraton Corp.
60 State St.
Boston, MA 02109
John Kapilotas, CEO

Sherman Grinberg Film
Library
1040 N. McCadden Pl.
Hollywood, CA 90038

Sherwin-Williams
John G. Breen, CEO
101 Prospect Ave. NW.
Cleveland, OH 44115
World's largest paint producer

Shevardnadze, Edward
Amvrosiyevich
Ministry of Foreign Affairs
Smolenskaya-Sennaya Pl 32/34
Moscow, U.S.S.R.
Foreign Minister of U.S.S.R.

Shields, Brooke
P.O. Box 147
Harrington Park, NJ 07640
Actress/model

Shields, Jerry A., Dr.
Wills Eye Hospital
Philadelphia, PA 19107
Eye cancer specialist

Shields, Thomas W., Dr.
Northwestern Memorial Hospital
Chicago, IL 60611
Thoracic surgeon

Shire, Talia Rose
2121 Ave. of the Stars (#410)
Los Angeles, CA 90067
"Rocky" actress

Shirer, William L.
P.O. Box 487
Lennox, MA 01240
Author

Shocked, Michelle
(Johnston)
% Polygram Records
450 Park Ave.
New York, NY 10022
Pop singer

Shoemaker, Willie
(William Lee)
1900 Ave. of the Stars (#2820)
Los Angeles, CA 90067
Horseracing's "Shoe"

Shore, Dinah
3552 Federal Ave.
Los Angeles, CA 90066
Kay Daly, fan club president

Short, Martin
9830 Wilshire Blvd.
Beverly Hills, CA 90212
Comic actor

Shriver, Maria
% CBS News
524 W. 57th St.
New York, NY 10019
Television journalist

Shriver, Pamela Howard
% ProServ
888 17th St. NW.
Washington, DC 20006
Tennis star

Shumway, Norman E., Dr.
Stanford University Hospital
Stanford, CA 94305
Heart surgeon

Siegel, Bernie S.
% Harper & Row
10 E. 53rd St.
New York, NY 10022
Self-help author

Sierra, Ruben
% Texas Rangers
Arlington Stadium
Arlington, TX 76010
Baseball star

Sierra Club
530 Bush St.
San Francisco, CA 94108
Michael McCloskey, executive
  director

**Sierra Club Legal Defense
  Fund**
2044 Fillmore St.
San Francisco, CA 94115
Frederic P. Sutherland,
  executive director

Sikh Church
1649 S. Robertson Blvd.
Los Angeles, CA 90035
Siri Singh Sahib, administrator

Silber, John Robert
% Boston University
147 Bay State Rd.
Boston, MA 02215
University president

**Sills, Beverly
(Belle Silverman)**
% New York City Opera
N.Y. State Theatre, Lincoln
  Center
New York, NY 10023
Former opera star

Silver, Joan Micklin
600 Madison Ave. (18th floor)
New York, NY 10022
Film director

Silver, Joel
% Silver Pictures Company
10201 W. Pico Blvd.
Los Angeles, CA 90035
Film producer

Silver, Ron
8899 Beverly Blvd.
Los Angeles, CA 90048
Actor

Silverstone, Paul H.
330 W. 58th St.
New York, NY 10019
Naval history expert

Simmons, Andrew
3530 Pine Valley Dr.
Sarasota, FL 34239
Wildlife expert

Simms, Phil
% New York Giants
Giants Stadium
East Rutherford, NJ 07073
Football quarterback

Simon, Carly
130 W. 57th St. (#12B)
New York, NY 10019
Pop singer

Simon, Neil
% A. DaSilva
502 Park Ave.
New York, NY 10022
Playwright

Simon, Norton
P.O. Box 2248
Beverly Hills, CA 90213
Philanthropist

Simon, Paul
1619 Broadway (#500)
New York, NY 10019
Singer/songwriter

Simon, Paul
462 Senate Dirksen Bldg.
Washington, DC 20510
Senator from Illinois

Simon & Schuster
1230 6th Ave.
New York, NY 10020
Richard E. Snyder, chairman

Simone, Joseph V., Dr.
St. Jude's Hospital
Memphis, TN 38101
Pediatric cancer specialist

Simple Minds
63 Frederic St.
Edinburgh EH2 1LH Scotland
Rock group

Simplesse Co.
P.O. Box 830
Deerfield, IL 60015
Makers of fat substitute

Simpson, Alan Kooi
261 Senate Dirksen Bldg.
Washington, DC 20510
Senator from Wyoming

**Simpson, O.J.
(Orenthal James)**
% NBC Sports
30 Rockefeller Plaza
New York, NY 10019
Sportscaster/former football great

**Simpsons, The (Homer,
Marge, Lisa, Maggie,
Bart)**
W. Pico Blvd.
Los Angeles, CA 90035
The Nineties' nuclear family

**Sinatra, Frank
(Francis Albert)**
1041 N. Formosa Ave.
Hollywood, CA 90046
"Ol' Blue Eyes" singer/actor

Singer, Isaac Bashevis
% Farrar, Straus and Giroux
19 Union Square West
New York, NY 10003
Author

Single Mothers By Choice
P.O. Box 1642, Gracie Sq. St.
New York, NY 10028
Jane Mattes, founder

Singletary, Mike
% Chicago Bears
250 North Washington, Halas
  Hall
Lake Forest, IL 60045
Football defensive star

Sirhan, Sirhan
Soledad State Prison
Soledad, CA 93960
Assassin of Robert F. Kennedy

Siskel, Gene
(Eugene Kal)
% Chicago Tribune
435 Michigan Ave., Tribune
  Tower
Chicago, IL 60611
Film critic

Six of One
2426 Lexington Rd.
Hatfield, PA 19440
"The Prisoner" fan club

Skaggs, Ricky
P.O. Box 15781
Nashville, TN 37215
Country musician

Skeptical Inquirer, The
P.O. Box 229
Buffalo, NY 14215
Debunkers

Skerritt, Tom
10100 Santa Monica Blvd.
  (#1600)
Los Angeles, CA 90067
Actor

Skid Row
% Atlantic Records
75 Rockefeller Plaza
New York, NY 10019
Rock band

Skinner, Samuel
400 Seventh St. SW.
Washington, DC 20590
Secretary of Transportation

Slim Whitman Appreciation
  Society
1002 W. Thurber
Tucson, AZ 85705
Loren Knapp,
  president

Small Business
  Administration
1441 L St. NW.
Washington, DC 20416
James Abdnor,
  administrator

Smart, Jean
8899 Beverly Blvd.
Los Angeles, CA 90048
Actress

Smith, Buffalo Bob
Big Lake
Princeton, ME 04619
Howdy Doody's partner

Smith, J. Lawton, Dr.
Bascom Palmer Eye Institute
University of Miami
Miami, FL 33101
Neuro-ophthalmologist

Smith, Jaclyn
151 El Camino Dr.
Beverly Hills, CA 90212
Actress

Smith, Jeff
% William Morrow & Co.
105 Madison Ave.
New York, NY 10016
"The Frugal Gourmet"

Smith, Joe
% Capitol Records
1750 N. Vine St.
Hollywood, CA 90028
Record company executive

Smith, Liz
% New York Daily News
220 E. 42nd St.
New York, NY 10017
Newspaper columnist

Smith, Maggie Natalie
% ICM Ltd.
388 Oxford St.
London W1N 9HE England
Actress

Smith, Margaret Chase
Norridgewock Ave.
Skowhegan, ME 04976
Former senator from Maine

Smith, Ozzie
% St. Louis Cardinals
250 Stadium Plaza
St. Louis, MO 63102
Baseball's "Wizard of Oz"

Smith, Ron
7060 Hollywood Blvd. (#1215)
Los Angeles, CA 90028
Celebrity look-alikes company

Smith, William French
% Gibson, Dunn & Crutcher
333 S. Grand Ave.
Los Angeles, CA 90071
Attorney

Smith & Wesson
2100 Roosevelt Ave.
Springfield, MA 01102
T.S. Melvin, president

Smith Family Foundation
Toukie Smith, president
1775 Broadway (7th floor)
New York, NY 10019
Educates youngsters about AIDS

Smithereens, The
P.O. Box 1665
New York, NY 10009
Rock group

Smithsonian Institution
1000 Jefferson Dr. SW.
Washington, DC 20560
Robert McCormick Adams,
  secretary

Smithsonian Magazine
900 Jefferson Dr.
Washington, DC 20560
Don Moser, editor

Smits, Jimmy
9301 Wilshire Blvd. (#312)
Beverly Hills, CA 90210
Actor

Smothers, Tom and Dick
10100 Santa Monica Blvd.
(#1600)
Los Angeles, CA 90067
Comedy team

Snead, Sam
P.O. Box 777
Hot Springs, VA 24445
Legendary golfer

Snoopy
One Snoopy Place
Santa Rosa, CA 95401
Beagle/Joe Cool/WW I flying ace

Snowe, Olympia J.
2464 Rayburn House Office Bldg.
Washington, DC 20515
Congresswoman from Maine

Soap Opera Digest
45 W. 25th St. (8th floor)
New York, NY 10010
Meredith Brown, editor

Soap Opera Trading Cards
% Red Star
P.O. Box 3555
Hollywood, CA 90078
Baseball-type cards of soap stars

Soaring Society of America
Larry P. Sanderson, executive
director
P.O. Box E
Hobbs, NM 88241
Club for soaring/glider fans

Sobel, Barry
9000 Sunset Blvd. (#1200)
Los Angeles, CA 90069
Comedian

Socialist Party of the USA
516 West 25th St. (#404)
New York, NY 10001
Ann Rosenhaft, secretary

**Society for Preservation &
Encouragement of Barber
Shop Quartet Singing**
6315 3rd Ave.
Kenosha, WI 53140

**Society for the Eradication
of Television**
P.O. Box 1124
Alburquerque, NM 87103
Mary W. Dixon, director

Society For the Right to Die
250 W. 57th St.
New York, NY 10107
Shirley Neitlich, spokesperson

Society of Dirty Old Men
P.O. Box 18202
Indianapolis, IN 46218
D.M. Butler, spokesperson

Solarz, Stephen J.
1536 Longworth House Office
Bldg.
Washington, DC 20515
Congressman from New York

Soldier of Fortune Magazine
P.O. Box 693
Boulder, CO 80306
Robert K. Brown, editor

Solow, Robert Merton, Dr.
Massachusetts Inst. of
  Technology
Department of Economics
Cambridge, MA 02139
Nobel Prize economist

Solti, Georg, Sir
% Chicago Symphony Orchestra
220 S. Michigan Ave.
Chicago, IL 60604
Conductor

**Solzenitsyn, Alexandr
  Isayevich**
% Harper & Row
10 E. 53rd St.
New York, NY 10022
"Gulag" *author*

**Somers, Suzanne
(Mahoney)**
8730 Sunset Blvd. (6th floor)
Los Angeles, CA 90069
Actress/singer

Sondheim, Stephen Joshua
% Flora Roberts
65 E. 55th St. (#702)
New York, NY 10022
Theater composer

Sons of the Desert
% Lori Jones
P.O. Box 8341
Universal City, CA 91608
Laurel and Hardy fan club

Sontag, Susan
% Farrar, Straus, and Giroux
19 Union Square West
New York, NY 10003
Author

Sorensen, Jacki
19420 Business Center Dr.
  (#6600)
Northridge, CA 91328
Aerobic dancing pioneer

**Southeastern Conference
(SEC)**
3000 Galleria Tower (#990)
Birmingham, AL 35244
Dr. Harvey W. Schiller,
  commissioner

Southern, Terry
RFD
East Caanan, CT 06020
Screenwriter

**Southern Christian
  Leadership Conference
(SCLC)**
334 Auburn Ave. NE.
Atlanta, GA 30312
Dr. Joseph E. Lowery, president

**Southern Pacific
  Transportation Co.**
One Market Plaza (#220)
San Francisco, CA 94105
D.M. Mohan, president

Southland Corp. (7-Eleven)
2828 N. Haskell Ave.
Dallas, TX 75221
Jere W. Thompson, CEO

**Southwest Athletic
  Conference
(SWAC)**
P.O. Box 569420
Dallas, TX 75356
Fred Jacoby, commissioner

Southwest Museum
234 Museum Dr.
Los Angeles, CA 90065
Dr. Patrick T. Houlihan, director

Space Museum of Flight
4343 N. 73rd St.
Birmingham, AL 35206
Thurston W. Summer, chairman

**Spacek, Sissy
(Mary Elizabeth)**
9830 Wilshire Blvd.
Beverly Hills, CA 90212
Actress

Spader, James
151 El Camino Dr.
Beverly Hills, CA 90212
Actor

Sparks, Walter Chappel, Dr.
University of Idaho
Research and Extension Center
Aberdeen, ID 83210
Horticulturalist

Special Olympics
Sargent Shriver, president
1350 New York Ave. NW. (#500)
Washington, DC 20005
Athletics for mentally retarded

Specter, Arlen
303 State Hart Bldg.
Washington, DC 20510
Senator from Pennsylvania

Spector, Phil
P.O. Box 69529
Los Angeles, CA 90069
Record producer

Spelling, Aaron
1041 N. Formosa Ave.
Los Angeles, CA 90046
Television producer

Sperry, Roger Wolcott, Dr.
1201 E. California St.
Pasadena, CA 91125
Nobel Prize neurobiologist

Spiegel Catalog
1515 W. 22nd St.
Oak Brook, IL 60522
Henry A. Johnson, CEO

Spielberg, Steven
c/o Amblin Entertainment
100 Universal Plaza (#477)
Universal City, CA 91608
Film director/producer

**Spillane, Mickey
(Frank Morrison)**
2121 Ave. of the Stars (32nd
floor)
Los Angeles, CA 90067
Mystery novelist

Spinks, Michael
c/o Butch Lewis
250 W. 57th St.
New York, NY 10107
Boxer

Spock, Benjamin McLane
P.O. Box 1890
St. Thomas 00803 Virgin Islands
Pediatrician

Sports Car Club of America
9033 E. Easter Pl.
Englewood, CO 80112

Sports Illustrated Magazine
Time/Life Bldg.
New York, NY 10020
Mark Mulvoy, editor

Springsteen, Bruce
136 E. 57th St. (#1202)
New York, NY 10022
Rock's "The Boss"

Spruce Goose
c/o Darlene D. Lynch
P.O. Box 8, Pier J
Long Beach, CA 90801
Howard Hughes' wooden plane

Spy Magazine
295 Lafayette
New York, NY 10012
Graydon Carter, editor

Spyro Gyra
P.O. Box 239
Tallman, NY 10982
Jazz group

Stack, Robert Langford
2121 Ave. of the Stars (#410)
Los Angeles, CA 90067
Actor

Stadler, Craig
P.O. Box 3504
Rancho Santa Fe, CA 92067
Golfer

Stahl, Lesley
c/o CBS News
51 W. 57th St.
New York, NY 10019
Television journalist

Stallone, Jacqueline
2901 S. Las Vegas Bldg.
Las Vegas, NV 89109
Sly's mother/wrestling promoter

Stallone, Sylvester Enzio
9830 Wilshire Blvd.
Beverly Hills, CA 90212
Actor

Stalmaster, Lynn
P.O. Box 3282
Beverly Hills, CA 92012
Casting director

Stamey, Thomas A., Dr.
Stanford U. Medical Center
Stanford, CA 94305
Prostate surgeon

Stamos, John
c/o "Full House"
2040 Ave. of the Stars
Los Angeles, CA 90067
Actor

Stanley, Steven Mitchell, Dr.
Johns Hopkins University
Dept. of Earth & Planetary
Science
Baltimore, MD 21218
Paleobiologist

Stanley Tools
600 Myrtle St.
New Britain, CT 06050
C.S. Gentsch, president

Stanton, Harry Dean
151 El Camino Dr.
Beverly Hills, CA 90212
Actor

Stapleton, Jean
9220 Sunset Blvd. (#202)
Los Angeles, CA 90069
Actress

Star-Kist Foods
180 E. Ocean Blvd.
Long Beach, CA 90802
Richard L. Beattie, CEO

Star Search
P.O. Box Star
8033 Sunset Blvd.
Hollywood, CA 90046
Television talent show

**Star Trek: The Official Fan
   Club**
P.O. Box 111000
Aurora, CA 80011
Daniel H. Madsen, president

Stark, Ray
4000 Burbank Blvd.
Burbank, CA 91522
Film producer

Starlog
475 Park Ave. S.
New York, NY 10016
Science fiction magazine

**Starr, Ringo
(Richard Starkey)**
Tittenhurst Park, Ascot
Surrey, England
Drummer/former Beatle

Starship
1319 Bridgeway
Sausalito, CA 94965
Rock group

State Farm Insurance
One State Farm Plaza
Bloomington, IL 61701
Edward B. Rust, Jr., CEO

Staubach, Roger
6750 LBJ Freeway
Dallas, TX 75230
Former football star

Steele, Danielle
c/o Janklow and Assoc.
598 Madison Ave.
New York, NY 10022
Romance novelist

Steenburgen, Mary
8899 Beverly Bldg.
Los Angeles, CA 90048
Actress

Steere, Allen C., Dr.
Tufts-New England Medical
   Center
Boston, MA 02111
Lyme disease specialist

Steib, Dave
c/o Toronto Blue Jays
Exhibition Stadium
Toronto, ON Canada
M5C 2K7
Baseball pitcher

Steiger, Rod
P.O. Box 5617
Beverly Hills, CA 90210
Actor

Steinberg, David
151 El Camino Dr.
Beverly Hills, CA 90212
Comedian

Steinberg, Leigh
2737 Dunleer Pl.
Los Angeles, CA 90064
Sports agent/attorney

Steinberger, Jack, Dr.
European Center for Nuclear
Research
1211 Geneva 23, Switzerland
Nobel Prize physicist

Stella, Frank
c/o Knoedler
19 E. 70th St.
New York, NY 10022
Painter

Stenmark, Ingemar
Tarnaby, Sweden
Skier

Stern, Howard
c/o WXRK
600 Madison Ave.
New York, NY 10022
Disc jockey

Stern, Isaac
c/o ICM
40 W. 57th St.
New York, NY 10019
Violinist

Stern, Kenneth
c/o American Jewish Committee
165 E. 56th St.
New York, NY 10022
Expert on anti-Semitism

Sterrett, Samuel B.
U.S. Tax Court
Washington, DC 20217
Chief Judge

**Steve's Homemade Ice
Cream**
424 E. John St.
Lindenhurst, NY 11757
R.E. Smith, CEO

Stevens, John Paul
U.S. Supreme Court Bldg.
One 1st Street NE.
Washington, DC 20543
Supreme Court Justice

Stevens, Shadoe
9000 Sunset Blvd. (12th floor)
Los Angeles, CA 90069
Actor

Stevenson, Teofilo
c/o Comite Olympico
Hotel Habana Libre
Havana, Cuba
Former Olympic boxing great

Stewart, Catherine Mary
8899 Beverly Blvd.
Los Angeles, CA 90048
Actress

Stewart, Dave
c/o Oakland Athletics
Oakland-Alameda County
Stadium
Oakland, CA 94612
Baseball pitcher

**Stewart, Harris Bates, Jr.,
Dr.**
966 Jamestown Crescent
Norfolk, VA 23508
Oceanographer

Stewart, Jimmy
(James Maitland)
8899 Beverly Blvd.
Los Angeles, CA 90048
Actor

Stewart, Rod
(Roderick)
9200 Sunset Blvd. (#415)
Los Angeles, CA 90069
Rock singer

Steyermark, Julian Alfred,
Dr.
Missouri Botanical Garden
P.O. Box 299
St. Louis, MO 63166
Botanist

Stigler, George Joseph, Dr.
U. of Chicago, Dept. of
Economics
1101 E. 58th St.
Chicago, IL 60637
Nobel Prize economist

Sting
(Gordon Matthew Sumner)
250 E. 57th St. (#603)
New York, NY 10107
Rock singer

Stock, James
Enforcement & Compliance
Mgmt.
U.S. Environmental Protection
Agency
Washington, DC 20460

Stockman, David
c/o Salomon Brothers
One New York Plaza
New York, NY 10004
Financial consultant

Stockton, John
c/o Utah Jazz
5 Triad Center (#500)
Salt Lake City, UT 84160
Basketball star

Stockwell, Dean
P.O. Box 2835
Carmel, CA 93921
Actor

Stokes, Louis
2365 Rayburn House Office Bldg.
Washington, DC 20515
Congressman from Ohio

Stoltz, Eric
9830 Wilshire Blvd.
Beverly Hills, CA 90212
"Mask" actor

Stone, Oliver
P.O. Box 43
Sagaponack, NY 11962
Film director/writer

Stone, Peter
c/o Dramatists Guild
234 West 44th St.
New York, NY 10036
Playwright

Stop Equal Rights
Amendment
c/o Eagle Forum
P.O. Box 618
Alton, IL 62002
Phyllis Schlafly, chairman

Stoppard, Tom
c/o Fraser
91 Regent St.
London, W1R 8RU England
Playwright

Strait, George
c/o Erv Woolsey
1000 18th Ave. S.
Nashville, TN 37212
Country singer

Strange, Curtis Northrup
c/o PGA
100 Ave. of the Champions
Palm Beach Gardens, FL 33401
Golfer

Straub, Peter
P.O. Box 395
Greens Farms, CT 06436
Author

Strauss, Annette
City Hall
1500 Marilla
Dallas, TX 75201
Mayor of Dallas

Strauss, John S., Dr.
University Hospitals
Iowa City, IA 52240
Acne specialist

Strauss, Peter
9830 Wilshire Blvd.
Beverly Hills, CA 90212
Actor

Strawberry, Darryl
c/o New York Mets
126th and Roosevelt Ave.
Flushing, NY 11368
Baseball star

**Streep, Meryl
(Mary Louise)**
P.O. Box 105
Taconic, CT 06079
Actress

Streetwork Project
2 Lafayette St.
New York, NY 10003
Outreach for runaway children

Streisand, Barbra Joan
1040 N. Las Palmas (Bldg. 17)
Los Angeles, CA 90038
Singer/actress

Stritch, Elaine
9301 Wilshire Blvd. (#312)
Beverly Hills, CA 90210
Actress

Stroh Brewery
100 River Pl.
Detroit, MI 48207
Peter W. Stroh, chairman

Studd, Big John
P.O. Box 3859
Stamford, CT 06905
Professional wrestler

Studds, Gerry E.
237 Cannon House Office Bldg.
Washington, DC 20515
*Congressman from
  Massachusetts*

Stuntmen's Association
4810 Whitsett Ave.
N. Hollywood, CA 91607

Styron, William
RFD
Roxbury, CT 06783
Author

Suarez, Xavier
3500 Pan American Dr.
Miami, FL 33133
Mayor of Miami

Sugarman, Burt
150 El Camino Dr. (#303)
Beverly Hills, CA 90212
Financier

Suit, Herman, Dr.
Massachusetts General Hospital
Boston, MA 02114
Cancer radiation specialist

Sullivan, Louis
200 Independence Ave. SW.
Washington, DC 20201
*Sec. of Health and Human
Services*

Sullivan, Susan
9301 Wilshire Blvd. (#312)
Beverly Hills, CA 90210
Actress

Sullivan, Tom
8730 Sunset Blvd. (#400)
Los Angeles, CA 90069
Inspirational entertainer/author

**Summer, Donna
(La Donna Andrea Gaines)**
c/o Munao Mgmt.
1224 N. Vine St.
Los Angeles, CA 90038
Pop Singer

**Summerall, Pat
(George)**
c/o CBS Sports
51 W. 52nd St.
New York, NY 10019
Sportscaster

Sunia, Fofo I.F.
1206 Longworth House Office
Bldg.
Washington, DC 20515
*Congressional delegate from
Samoa*

Sunkist Growers
P.O. Box 7888
Van Nuys, CA 91409
J.V. Newman, chairman

Sununu, John H.
c/o The White House
1600 Pennsylvania Ave. NW.
Washington, DC 20500
Chief of Staff to the President

Suomi, Verner Edward, Dr.
University of Wisconsin
1225 W. Dayton St. (Space
Science)
Madison, WI 53706
Meteorologist

**Superintendent of
Documents**
U.S. Government Printing Office
Washington, DC 20402

**Sutherland, Donald
McNichol**
760 N. La Cienega Blvd.
Los Angeles, CA 90069
Actor

Sutherland, Joan, Dame
c/o Colbert
111 W. 57th St.
New York, NY 10019
Opera singer

Sutherland, Keifer
9200 Sunset Blvd. (#25)
Los Angeles, CA 90069
Actor

Suzman, Helen
c/o House of Assembly
P.O. Box 15 (#281)
Capetown 8000 Republic of South
   Africa
Anti-apartheid activist

Suzuki, Osamu
Hamamatsu-nishi, P.O. Box 1
Hamamatsu, Japan
Suzuki Motor Co., president

Svenson, Bengt
Trollhattan, Sweden
*Lived 48 years with screw in
   head*

Swaggart, Jimmy Lee
P.O. Box 2550
Baton Rouge, LA 70821
Televangelist

Swan, Lynn Curtis
10000 Santa Monica Blvd. (#305)
Los Angeles, CA 90067
Sportscaster/former football star

Swayze, Patrick
8436 W. 3rd St. (#650)
Los Angeles, CA 90048
Actor

Sweet, William Herbert, Dr.
Massachusetts General Hospital
Boston, MA 02114
Neurosurgeon

Swensens
P.O. Box 9008
Andover, MA 01810
Richard Smith, chairman

Swit, Loretta
151 El Camino Dr.
Beverly Hills, CA 90212
Actress

Sydnor, Rebecca
c/o Korbel Champagne Cellars
1922 Pierce
San Francisco, CA 94115
Entertaining expert

T

Taft, William Howard IV
c/o North Atlantic Treaty
  Organization
1110 Brussels, Belgium
U.S. Representative to NATO

Taittinger, Jean
58 Boulevard Gouvion, St. Cyr
75017 Paris, France
Champagne maker

Talbot, Lee Merriam
6656 Chilton Ct.
McLean, VA 22101
Ecologist

Tambo, Oliver
c/o African National Congress
P.O. Box 2239
Dar Es Salaam, Tanzania
Politician

Tamburin, Henry J., Dr.
6920 Airport Blvd. (#117-111)
Mobile, AL 36608
Authority on casino gambling

Tampa Bay Buccaneers
One Buccaneer Place
Tampa, FL 33607
Hugh F. Culverhouse, president

Tampax
One Marcus Ave.
Lake Success, NY 11042
M.F. Emmett, CEO

Tandy, Jessica
8899 Beverly Blvd.
Los Angeles, CA 90048
Actress

Taraborrelli, J. Randy
7510 Sunset Blvd. (#100)
Los Angeles, CA 90046
Diana Ross and Cher expert

Tarkanian, Jerry
University of Nevada—Las
  Vegas
Las Vegas, NV 89154
Basketball's "Tark the Shark"

Tartikoff, Brandon
c/o NBC
3000 W. Alameda Blvd.
Burbank, CA 91523
Entertainment executive

Taubman, Alfred
200 E. Long Lake Rd.
Bloomfield Hills, MI 48013
Real estate developer

Tausch, Gerry and Roland
3530 Pine Valley Dr.
Sarasota, FL 34239
Speakers bureau

Tavernier, Bertrand
c/o Little Bear Productions
66 Boulevard Malesherdes
75008 Paris, France
Film director

Taylor, Elizabeth
c/o Chen Sam and Associates
315 E. 72nd St.
New York, NY 10021
Actress

Taylor, James Vernon
644 N. Doheny Dr.
Los Angeles, CA 90069
Pop singer

Taylor, Lawrence
c/o New York Giants
Giants Stadium
East Rutherford, NJ 07073
Football star

Teamsters (Brotherhood of Teamsters, Chauffeurs, Warehousemen and Helpers)
25 Louisiana Ave. NW.
Washington, DC 20001
William J. McCarthy, president

Tears for Fears
P.O. Box 4ZN
London W1A 4ZN England
Rock group

Teddy Bear Review
A. Christian Revi, editor
170 5th Ave.
New York, NY 10010
Magazine about teddy bears

Tedrow, John Charles Fremont, Dr.
Rutgers University
P.O. Box 231, College Farm Rd.
New Brunswick, NJ 08903
Soil scientist

Teen Beat Magazine
215 Lexington Ave.
New York, NY 10016
Karen L. Williams, editor

Teenage Mutant Ninja Turtles
c/o New Line Cinema
116 N. Robertson Blvd. (#200)
Los Angeles, CA 90048
Pizza-eating crime fighters

Teirstein, Alvin S., Dr.
Mount Sinai Medical Center
New York, NY 10029
Pulmonary specialist

Teledyne
George A. Roberts, CEO
1901 Ave. of the Stars
Los Angeles, CA 90067
Electronics company

Teller, Edward U., Dr.
Radiation Lab (Box 80)
Livermore, CA 94550
Nuclear physicist

10,000 Maniacs
P.O. Box 642
Jamestown, NY 14701
Rock band

Tensing, Sharpa
One Tonga Rd., Ghang-La
Darjeeling
West Bengal, India
First man to climb Mt. Everest

Teresa, Mother
(Agnes Gonxha Bojaxhia)
54A Acharya Jagadish, Chandra
  Bose Rd.
Calcutta, India
*Missionary/Nobel–Peace Prize
  winner*

Tereshkova, Valentina
  Vladimirovna Nikolayeva
c/o Soviet Women's Committee
6 Nemirovich-Danchenko St.
Moscow 103009 U.S.S.R.
First woman in space

Terkel, Studs Louis
500 N. Michigan Ave.
Chicago, IL 60656
Author

Tesh, John
c/o "Entertainment Tonight"
5555 Melrose Ave.
Los Angeles, CA 90038
*Entertainment journalist/
  musician*

Tesich, Steve
40 W. 57th St.
New York, NY 10019
Playwright

Tesla
P.O. Box 3070 Uptown
Hoboken, NJ 07030
Rock group

Tesla Memorial Society
453 Martin Rd.
Lackawanna, NY 14218
Promotes inventor Nikola Tesla

Testaverde, Vinny
c/o Tampa Bay Buccaneers
One Buccaneer Place
Tampa, FL 33607
Football quarterback

Texaco
2000 Westchester Ave.
White Plains, NY 10650
Alfred C. DeCrane, Jr.,
  president

Texas Instruments
P.O. Box 225474
Dallas, TX 75265
Jerry R. Junkins, president

Texas Rangers
Arlington Stadium
Arlington, TX 76010
George Bush III, owner

TGI Friday's
14665 Midway Rd.
Dallas, TX 75380
Curtis L. Carlson, chairman

Thalheimer, Richard
c/o Sharper Image
650 Davis St.
San Francisco, CA 94111
Adult toys mail order cofounder

Thatcher, Margaret Hilda
10 Downing St.
London, SW1 England
Prime Minister of England

The Kinks
c/o Larry Page
29 Ruston Mews
London W11 1RB England
Rock band

Thicke, Alan
P.O. Box 724
Altadena, CA 91001
Actor

Thirtysomething
4024 Radford Ave. (#310)
Studio City, CA 91604
Television series

Thomas, Andria Act, Dr.
St. Thomas/St. John Medical
  Society
4 Norre Gade, Charlotte Amalie
St. Thomas 00801 VI
Allergist/immunologist

Thomas, Cal
c/o Los Angeles Times
Times Mirror Square
Los Angeles, CA 90053
Religion journalist

**Thomas, Danny
(Amos Jacobs)**
c/o St. Jude Children's Hospital
332 N. Lauderdale
Memphis, TN 38105
Comic actor

Thomas, Isiah Lord
c/o Detroit Pistons
3777 Lapeer Rd.
Auburn Hills, MI 48057
Basketball star

Thomas, Jay
c/o KPWR
6430 Sunset Blvd. (#418)
Los Angeles, CA 90028
Disc jockey/actor

Thomas, Kurt
6430 Sunset Blvd. (#701)
Los Angeles, CA 90028
Former gymnast/actor

Thomas, Marlo (Margaret)
9830 Wilshire Blvd.
Beverly Hills, CA 90212
Actress

Thomas, Michael Tilson
c/o Carson Office
1414 6th Ave.
New York, NY 10019
Conductor

Thomas, Richard
9000 Sunset Blvd. (12th floor)
Los Angeles, CA 90069
Actor

Thomas, Tony
c/o Witt/Thomas Productions
1438 N. Gower St. (4th floor)
Los Angeles, CA 90028
Television producer

Thompson, Charlotte E., Dr.
2000 Van Ness Ave. (#307)
San Francisco, CA 94109
Handicapped-children expert

Thompson, Hunter S.
c/o Rolling Stone
745 5th Ave.
New York, NY 10022
Gonzo journalist

Thompson, James R.
State Capitol
Springfield, IL 62706
Governor of Illinois

Thompson, John
Georgetown University
Washington, DC 20057
Basketball coach

Thompson, Lea
222 N. Canon Dr. (#202)
Beverly Hills, CA 90210
Actress

Thorgeirsson, Snovri Sveinn, Dr.
National Cancer Institute
National Institutes of Health
Bethesda, MD 20205
Cancer researcher

Thornburgh, Richard Lewis (Dick)
c/o Department of Justice
10th and Constitution Ave. NW.
Washington, DC 20530
U.S. Attorney General

Three Stooges Journal
710 Collins Ave.
Lansdale, PA 19466
Fan club

Thrifty Drug
615 Alpha Dr.
Pittsburgh, PA 15238
Robert W. Hannan, president

Thurmond, Strom
218 Senate Russell Bldg.
Washington, DC 20510
Senator from South Carolina

Thurow, Lester
c/o Economic Policy Institute
1730 Rhode Island Ave. NW.
  (#812)
Washington, DC 20036
Economist

Tiegs, Cheryl
7060 Hollywood Blvd. (#1010)
Los Angeles, CA 90028
Model

Tiffany (Darwish)
c/o George Tobin
11337 Burbank Blvd.
N. Hollywood, CA 91601
Pop singer

Tiffany & Co.
727 5th Ave.
New York, NY 10022
William B. Chaney, chairman

Tiger Beat Magazine
1086 Teaneck Rd.
Teaneck, NJ 07666
Mary J. Edrei, editor

Tilly, Jennifer
151 El Camino Dr.
Beverly Hills, CA 90212
Actress

Tilly, Meg
9830 Wilshire Blvd.
Beverly Hills, CA 90212
Actress

Timberland Co.
11 Merrill Industrial Dr.
Hampton, NH 03842
S.W. Swartz, CEO

Time-Life Books
777 Duke St.
Alexandria, VA 22314
Kelso F. Sutton, chairman

Time Warner Inc.
Time/Life Bldg.
New York, NY 10020
J. Richard Munro, CEO

Timex Group, Ltd.
Waterbury, CT 06720
T.F. Olsen, chairman

Tippers Anonymous
P.O. Box 178
Cochituate, MA 01778
Robert S. Farrington, president

Titanic Historical Society
P.O. Box 53
Indian Orchard, MA 01151

T.J.'s Fans of Soul
Marian H. Shannon, president
2191 N.W. 58th St.
Miami, FL 33142
Tom Jones fan club

Tobacco Institute
1875 I Street NW.
Washington, DC 20006
*Represents cigarette
manufacturers*

Tobin, James, Dr.
Yale University
P.O. Box 2125
New Haven, CT 06520
Nobel Prize economist

Todaro, George Joseph, Dr.
c/o Oncogen
3005 1st Ave.
Seattle, WA 98121
Pathologist

Tom and Jerry
3400 Cahuenga Blvd. W.
Hollywood, CA 90068
Cat and mouse

Toma, David
P.O. Box 854
Clark, NJ 07056
Drug abuse expert

Tomba, Alberto
Rete di San Giorgio di Piano
San Lazzaro di Lavena
Bologna, Italy
Skier

Tomlin, Lily
P.O. Box 27700
Los Angeles, CA 90027
Comedienne

**Tone Loc
(Tony Smith)**
c/o Island Records
14 E. Fourth St.
New York, NY 10012
Rapper

**Tonka Corp. (Trivial
    Pursuit, Monopoly, Play-
    Doh)**
6000 Clearwater Dr.
Minnetonka, MN 55343
Stephen G. Shank, CEO

Tony Lama Co.
1137 Tony Lama St.
El Paso, TX 79915
Anthony B. Lama, Jr., CEO

Tony the Tiger
c/o Kellogg Co.
235 Porter
Battle Creek, MI 49017
Kellogg's "Gr-r-reat" mascot

Toomey, Bill
1930 Century Park W. (#303)
Los Angeles, CA 90067
Former Olympic decathlon champ

Tootsie Roll
7401 Cicero Ave.
Chicago, IL 60629
M.J. Gordon, president

**Torme, Mel
(Melvin Howard)**
10100 Santa Monica Blvd.
(#1600)
Los Angeles, CA 90067
Jazz singer

**Torn, Rip
(Elmore, Jr.)**
9200 Sunset Blvd. (#710)
Los Angeles, CA 90069
Actor

Toro Company
8111 Lyndale Ave. S.
Minneapolis, MN 55420
Kondrick B. Melrose, CEO

Toronto Blue Jays
Exhibition Stadium
Exhibition Place
Toronto, ON Canada M5C 2K7
Pat Gillick, general manager

Toronto Maple Leafs
60 Carlton St.
Toronto, ON Canada M5B 1L1
Gerry McNamara, general
  manager

Toshiba Corp.
1-1 Shibaura 1-chome, Minato-ku
Tokyo, Japan
J. Aoi, CEO

Total Organization
4250 Parks Ave. (#8)
La Mesa, CA 92041
Consultants on organization

**Toulmin, Stephen Edelston,
  Dr.**
Northwestern University
1818 Hinman, Brentano Hall
Evanston, IL 60208
Humanities educator

Town and Country Magazine
959 8th Ave.
New York, NY 10019
Frank Zachary, editor

Towne, Robert
8899 Beverly Blvd.
Los Angeles, CA 90048
Screenwriter/director

Townsend, Robert
445 N. Bedford Dr. (PH)
Beverly Hills, CA 90210
Actor/film director

Townshend, Peter Dennis Blandford
c/o The Boathouse
Ranelagh Dr.
Twickenham TW1 1Q2 England
Rock musician

Toys "Я" Us
395 W. Passaic St.
Rochelle Park, NJ 07662
Charles Lazarus, CEO

Trabulus, Joshua, Dr.
435 N. Roxbury Dr. (#300)
Beverly Hills, CA 90212
Physician

Tracy, Mary Ellen
Church of the Most High
Goddess
1803 Griffith Park Blvd.
Los Angeles, CA 90026
High priestess of sex religion

TransAfrica
Randall Robinson, president
545 8th St. SE. (#200)
Washington, DC 20003
Pro-Africa lobby

Transamerica
600 Montgomery St.
San Francisco, CA 94111
James R. Harvey, CEO

Trans World Airlines (TWA)
100 S. Bedford Rd.
Mt. Kisco, NY 10549
Carl C. Icahn, chairman

Travalena, Fred
8899 Beverly Blvd.
Los Angeles, CA 90048
Impressionist

Travelers Insurance
One Tower Sq.
Hartford, CT 06183
Edward H. Budd, CEO

Travis, Randy
P.O. Box 121712
Nashville, TN 37212
Country singer

Travolta, John
c/o M.C.E.G.
11355 W. Olympic Blvd. (#500)
Los Angeles, CA 90064
Actor

Trebek, Alex
c/o Jeopardy!
1541 N. Vine St.
Hollywood, CA 90028
T.V. game show host

TreePeople
Andy Lipkis, president
12601 Mulholland Dr.
Beverly Hills, CA 90213
Plants trees to help environment

TreeSweet
9801 Westheimer
Houston, TX 77042
C.E. Owens, CEO

Trevino, Lee Buck
14901 Quorum Dr. (#170)
Dallas, TX 75240
Golf's "Super Mex"

Tropicana Products
1001 13th Ave. E.
Bradenton, FL 34208
R.L. Soran, CEO

Troutman, Richard, Dr.
755 Park Ave.
New York, NY 10021
Cornea specialist

Troyer, Alvah Forrest, Dr.
c/o DeKalb-Pfizer Genetics
3100 Sycamore Rd.
DeKalb, IL 60115
*Geneticist/seed company
executive*

Trudeau, Garry B.
c/o Universal Press Syndicate
4400 Johnson Dr.
Fairway, KS 66205
"Doonesbury" cartoonist

Trump, Donald John
721 5th Ave.
New York, NY 10022
Entrepreneur

TRW
1900 Richmond Rd.
Cleveland, OH 44124
Joseph T. Gorman, CEO

Tucker, Michael
11726 San Vicente Blvd. (#300)
Los Angeles, CA 90049
Actor

Tucker, Tanya
2325 Crestmoor Dr. (#15245)
Nashville, TN 37215
Country singer

Tune, Tommy
c/o Marvin Schulman
890 Broadway
New York, NY 10003
Broadway singer/dancer

Tupou IV, King
Palace Officiale
Nuku'alofa, Tonga
King of Tonga

Turner, Debbye
1325 Boardwalk
Atlantic City, NJ 08401
Miss America 1990

Turner, Kathleen
P.O. Box 5617
Beverly Hills, CA 90213
Actress

**Turner, Ted
(Robert Edward, III)**
P.O. Box 4064
Atlanta, GA 30302
Communications executive

**Turner, Tina
(Annie Mae Bullock)**
3575 Cahuenga Blvd. W. (#580)
Los Angeles, CA 90068
Rock singer

Turow, Scott
c/o Warner Books
4000 Warner Blvd.
Burbank, CA 91522
Author

257

**Tutu, Desmond Mpelo,
Archbishop**
P.O. Box 31190, Braamfontein
Johannesburg, Republic of South
Africa
Anti-apartheid leader

Tutwiler, Margaret DeB.
2201 C St. NW.
Washington, DC 20520
State Dept. spokesperson

TV Guide
Radnor, PA 19088
Joseph William Cece, publisher

Twentieth Century Fox
P.O. Box 900
Beverly Hills, CA 90213
Barry Diller, chairman

**Twiggy
(Leslie Lawson)**
c/o Neville Shulman
4 St. George's House, 15
Hanover Sq.
London W1R 9AJ England
Actress/former model

Tyson, Mike
9 W. 57th St. (#4800)
New York, NY 10019
Boxing's "Iron Mike"

U

Udall, Mo (Morris K.)
235 Cannon House Office Bldg..
Washington, DC 20515
Congressman from Arizona

Uecker, Bob
c/o Milwaukee Brewers
County Stadium
Milwaukee, WI 53214
Sportscaster-personality

U-Haul
2727 N. Central
Phoenix, AZ 85404
Edward J. Shoen, CEO

Ullman, Tracey
20th Century Fox Television
10201 W. Pico Blvd.
Los Angeles, CA 90035
Comedienne/actress

Ullmann, Liv Johanne
c/o London Management
235 Regent St.
London W1 England
Actress/activist

Ultimate Players Association
P.O. Box 2331
Silver City, NM 88062
Creators of Ultimate Frisbee

U.N.C.L.E.
Lynda Mendoza, HQ
P.O. Box 165
Downers Grove, IL 60515
"Man from U.N.C.L.E." fan club

Underground Film Bulletin
P.O. Box 1589
New York, NY 10009

Unger, Jim
4900 Main St. (9th floor)
Kansas City, MO 62114
"Herman" cartoonist

Union Carbide
39 Old Ridgebury Rd.
Danbury, CT 06817
Robert D. Kennedy, CEO

Union of American Hebrew Congregations
838 5th Ave.
New York, NY 10021
Rabbi Alexander M. Schindler, president

Union of Orthodox Jewish Congregations
45 W. 36th St.
New York, NY 10018
Sidney Kwestel, president

Uniroyal
World Headquarters
Middlebury, CT 06762
Joseph P. Flannery, president

Unisys Corporation
P.O. Box 500
Blue Bell, PA 19424
W. Michael Blumenthal, CEO

Unitarian Universalist Assn.
25 Beacon St.
Boston, MA 02108
Rev. William Schultz, president

Unitas, John Constantine
Johnny Unitas Golden Arm
Restaurant
6345 York Rd.
Baltimore, MD 21212
Former football great

United Air Lines
P.O. Box 66100
Chicago, IL 60666
Stephen Wolf, chairman

**United Cerebral Palsy
Association**
66 E. 34th St.
New York, NY 10016
James E. Introne, director

United Church of Christ
105 Madison Ave.
New York, NY 10016
Rev. Avery D. Post, president

United Methodist Church
168 Mt. Vernon St.
Newtonville, MA 02160
Faith Richardson, secretary

United Negro College Fund
500 E. 62nd St.
New York, NY 10021
Christopher Edley, president

**United Parcel Service
(UPS)**
Greenwich Office Park 5
Greenwich, CT 06831
John W. Rogers, chairman

**United Press International
(UPI)**
1200 I Street NW.
Washington, DC 20005
Bill Ferguson, chairman

**United States Auto Club
(USAC)**
4910 W. 16th St.
Indianapolis, IN 46224

**United Synagogue of
America**
155 5th Ave.
New York, NY 10010
Franklin D. Kreutzer, president

**United Technologies
Corporation**
United Technologies Bldg.
Hartford, CT 06101
Robert F. Daniell, CEO

United Van Lines
One United Dr.
Fenton, MO 63026
Maurice Greenblatt, chairman

United Way
801 N. Fairfax St.
Alexandria, VA 22309
Erwin Field/Ernest Loebbecke,
chairmen

Universal Autograph
Collectors Club
P.O. Box 6181
Washington, DC 20044

Universal City Studios
100 Universal City Plaza
Universal City, CA 91608
Sidney Jay Sheinberg, president

Universal Fan Mail
14842 Strathern St.
Van Nuys, CA 91402

Universal Life Church, Inc.
601 3rd St.
Modesto, CA 95351
Become a minister by mail

Unknown Museum
Mickey McGowan, curator
243 E. Blithdale Ave.
Mill Valley, CA 94941
Pays tribute to "everyone in America"

Unocal
Unocal Center
Los Angeles, CA 90017
Richard J. Stegemeier, CEO

Unser, Bobby
7700 Central Ave. SW.
Albuquerque, NM 87105
Racecar driver

Updike, John Hoyer
Beverly Farms, MA 01915
Author

Upjohn Co.
7000 Portage Rd.
Kalamazoo, MI 49001
T. Cooper, CEO

Urich, Robert
2121 Ave. of the Stars (#410)
Los Angeles, CA 90067
Actor

Uris, Leon
P.O. Box 1559
Aspen, CO 81611
Novelist

US Air
National Airport
Washington, DC 20001
Edwin I. Colodny, chairman

U.S. Air Force Academy
Colorado Springs, CO 80840
Lt. Gen. Charles Hamm

US Magazine
Dag Hammarskjold Plaza
New York, NY 10017
Jann S. Wenner, editor

U.S. Borax
3075 Wilshire Blvd.
Los Angeles, CA 90010
Lord Clitherol, chairman

U.S. Coast Guard Academy
New London, CT 06320
Rear Adm. Richard P. Cueroni

U.S. Cycling Federation
1750 E. Boulder
Colorado Springs, CO 80909
Jerry E. Lace, exec. director

U.S. Hang Gliding
Association
P.O. Box 8300
Colorado Springs, CO 80907

USA Today
P.O. Box 500
Washington, DC 20044
John C. Quinn, editor

U.S. Marine Corps
Arlington Annex
Washington, DC 20380
Gen. A.M. Gray, commandant

U.S. Merchant Marine Academy
Kings Point, NY 11024
Rear Adm. P.L. Krinsky

U.S. Military Academy
West Point, NY 10996
Lt. Gen. Dave R. Palmer, commandant

U.S. Naval Academy
Annapolis, MD 21402
Rear Adm. Virgil Hill, Jr., superintendent

U.S. News and World Report Magazine
2400 N St. NW.
Washington, DC 20037
Roger Rosenblatt, editor

U.S. Olympic Committee (USOC)
1750 E. Boulder St.
Colorado Springs, CO 80909
Barron Pittenger, executive director

U.S. Paddle Tennis Association
189 Seeley St.
Brooklyn, NY 11218
Greg Lawrence, president

U.S. Professional Tennis Assoc.
P.O. Box 7077
Wesley Chapel, FL 34249

U.S. Secret Service
c/o Office of Government Liaison
1800 G St. NW.
Washington, DC 20223
John R. Simpson, director

U.S. Stickball League
P.O. Box 363
East Rockaway, NY 11518
Ronald B. Babineau, president

USO (United Service Organizations)
601 Indiana Ave. NW
Washington, DC 20004

Ustinov, Peter Alexander
11 Rue de Silly
Boulogne, France 92100
Actor/author

USX Corp.
600 Grant St.
Pittsburgh, PA 15219
Charles A. Corry, CEO

Utah Jazz
5 Triad Center (#500)
Salt Lake City, UT 84160
Jerry Sloan, coach

Utne Reader
Eric Utne, editor
2732 W. 43rd St.
Minneapolis, MN 55410
Alternative press publisher

U2
4 Windmill Lane
Dublin 4, Ireland
Rock group

V

Vadim, Roger (Roger Vadim Plemiannikov)
2429 Beverly Ave.
Santa Monica, CA 90406
Film director

Valenti, Jack Joseph
1600 I Street NW.
Washington, DC 20006
Motion Picture Assn., president

Valenzuela, Fernando
% Los Angeles Dodgers
1000 Elysian Park Ave.
Los Angeles, CA 90012
Baseball pitcher

Vampire Research Center
P.O. Box 252
Elmhurst, NY 11373

Van Ark, Joan
151 El Camino Dr.
Beverly Hills, CA 90212
Actress

**Van Buren, Abigail
(Pauline Friedman Phillips)**
9200 Sunset Blvd. (#1003)
Los Angeles, CA 90069
Abby of "Dear Abby"

Vance, Cyrus Roberts
% Simpson, Thacher and Bartlett
455 Lexington Ave.
New York, NY 10017
Foreign affairs expert

Vancouver Canucks
100 North Renfrew St.
Vancouver, BC Canada
V5K 3N7
Jack Gordon, general manager

Van Damme, Jean-Claude
P.O. Box 69A05
Los Angeles, CA 90069
Actor/martial arts star

Vander Jagt, Guy
2409 Rayburn House Office Bldg.
Washington, DC 20515
Congressman from Michigan

Van Doren, Mamie
8340 Rush St.
Rosemead, CA 91770
Joe Doyle, fan club president

Vandross, Luther
8271 Melrose Ave.
Los Angeles, CA 90046
R&B singer

Van Dyke, Dick
151 El Camino Dr.
Beverly Hills, CA 90212
Actor/comedian

Van Halen
10100 Santa Monica Blvd.
(#2460)
Los Angeles, CA 90067
Rock group

Vanity
(Denise Matthews)
151 El Camino Dr.
Beverly Hills, CA 90212
Actress/singer

Vanity Fair Magazine
350 Madison Ave.
New York, NY 10017
Tina Brown, editor

Van Peebles, Mario
151 El Camino Dr.
Beverly Hills, CA 90212
Actor

Van Zandt, Steven
("Little Steven")
9200 Sunset Blvd. (#915)
Los Angeles, CA 90069
Rock musician

Vargas Llosa, Mario
% PEN
62-63 Glebe Place
London SW3 England
Author/Peruvian politician

Vaughn, Robert
8899 Beverly Blvd.
Los Angeles, CA 90048
Actor

Vega, Suzanne
P.O. Box 4221, Grand Central St.
New York, NY 10163
Folk/pop singer

Vegetarian Society
P.O. Box 926
Joshua Tree, CA 92252
Bianca Leonardo, president

Vegetarian Times
P.O. Box 570
Oak Park, IL 60303
Paul Obis, editor

Vereen, Ben
8730 Sunset Blvd. (#600)
Los Angeles, CA 90069
Actor/entertainer

Versace, Gianni
Via della Spiga 25
20121 Milan, Italy
Fashion designer

Veterans of Foreign Wars
(VFW)
406 W. 34th St.
Kansas City, MO 64111
Larry W. Rivers, executive
director

Veterans of the Vietnam
War
2090 Bald Mountain Rd.
Wilkes-Barre, PA 18702

Vetter, Robert
P.O. Box 929
Westhampton Beach, NY 11978
Anthropologist of American
Indians

Victoria's Secret
% The Limited
Two Limited Pkwy.
Columbus, OH 43216
Sexy lingerie stores

Vidal, Gore
% Random House
201 E. 50th St.
New York, NY 10022
Author

Viera, Meredith
% CBS News
55 W. 57th St.
New York, NY 10019
Television journalist

Village Voice
842 Broadway
New York, NY 10003
Martin Gottlieb, editor

Villechaize, Herve Jean Pierre
P.O. Box 1305
Burbank, CA 91507
Actor

Vincent, Jan-Michael
151 El Camino Dr.
Beverly Hills, CA 90212
Actor

Vinton, Bobby (Stanley Robert)
P.O. Box 906
Malibu, CA 90265
Pop singer

Viorst, Judith
% Simon & Schuster
1230 6th Ave.
New York, NY 10020
Author

Viscott, David, Dr.
% KABC
3321 S. La Cienega Blvd.
Los Angeles, CA 90016
Psychologist

Vitale, Dick
% ESPN
935 Middle St.
Bristol, CT 06010
Basketball announcer

Vogue Magazine
350 Madison Ave.
New York, NY 10017
Anna W. Wintour, editor

Voight, Jon
9830 Wilshire Blvd.
Beverly Hills, CA 90212
Actor

Voinovich, George V.
City Hall
601 Lakeside Ave.
Cleveland, OH 44114
Mayor of Cleveland

Volcker, Paul
Princeton University
Princeton, NJ 08540
Economist

Volkswagen of America
888 W. Big Beaver
Troy, MI 48007
Hans-Joerg Hungerland, CEO

Volvo North American Corp.
Rockleigh Industrial Park
Rockleigh, NJ 07647
Bjorn Ahlstrom, CEO

Von Bulow, Claus
960 5th Ave.
New York, NY 10021
Socialite

Vonnegut, Kurt
% Donald C. Farber
99 Park Ave. (25th floor)
New York, NY 10016
Author

Von Stade, Frederica
165 W. 57th St.
New York, NY 10019
Opera star

Von Sydow, Max Carl Adolf
Avd C/G Risberg, Strandveegen B
114-56 Stockholm, Sweden
Actor

Von Thurn und Taxis, Johannes Prince (and Princess Gloria)
Emmeramsplatz 5, Schloss
D-8400 Regensburg, Germany
Socialites

Vos Savant, Marilyn Mach
124 W. 60th St.
New York, NY 10023
World's highest IQ (228)

Vuckovich, Dragomir M., Dr.
% Neuroscience Center
720 Osterman Ave.
Deerfield, IL 60015
Neurologist

W

Women's Wear Daily
7 E. 12th St.
New York, NY 10003
Michael F. Coady, ed.

Wade, Virginia
Sharstead Court
Sittingbourne
Kent, England
Former tennis star

Wages and Not Tips
Richard Busemeyer, president
10044 Princeton Rd.
Cincinnati, OH 45246
Group seeks to abolish tipping

Wagner, Jane
P.O. Box 27700
Los Angeles, CA 90027
Comedy writer

Wagner, Lindsay J.
11500 W. Olympic Blvd. (#300)
Los Angeles, CA 90064
Actress

Wagner, Robert
151 El Camino Dr.
Beverly Hills, CA 90212
Actor

Wahl, Ken
151 El Camino Dr.
Beverly Hills, CA 90212
Actor

**Waits, Tom
(Thomas Alan)**
% Rothberg-Gerber Management
145 Central Park W.
New York, NY 10023
Singer/songwriter/actor

Wajda, Andrzej
% Film Polski
ul. Mazowieckei 6/8
Warsaw, Poland
Film director

Wald, Patricia M.
U.S. Court of Appeal
District of Columbia
Washington, DC 20001
Chief Judge

Waldheim, Kurt
Hofburg, Ballhausplatz
1010 Vienna, Austria
President of Austria

Walesa, Lech
Ul. Pilotow 17/D3
Gdansk-Zaspa, Poland
Solidarity founder

Walker, Alice Malsenior
% Harcourt Brace Jovanovich
111 5th Ave.
New York, NY 10003
Novelist

Walker, Herschel
% Minnesota Vikings
9520 Viking Dr.
Eden Prairie, MN 55344
Football star

Walker, Jimmie
9000 Sunset Blvd. (#909)
Los Angeles, CA 90069
Comedian

Wallace, George Corley
P.O. Box 17222
Montgomery, AL 36104
Former governor of Alabama

Wallace, Mike
55 W. 57th St.
New York, NY 10019
Television journalist

Wallach, Eli
8899 Beverly Blvd.
Los Angeles, CA 90048
Actor

Walsh, John and Reve
Adam Walsh Child Resource
   Center
3111 S. Dixie Highway (#244)
West Palm Beach, FL 33405
Lobbyists for children's rights

Wall St. Journal
200 Liberty St.
New York, NY 10281
Robert L. Bartley, editor

Walters, Barbara
% ABC News
1330 6th Ave.
New York, NY 10019
Television journalist

Walton, Sam M.
Wal-Mart, president
702 SW. 8th St.
Bentonville, AR 72716
*Formerly wealthiest man in
America*

Wambaugh, Joseph
% William Morrow & Co.
105 Madison Ave.
New York, NY 10016
Cop author

Wanamaker, Marc
Bison Archives
650 N. Bronson Ave. (#146)
Hollywood, CA 90004
Hollywood historian

Wanamaker, Sam
40 Bankside
London SE1 England
*Reconstructing Shakespeare's
   Globe*

Wang Laboratories
One Industrial Ave.
Lowell, MA 01851
Computer manufacturer

**Wapner, Joseph
(Albert)**
1717 N. Highland Ave.
Hollywood, CA 90028
"People's Court" judge

Ward, Burt
8444 Wilshire Blvd. (#313)
Beverly Hills, CA 90211
"Batman's" Robin

Ward, Fred
9301 Wilshire Blvd. (#312)
Beverly Hills, CA 90210
Actor

Ward, Rachel
10100 Santa Monica Blvd.
(#1600)
Los Angeles, CA 90067
Actress

Warfield, Marsha
P.O. Box 691713
Los Angeles, CA 90069
Comedienne

Warner, David
60 Saint James's St.
London SW1 England
Actor

Warner, John William
Akota Farms
Middleburg, VA 22177
Senator from Virginia

Warner, Malcolm Jamal
% NBC
3000 W. Alameda Blvd.
Burbank, CA 91523
Actor

Warner Brothers Films
4000 Warner Blvd.
Burbank, CA 91522
Robert A. Daly, chairman

**Warner Communications,
  Inc.**
75 Rockefeller Plaza
New York, NY 10019
Stephen J. Ross, chairman

Warrant
% CBS Records
1801 Century Park W.
Los Angeles, CA 90067
Rock group

Warren, Lesley Ann
9830 Wilshire Blvd.
Beverly Hills, CA 90212
Actress

**Warwick, Dionne
(Marie Dionne Warrick)**
9200 Sunset Blvd. (#420)
Los Angeles, CA 90069
Pop singer

Washington, Denzel
151 El Camino Dr.
Beverly Hills, CA 90212
Actor

Washington, Grover, Jr.
% Lloyd Z. Remick
700 Three Penn Center
Philadelphia, PA 19102
Jazz saxophonist

Washington Bullets
Capitol Centre
Landover, MD 20785
Bob Ferry, general manager

Washington Capitals
Capital Centre
Landover, MD 20785
David Poile, general manager

Washington Post
1150 15th St. NW.
Washington, DC 20071
Benjamin C. Bradlee, editor

Washington Redskins
P.O. Box 17247
Dulles International Airport
Washington, DC 20041
Jack Kent Cooke, chairman

Wasserburg, Gerald Joseph, Dr.
California Institute of Technology
Geology and Planetary Science
Div.
Pasadena, CA 91125
Geologist

Wasserman, Lew
% Universal Studios
100 Universal City Plaza
Universal City, CA 91608
Entertainment executive

Wasserstein, Wendy
% Luis Sanjurgo
40 W. 57th St.
New York, NY 10019
Playwright

Water Baby
Karil Daniels, spokesperson
2477 Folsom St.
San Francisco, CA 94110
Promotes births in water

Waterston, Sam
(Samuel Atkinson)
9000 Sunset Blvd. (#1200)
Los Angeles, CA 90069
Actor

Watkins, James
1000 Independence Ave. SW.
Washington, DC 20585
Secretary of Energy

Watley, Jody
8439 Sunset Blvd. (#103)
Los Angeles, CA 90069
Pop singer

Watson, Tom
(Thomas Sturges)
1313 Commerce Tower
Kansas City, MO 64105
Golfer

Watt, James Gaius
P.O. Box 3705
Jackson Hole, WY 83001
Former Secretary of the Interior

Watterson, Bill
% Andrew & McMeel
4900 Main St.
Kansas City, MO 64112
"Calvin and Hobbs" cartoonist

Wattleton, Faye Alyce
810 7th Ave.
New York, NY 10019
Planned Parenthood, president

Watts, Charlie
Halsdon House, Near Barnstable
Devon, England
Rock drummer

Waxman, Henry
2411 Rayburn House Office Bldg.
Washington, DC 20515
Congressman from California

Weaver, Dennis
% Nashville International
116 17th Ave. S.
Nashville, TN 37203
Actor/country singer

Weaver, Sigourney (Susan)
8899 Beverly Blvd.
Los Angeles, CA 90048
Actress

Webb, Spud
% Atlanta Hawks
One CNN Center, South Tower
 (#405)
Atlanta, GA 30303
Basketball star

Webber, Andrew Lloyd
20 Greek St.
London W1V 5LF England
Theatrical composer

Weber, Arnold R., Dr.
Northwestern University
Evanston, IL 60201
University president

Weight Watchers
800 Community Dr.
Manhasset, NY 11030
Albert Lippert, chairman

Weir, Benjamin, Rev.
% Presbyterian Church of USA
475 Riverside Dr. (#1201)
New York, NY 10115
Former hostage in Lebanon

Weir, Morton W., Dr.
University of Illinois
Champaign-Urbana, IL 61801
University president

Weir, Peter
% DGA
7920 Sunset Blvd.
Los Angeles, CA 90046
Film director

Weirdbook
W. Paul Ganley, editor
P.O. Box 149, Amherst Branch
Buffalo, NY 14226
Fantasy fiction magazine

Weiss, Ted
2467 Rayburn House Office Bldg.
Washington, DC 20515
Congressman from New York

Welch, Raquel
P.O. Box 26472
Prescott, AZ 85253
Actress

Welch Foods
100 Main St.
Concord, MA 01742
Everett N. Baldwin, president

Weldon, Fay
% Anthony Sheil Associates
43 Doughty St.
London WC1 N2LF England
Author

Weller, Peter
9830 Wilshire Blvd.
Beverly Hills, CA 90212
"Robocop" actor

Wellman, Frieda "Freddie"
% F.U.N. Products, Inc.
11702 Trask Ave.
Garden Grove, CA 92643
*Sex aids via in-home demos for
   women*

Wellman, Inc.
1040 Broad St. (#302)
Shrewsbury, NJ 07702
Largest plastics recycler in U.S.

Wendelstedt, Harry Hunter, Jr.
% Major League Umpires Assoc.
88 South St.
Ormond Beach, FL 32074
Baseball umpire

Wenders, Wim
% Jess S. Morgan & Co.
6420 Wilshire Blvd.
Los Angeles, CA 90048
Film director

Wendy's
4288 W. Dublin Granville Rd.
Dublin, OH 43017
R. David Thomas, founder

We Remember Dean
% Sylvia Bongiovanni
P.O. Box 5025
Fullerton, CA 92635
James Dean fan club

Wesleyan Church
10880 State Rt. 170
Negley, OH 44441
Rev. J. Steven Manley,
   superintendent

**West, Adam
(William Anderson)**
P.O. Box 3446
Ketchum, ID 83340
Television's "Batman"

**Western Heroes
   Appreciation Society**
743 Harvard
St. Louis, MO 63130
Fan club

Western Union
One Lake St.
Upper Saddle River, NJ 07458
Robert S. Leventhal, chairman

Westheimer, Ruth, Dr.
3575 Cahuenga Blvd. W.
Los Angeles, CA 90068
Sex expert

Westinghouse Electric
6 Gateway Ctr., Westinghouse
   Bldg.
Pittsburgh, PA 15222
J.C. Marous, CEO

Westin Hotel Company
The Westin Bldg.
Seattle, WA 98121
Larry B. Magnan, CEO

**Westmoreland, William
   Childs, Gen.**
P.O. Box 1059
Charleston, SC 29402
*Former commanding general in
   Vietnam*

Weyerhaeuser Co.
Tacoma, WA 98477
George H. Weyerhaeuser, CEO

Wheel of Fortune
Studio Plaza
3400 Riverside Dr. (2nd floor)
Burbank, CA 91505
Television game show

Whelan, Elizabeth, Dr.
American Council on Science &
   Health
1995 Broadway (16th floor)
New York, NY 10023
Chemical industry spokesperson

Whipple, Fred Lawrence, Dr.
60 Garden St.
Cambridge, MA 02138
Astronomer

Whirlpool
Administrative Center
Benton Harbor, MI 49022
David R. Whitwam, CEO

Whitaker, Thomas Wallace, Dr.
P.O. Box 150
La Jolla, CA 92037
Botanist

Whitburn, Joel
P.O. Box 200
Menomonee Falls, WI 53501
Pop music expert

White, Augustus A., III, Dr.
Beth Israel Hospital
Boston, MA 02215
Spinal surgeon

White, Betty
151 El Camino Dr.
Beverly Hills, CA 90212
Actress

White, Bill (William DeKova)
350 Park Ave.
New York, NY 10022
National League, president

White, Byron R.
U.S. Supreme Court Bldg.
One 1st Street NE.
Washington, DC 20543
Supreme Court Justice

White, Carrie
% Putnam Memorial Nursing Home
Palatka, FL 32077
World's oldest person (114)

White, Vanna
8306 Wilshire Blvd. (#75)
Beverly Hills, CA 90211
Letter turner on "Wheel of Fortune"

Whitesnake
15 Poulton Rd., Wallasey
Cheshire, England
Rock group

Whitmire, Kathryn Jean
901 Bagby St.
Houston, TX 77251
Mayor of Houston

Whitney Museum of American Art
945 Madison Ave.
New York, NY 10021
William S. Woodside, president

Who, The
112 Wardour
London W1V 3LD England
Rock group

Wick, Charles Z.
400 C Street SW.
Washington, DC 20547
U.S. Information Agency, director

Widmark, Richard
8899 Beverly Blvd.
Los Angeles, CA 90048
Actor

Wieland, Bob
3530 Pine Valley Dr.
Sarasota, FL 34239
World record wheelchair athlete

Wiesel, Elie
% Boston University
745 Commonwealth Ave.
Boston, MA 02215
Author and Nobel–Peace Prize winner

Wiesel, Tosten N., Dr.
Rockefeller University
1230 York Ave.
New York, NY 10021
Nobel Prize neurobiologist

Wilder, Billy (William)
P.O. Box 93877
Hollywood, CA 90093
Film director

Wilder, Douglas
State Capitol
Richmond, VA 23219
Governor of Virginia

Wilder, Gene (Jerome Silberman)
9350 Wilshire Blvd. (#400)
Beverly Hills, CA 90212
Comic actor

Wilderness Academy
% Douglas Nelson
1103 S. Orem Blvd.
Orem, UT 84058
Nature trips for troubled teens

Wildlife Legislative Fund
50 W. Broad St.
Columbus, OH 43215
Lobbyist for sportsmen's groups

Wildmon, Donald Ellis, Rev.
National Federation for Decency
P.O. Box 1398
Tupelo, MS 38801
TV "decency" watchdog group

Wilkins, Dominique
% Atlanta Hawks
One CNN Center, South Tower (#405)
Atlanta, GA 30303
Basketball's "Human Highlight Film"

Will, George F.
% Washington Post
1150 15th St. NW.
Washington, DC 20071
Political columnist

Willard, Fred
151 El Camino Dr.
Beverly Hills, CA 90212
Comedian

William Holden Wildlife Assoc.
P.O. Box 67981
Los Angeles, CA 90067

William Morrow & Co.
105 Madison Ave.
New York, NY 10016
Allen Marchioni, president

Williams, Billy Dee
151 El Camino Dr.
Beverly Hills, CA 90212
Actor

**Williams, Hank, Jr.
(Randall)**
P.O. Box 850
Paris, TN 38242
Country singer

Williams, JoBeth
8899 Beverly Blvd.
Los Angeles, CA 90048
Actress

Williams, John Towner
301 Massachusetts Ave.
Boston, MA 02115
Conductor/film music composer

Williams, Mary Alice
% NBC News
30 Rockefeller Plaza
New York, NY 10020
Television journalist

Williams, Paul
% Denny Bond
4570 Encino Ave.
Encino, CA 91316
Songwriter/actor

Williams, Robin
9830 Wilshire Blvd.
Beverly Hills, CA 90212
Actor/comedian

**Williams, Ted
(Theodore Samuel)**
P.O. Box 481
Islamorada, FL 33036
Baseball's "Teddy Ballgame"

Williams, Treat
888 7th Ave. (6th floor)
New York, NY 10106
Actor

Williams, Vanessa
P.O. Box 40
Millwood, NY 10546
Singer/former Miss America

Williamson, Myrna H.
Brig. Gen., U.S. Army (Ret.)
3530 Pine Valley Dr.
Sarasota, FL 34239
*Senior female officer on
retirement*

Willis, Allee
% Unicity Music
90 Universal City Plaza
Universal City, CA 91608
Songwriter

Willis, Bruce
10100 Santa Monica Blvd.
(#1600)
Los Angeles, CA 90067
Actor/singer

Wilson, Gahan
P.O. Box 4023
New York, NY 10017
Cartoonist

**Wilson, Kenneth Geddes,
Dr.**
Cornell University
316 Newman Lab
Ithaca, NY 14853
Nobel Prize physicist

Wilson, Pete Barton
720 Hart Office Bldg.
Washington, DC 20510
Senator from California

Wilson, Robert M.
% Byrd Hoffman Foundation
325 Spring St. (#228)
New York, NY 10013
Theatrical artist

Wilton, James Quinn, Dr.
UCLA Graduate School of
  Management
405 Hilgard Ave.
Los Angeles, CA 90024
Political scientist

**Wimbledon/The
  Championships**
All England Lawn Tennis &
  Croquet Club
Church Road
Wimbledon SW19 5AE England

Winfield, Dave
% New York Yankees
Yankee Stadium
Bronx, NY 10451
Baseball star

Winfield, Paul Edward
10000 Santa Monica Blvd. (#305)
Los Angeles, CA 90067
Actor

Winfrey, Oprah
% Harpo Productions
35 E. Wacker St. (#1782)
Chicago, IL 60601
Talk show host/actress

Winger, Debra
P.O. Box 4306
Malibu, CA 90265
Actress

Winkler, Henry Franklin
P.O. Box 1764
Studio City, CA 91604
Actor

Winkler, Irwin
10125 W. Washington Blvd.
Culver City, CA 90230
Film producer

Winnebago Industries
P.O. Box 152
Forest City, IA 50436
J.K. Hanson, president

Winningham, Mare
151 El Camino Dr.
Beverly Hills, CA 90212
Actress

Winnipeg Jets
15-1430 Maroons Rd.
Winnipeg, MB Canada
R3G 0L5
John Ferguson, general manager

Winokur, Jon
% New American Library
1633 Broadway
New York, NY 10019
Curmudgeon/author

Winslow, Scott J.
P.O. Box 6033
Nashua, NH 03063
*Obsolete, historic stocks and
  bonds*

**Winter, Johnny
(John Dawson Winter III)**
P.O. Box 60234
Chicago, IL 60660
Blues rock guitarist

Winters, Jonathan
% George Spota
11151 Ophir Dr.
Los Angeles, CA 90024
Comedian/painter

**Winters, Shelley
(Shirley Schrift)**
P.O. Box 10269
Beverly Hills, CA 90210
Actress

**Winwood, Steve
(Stephen Lawrence)**
9200 Sunset Blvd. (PH 15)
Los Angeles, CA 90069
Pop singer

Wirth, Tim
380 Russell Senate Office Bldg.
Washington, DC 20510
Senator from Colorado

Witt, Katarina
% Deutscher Turn-und
   Sportbund der DDR
Berlin, Germany
Ice skater

Wizard of Oz Club
P.O. Box 95
Kinderhook, IL 62345
Fan club

**Wohlschlag, Donald Eugene,
   Dr.**
University of Texas
Port Aransas Marine Lab
Port Aransas, TX 78373
Zoologist

**Wolanin, Barbara Ann
   Boese**
U.S. Capitol Office
Architect of the Capitol
Washington, DC 20515
Curator/art historian

**Wolfe, Tom
(Thomas Kennerly, Jr.)**
% Farrar Straus and Giroux
19 Union Sq.
New York, NY 10003
Author

Wolper, David Lloyd
% Warner Brothers
4000 Warner Blvd.
Burbank, CA 91522
Television producer

Woman's Day Magazine
1515 Broadway
New York, NY 10036
Ellen Levine, editor

**Women's Christian
   Temperance Union
(WCTU)**
1730 Chicago Ave.
Evanston, IL 60201

**Wonder, Stevie
(Steveland Judkins Morris)**
4616 Magnolia Blvd.
Burbank, CA 91505
Pop musician

Wood, William C., Dr.
Massachusetts General Hospital
Boston, MA 02114
Breast cancer surgeon

Woodard, Alfre
9301 Wilshire Blvd. (#312)
Beverly Hills, CA 90210
Actress

Woodbury, Chuck
% William Morrow & Co.
105 Madison Ave.
New York, NY 10016
*Newspaper on American small
  towns*

Woods, Icky
200 Riverfront Stadium
Cincinnati, OH 45202
Football star

Woods, James
9830 Wilshire Blvd.
Beverly Hills, CA 90212
Actor

**Woodward, Joanne
  Gignilliat**
P.O. Box 3090
Saugatuck, CT 06880
Actress

Woolf, Bob
4575 Prudential Tower
Boston, MA 02199
Sports agent

Woolworth Corp.
233 Broadway, Woolworth Bldg.
New York, NY 10279
Harold E. Sells, CEO

**World Association of
  Document Examiners**
111 N. Canal St.
Chicago, IL 60606
Edna Robertson, director

**World Boxing Association
(WBA)**
412 Colorado Ave.
Aurora, IL 60506
Nick P. Kerasiotis, treasurer

World Footbag Association
Greg Cortopassi, director
1317 Washington Ave. (#7)
Golden, CO 80401
Hackey Sack players

**World Professional
  Armwrestling Association**
3020 Earlmar Dr.
Los Angeles, CA 90064
Steve Simons, president

World Wildlife Fund
1250 24th St. NW. (Dept. 2F16)
Washington, DC 20037

Worldwide Curio House
P.O. Box 17095
Minneapolis, MN 55417
*World's largest occult supply
  house*

Woronov, Mary
400 S. Beverly Dr. (#216)
Beverly Hills, CA 90212
Actress

**Worrell, Ernest P.
(Jim Varney)**
P.O. Box 23325
Nashville, TN 37202
"Hey Vern!" actor

Worthy, James
% Los Angeles Lakers
P.O. Box 10
Inglewood, CA 90306
Basketball star

Wright, Don C.
% Miami News
P.O. Box 615
Miami, FL 33152
Editorial cartoonist

Wright, Robert C.
% NBC
30 Rockefeller Plaza
New York, NY 10112
Entertainment executive

Wright, Steven
9000 Sunset Blvd. (#1200)
Los Angeles, CA 90069
Comedian

Wrigley Co.
410 N. Michigan Ave.
Chicago, IL 60611
William Wrigley, CEO

Writers Guild of America, West
8955 Beverly Blvd.
Los Angeles, CA 90048
George Kirgo, president

W.W. Norton & Co.
500 Fifth Ave.
New York, NY 10110
Donald S. Lamm, chairman

Wyatt, Jane
151 El Camino Dr.
Beverly Hills, CA 90212
"Father Knows Best" actress

Wyeth, Andrew Newell
P.O. Box 247
Lookout Mtn, TN 37350
Artist

Wynn, Steve
% Mirage Hotel
3900 Las Vegas Blvd. S.
Las Vegas, NV 89109
Gambling casino entrepreneur

X

X, Laura
2325 Oak St.
Berkeley, CA 94708
Marital and date rape expert

Xerox Corporation
P.O. Box 1600
Stamford, CT 06904
David Kearns, CEO

Xtreme
Iram Zandl, president
325 Lafayette St.
New York, NY 10012
Youth market consultant

Y

Yalow, Rosalyn Sussman, Dr.
% VA Medical Center
130 W. Kingsbridge Rd.
Bronx, NY 10468
Physicist

Yamada, Tadataka, Dr.
U. of Michigan Medical School
Ann Arbor, MI 48109
Gastroenterology specialist

Yamamoto, Kenechi
3-1 Suinchi, Fucho-cho, Aki-gun
Hiroshima 730-91 Japan
Mazda Motor Corp., president

Yamaoka, Harus Seigen
% Buddhist Church of America
1710 Octavia St.
San Francisco, CA 94109
Religious leader

Yankovic, Weird Al
% Imaginary Entertainment
925 Westmount Dr.
Los Angeles, CA 90069
Song parodyist

Yao, Richard
P.O. Box 20324, Greeley Square
St.
New York, NY 10001
Fundamentalists Anonymous, founder

Yeager, Chuck (Charles Elwood)
P.O. Box 128
Cedar Ridge, CA 95924
First man to break sound barrier

Yetnikoff, Walter
% CBS Records
51 W. 52nd St.
New York, NY 10019
Music executive

Yeutter, Clayton
14th and Independence Ave. SW.
Washington, DC 20250
Secretary of Agriculture

YMCA (Young Men's Christian Association)
101 N. Wacker Dr.
Chicago, IL 60606

York, Michael (York-Johnson)
151 El Camino Dr.
Beverly Hills, CA 90212
Actor

Young, Andrew
68 Mitchell St. SW
Atlanta, GA 30335
Mayor of Atlanta

Young, Charles E.
U. of California, Los Angeles
Los Angeles, CA 90024
University chancellor

Young, Coleman Alexander
1126 City-County Bldg., 2
  Woodward
Detroit, MI 48226
Mayor of Detroit

Young, Neil
% Lookout Management
506 Santa Monica Blvd.
Santa Monica, CA 90401
Rock singer

Young, Sean
9830 Wilshire Blvd.
Beverly Hills, CA 90212
Actress

Young Astronaut Council
1211 Connecticut Ave. NW.
Washington, DC 20036
T. Wendell Butler, executive
  director

Younger, Julius Stuart, Dr.
U. of Pittsburgh School of
  Medicine
Department of Microbiology
Pittsburgh, PA 15261
Microbiologist

Youngman, Henny
77 W. 55th St.
New York, NY 10019
Comedian

Yount, Robin
% Milwaukee Brewers
County Stadium
Milwaukee, WI 53214
Baseball star

**Youth Ambassadors of
America**
Edwin R. Johnson, executive
  director
P.O. Box 5273
Bellingham, WA 98227
*Soviet-American cultural
  exchanges*

**Yurchenco, Henrietta Weiss,
Dr.**
139th St. and Convent Ave.
New York, NY 10031
Ethnomusicologist

**YWCA (Young Women's
Christian Association)**
726 Broadway
New York, NY 10003

Z

Zadora, Pia
725 5th Ave.
New York, NY 10022
Singer

Zal, H. Michael, Dr.
Two Bala Cynwyd Plaza
Bala Cynwyd, PA 19004
Psychiatrist

Zalusky, Ralph, Dr.
Beth Israel Medical Center
New York, NY 10003
Hematology/oncology specialist

**Zappa, Frank
(also Dweezil and Moon)**
P.O. Box 5265
N. Hollywood, CA 91616
Musicians/personalities

**Zeffirelli, Franco
(Corsi)**
Via Appia Pignatelli 448
Rome, Italy
Film director

Zeman, Jacklyn
9830 Wilshire Blvd.
Beverly Hills, CA 90212
Actress

Zenith Electronics
1000 Milwaukee Ave.
Glenview, IL 60025
Jerry K. Pearlman, CEO

Zsigmond, Vilmos
9229 Sunset Blvd. (#700)
Los Angeles, CA 90069
Cinematographer

**Zuckerman, Mortimer
Benjamin**
% Boston Properties
599 Lexington Ave.
New York, NY 10022
Business leader

Zuniga, Daphne
P.O. Box 1644
Pacific Palisades, CA 90272
Actress

ZZ Top
P.O. Box 19744
Houston, TX 77024
Rock group

Write to Me

The Address Book is updated every two years, and you can play an active role in this procedure. If you are notable in any field, or know someone who is, send the name, mailing address, and some documentation of the notability (newspaper clippings are effective) for possible inclusion in our next edition.

Also, we are very interested in learning of any success stories resulting from *The Address Book*.

During the last few years, I have received tens of thousands of letters, ranging from loving to vituperative, from owners of *The Address Book*. Despite the overwhelming task of answering this mail, I rather enjoy the letters. In fact, some have downright warmed me when the world was feeling especially cold.

But, please, remember a couple of rules if you write:

• Remember to include a self-addressed stamped envelope. For reasons of both time and expense, this is the only way I can respond to mail; so, unfortunately, I've had to draw the line—no S.A.S.E., no reply.
• I need your comments. While I confess I'm partial to success stories, comments from purchasers of the book have helped me a great deal for future editions; so fire away.
• Many people have written to request addresses of people not listed in the book. As much as I would like to, I simply can't open up this can of worms. Requests for additional addresses are carefully noted and considered for future editions.

Receiving a photo from someone who writes adds an entirely new dimension to the letter so feel free. That's right, enclose a photo of yourself. After all, from the photo on the back cover, you know what I look like, and I'm rather anxious to see you.

Keep those cards and letters coming.

Michael Levine
8730 Sunset Blvd., Sixth floor
Los Angeles, CA 90069